OPAQUE WATERCOLOR

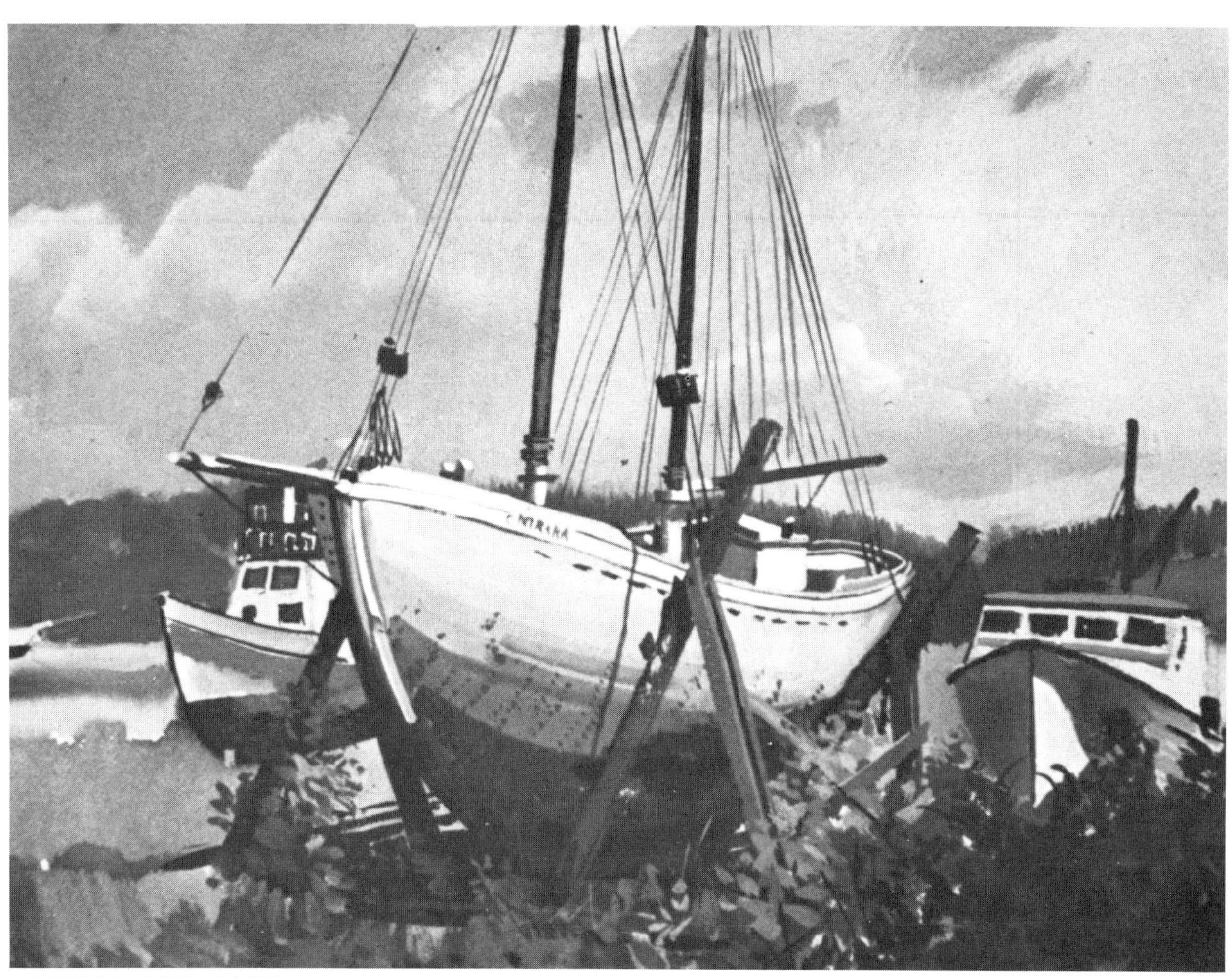

BADDECK, NOVA SCOTIA

Opaque Watercolor

Wallace Edmund Turner

NORTH LIGHT PUBLISHERS
37 Franklin Street · Westport, CT. 06880.

Published by NORTH LIGHT PUBLISHERS, a division of FLETCHER ART SERVICES, INC., 37 Franklin Street, Westport, Conn. 06880.

Distributed to the trade by Van Nostrand Reinhold Company, a division of Litton Educational Publishing, Inc., 135 West 50th Street, New York, N.Y. 10020.

Manufactured in U.S.A.
First Printing 1980

Library of Congress Cataloging in Publication Data

Turner, Wallace Edmund.
Opaque watercolor.

1. Water-color painting—Technique. I. Title.
ND2420.T87 751.42'2 80-22781
ISBN 0-89134-033-5

Edited by Fritz Henning
Designed by Fritz Henning
Composition by Stet/Shields, Inc.
Printed and bound by The Book Press
Color printed by Connecticut Printers

DEDICATION

To my wife, Trenna, whose help was invaluable in preparing this book.

To Ann, wife of my photographer, David Burton, who cooperated to the fullest.

To Kay, my wife's sister, and to her husband, Wilfred Holdridge, who drove me hither and yon to paint over a period of years.

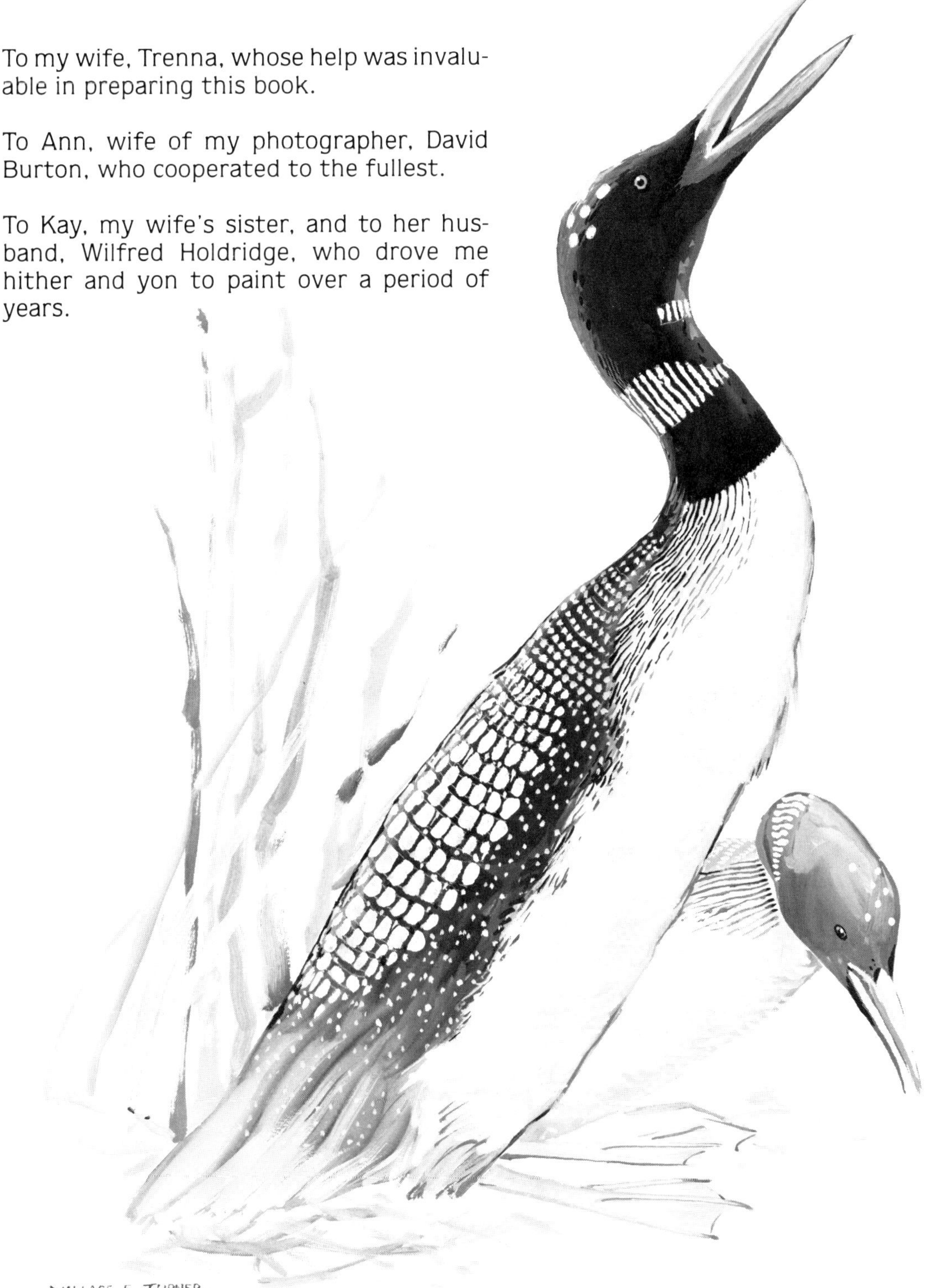

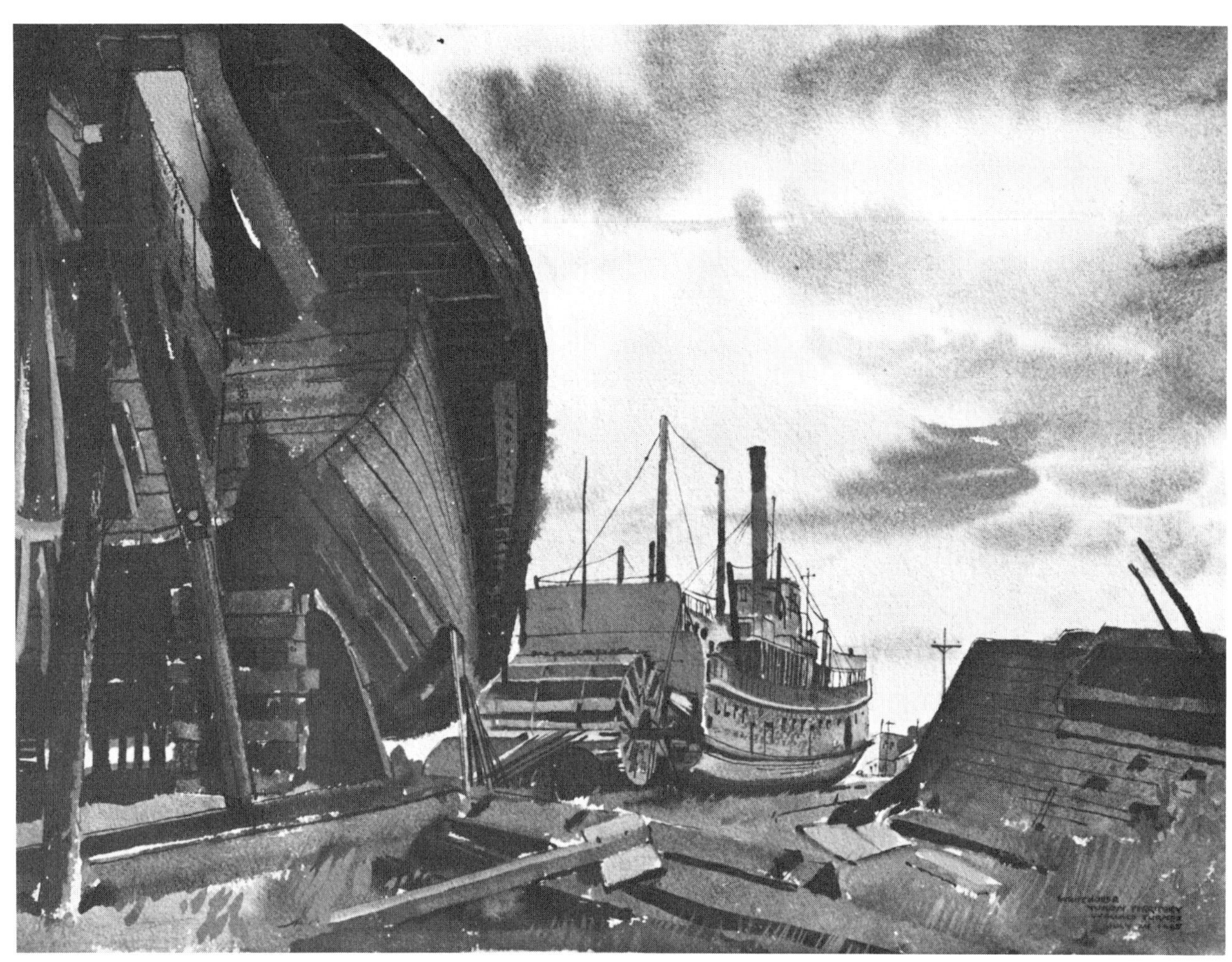

WHITEHORSE, YUKON TERRITORY

CONTENTS

Photography by David Burton

INTRODUCTION

One of my aims with this book is to share with you as a fellow artist a particular way of working with a particular kind of material:

opaque watercolor.

I shall not attempt to steer you into a philosophy of thinking or a way of interpreting what you set out to paint. Some of you will seek to portray the scene you look upon in the most literal, realistic way possible. Others will hope for a more interpretive impressionistic result. Both directions are valid—and art history has the records of scores of gifted artists who followed one or the other of those paths.

The important thing is for you to find out your own approach and preference. Decide on your point of view—then pursue it, but try to remain flexible and open to new ideas as you are exposed to them. This, plus solid learning from those who have come before, plus never-ending practice and looking and doing are the few simple guidelines to follow.

It's a pleasure to have you "with me," so to speak, as I introduce you to the medium of opaque watercolor and to show you paintings I have done in various parts of the world to demonstrate my procedures.

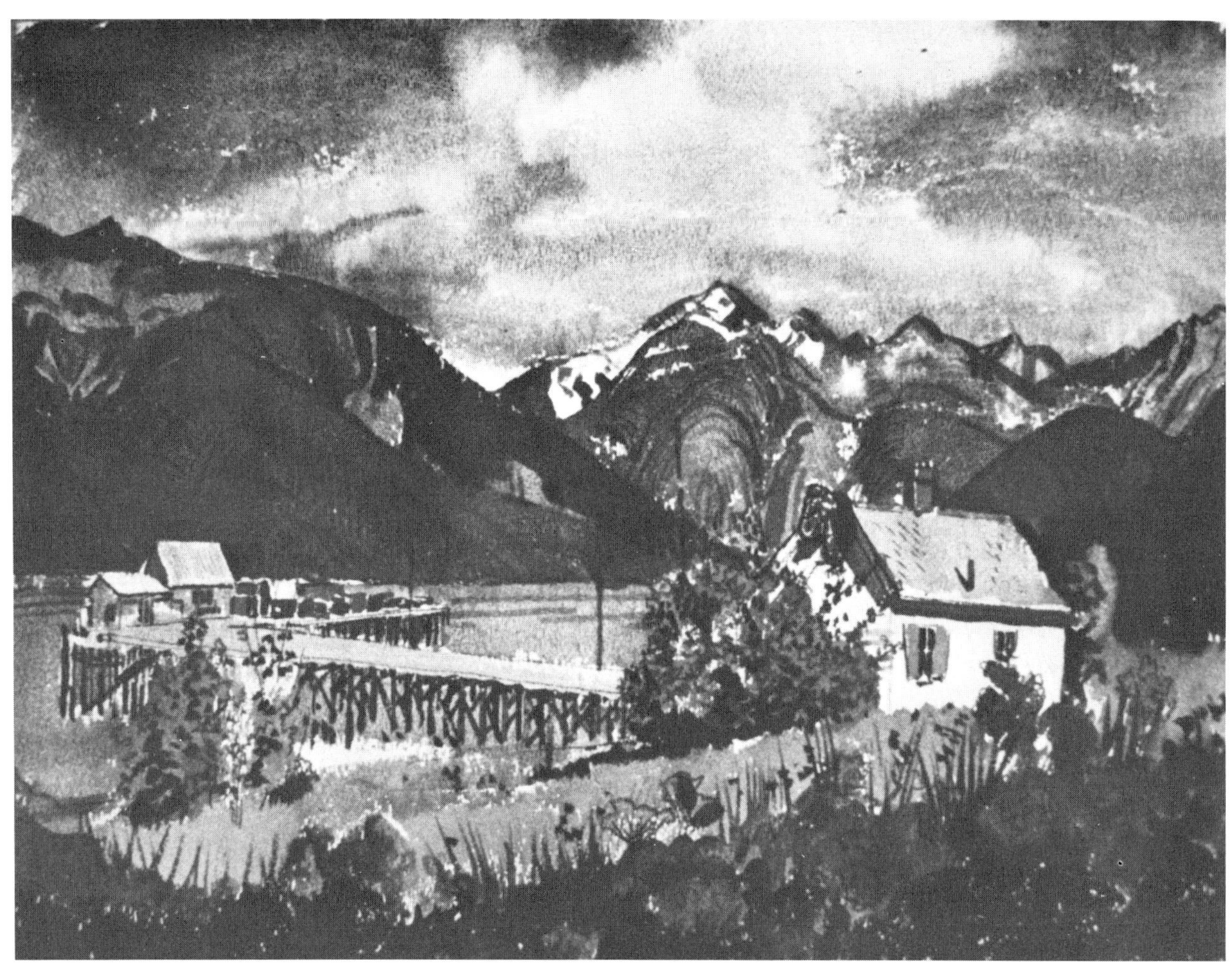

PORT CHILKOOT, ALASKA

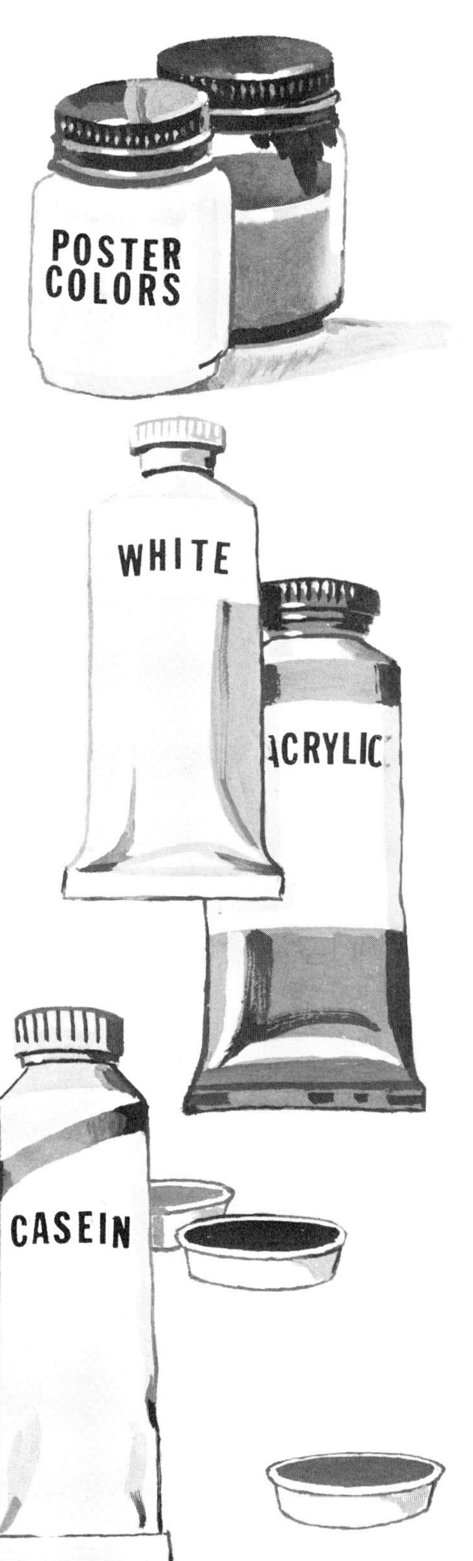

CHAPTER 1

The Materials

Perhaps the best way to laud the versatility and unique qualities of opaque watercolor is to remind you that in its simplest form it is the paint used in kindergarten to introduce youngsters to their first fling at self-expression. At that stage it is called Poster Paint and is most often used thickly and directly with spirited abandon on brown wrapping paper or newsprint. The results are mostly spectacular! Pure color is belted on. And wild and fanciful ideas come alive with no inhibitions. So you see, you probably used opaque watercolor long ago without knowing what to call it.

The other extreme is the fine professional form of opaques, sold mostly in tubes. Winsor & Newton's Designer Colors are usually considered superior. But these and the kid colors are basically the same in that they are both made with ground pigment and suspended in a binder. The difference, of course, is in the quality of the raw materials and the nature of the manufacture. You are apt to get what you pay for.

In between these extremes there exists a wide range of other brands and other forms. Opaque watercolor comes in jars, plastic bottles, tubes, and dried buttons. There also exist sets of graded grays in both warm (on the brown side) and cool (on the blue side). These are used extensively by illustrators working on black and white assignments and by photo retouchers who correct black and white photo prints. One or the other belongs in every painter's kit.

Before proceeding with "Opaques" (which I shall call them from here on) I should like to veer off a bit and briefly discuss the other forms and names of water base paints. They are:

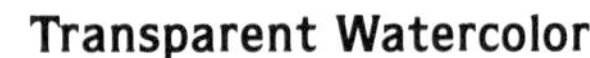

Transparent Watercolor

Transparent watercolor is made of finely ground pigment held in suspension by a binder. It contains no white. As it implies, it transparently stains the surface and uses the white of the paper for its luminosity. Values and intensities are controlled by the amount of dilution with water.

Gouache

Gouache is the French word for opaque watercolor. It means the addition of white to watercolor pigment, usually through the mixture of the two, either in manufacture or by the artist on his palette. The mixture can also be achieved by coating the painting surface with Chinese white (zinc white) and painting into it with transparent colors. Manufactured opaque gouache is produced with a gum arabic base. Since I use Designers Colors most of the time, most of my paintings are correctly referred to as gouache. However, I prefer to call them opaque watercolors as a simpler, broader, and more easily understood term.

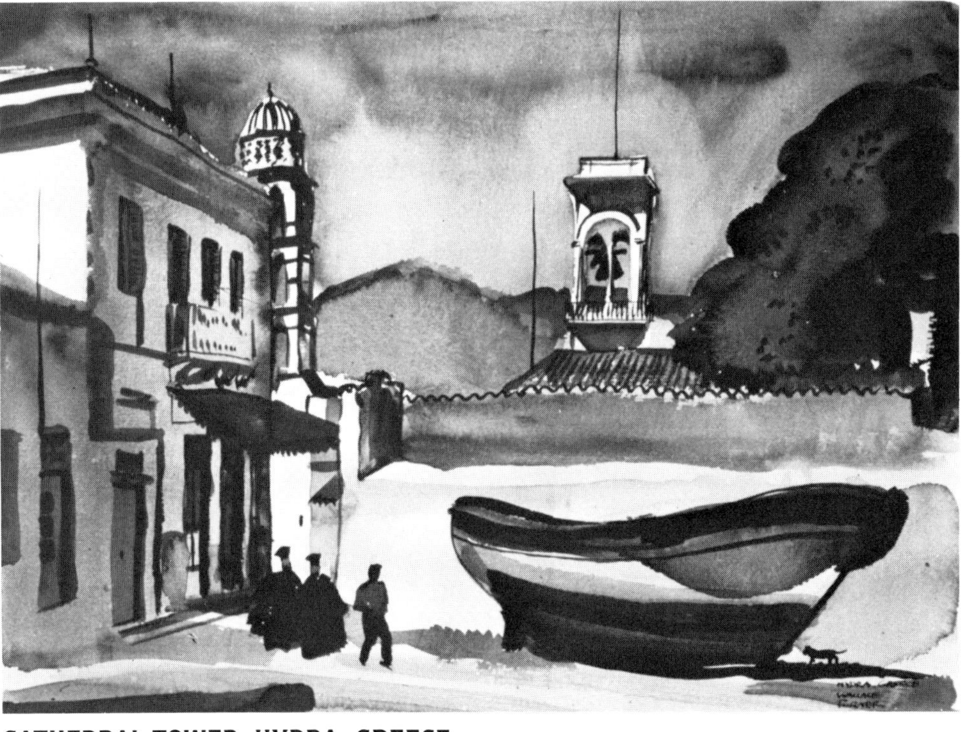

CATHEDRAL TOWER, HYDRA, GREECE

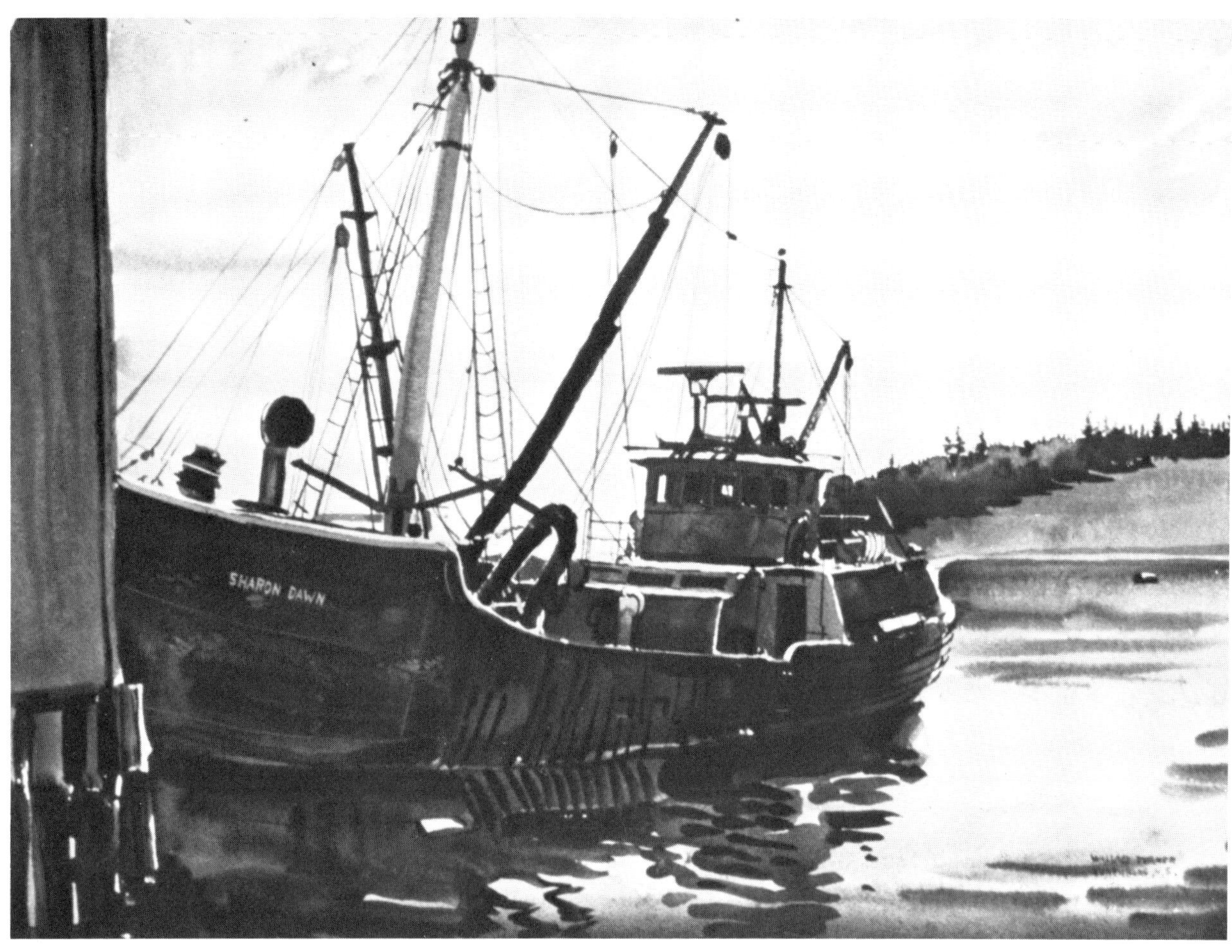

"SHARON DAWN," LUNENBERG, NOVA SCOTIA

Tempera

Tempera is a name rather loosely given by manufacturers to a number of products. Technically, tempera is a pigment bound together by an emulsifying agent. The emulsion allows the paint to be diluted, either by water or oil. A common emulsion is a mixture of gum arabic, varnish, and water. Among the oldest and most perfect emulsions is the egg. Sometimes the whole egg is used, or it can be mixed with linseed oil and water. Paint using egg yolk as a binder becomes a special kind of tempera— it is called egg tempera. It is a wonderful medium in the hands of a master craftsman, but it offers a number of limitations that make it difficult to prepare and use. Its use requires special study and it is not the medium we will discuss in this book.

Casein

For those painters who may not feel comfortable with the quick flooding property of transparent watercolor, casein with its heavier body and some attributes of oil painting may be the answer. Casein pigment is derived from skimmed milk. It has a long history, going back to early Roman times.

Casein has a heavier body than opaque watercolor or gouache, and can be used with as much vigor and assurance as oils. Unlike opaque, casein, when dry, can be overpainted or glazed. Casein, like acrylics, dries rapidly. Your brushes, however, will need special care when working with acrylics or casein. When varnished, casein can have a strong similarity to oils. It is truly a versatile medium.

Some caseins have a tendency to yellow somewhat, and if piled up on the paper may crack. Because of this casein should be applied to paper or illustration board rather than canvas.

Casein mingles well with opaque colors. I have used casein white when opaque white was unavailable. I find Designers Permanent White, Grumbacher White and others admirable for the job. Occasionally, the only white available would be too watery for my type of working, so I would fall back on Titanium Casein White instead.

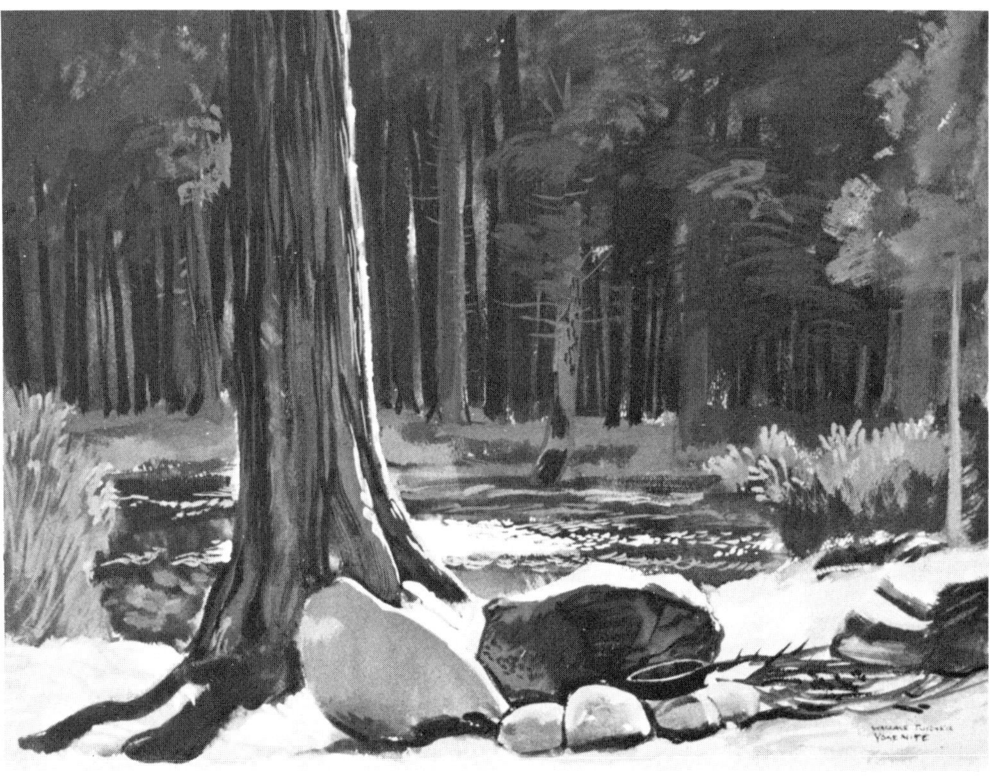

CAMPSITE, YOSEMITE, CALIFORNIA

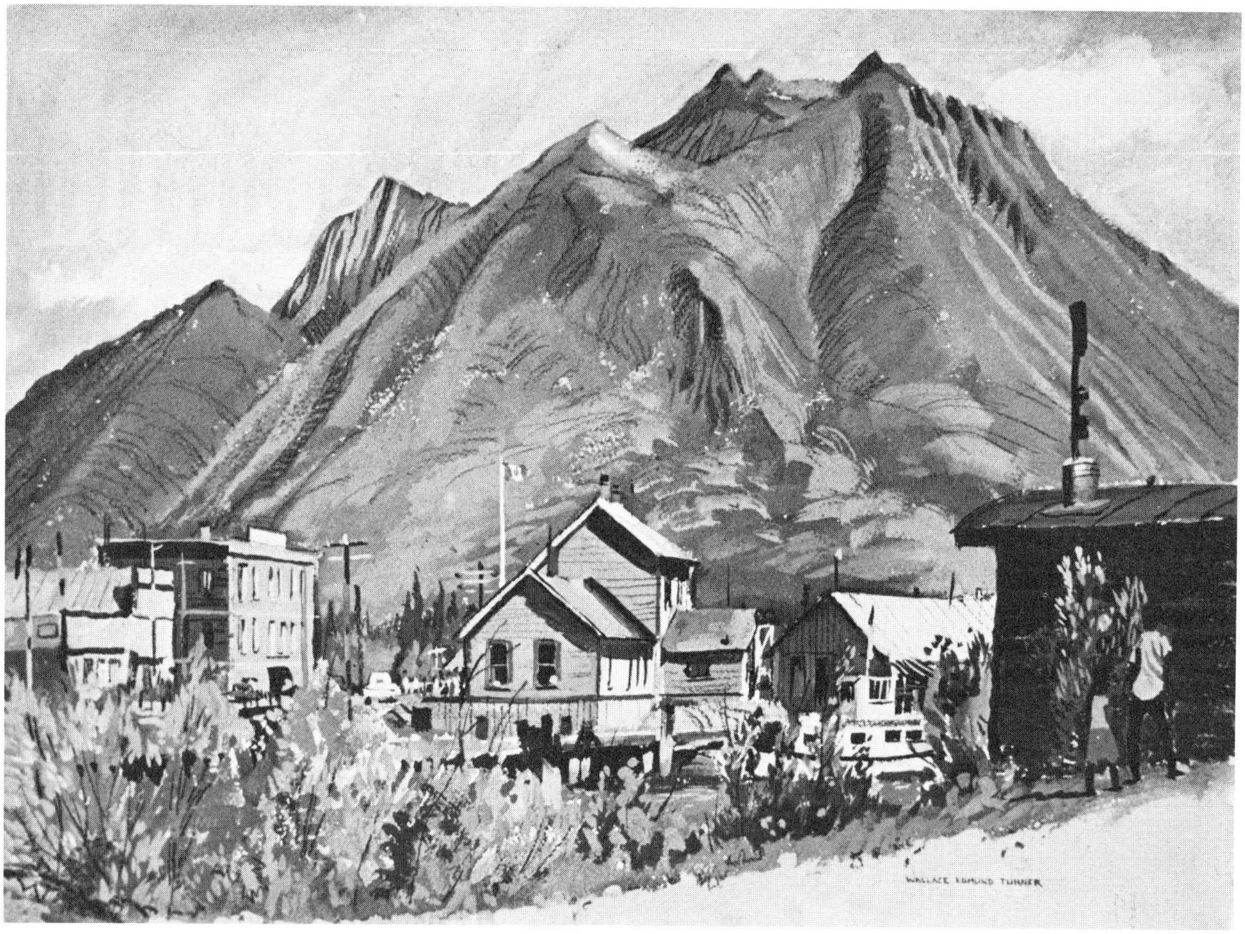

CARCROSS, YUKON TERRITORY

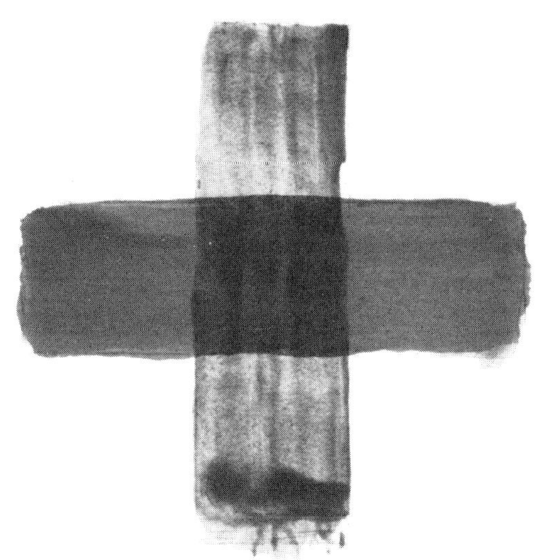

Acrylics

Acrylics are a newer water base paint with characteristics quite different from the others. They became popular some 20 years ago, when they were first commercially promoted.

Many artists now prefer acrylics to oils as they are more quickly and easily handled. They dry faster and are less affected by heat and other adverse features of oils, while producing the brilliancy of transparent watercolor. Although they have these features with the addition of being waterproof, they have the disadvantage of being altered only by painting over the underlying paint, whereas opaque watercolors can be quite successfully removed if one wishes to make changes or additions. Too, the brushes take more care than for other water base paints.

Opaque watercolor is the medium we shall be dealing with in this book. . . or call it gouache or tempera or poster paint or even show card color. It is an easily handled medium with many very attractive properties: it flows beautifully from your brush—any kind of brush. It dries rapidly. It covers well. It lays flat and matte (if you don't thin it too much). It is accepted well on paper, cardboard, and canvas surfaces. It takes fixative well. It can be thinned down to use in ruling pens, speedball pens, and lettering pens. With some care, it is harmless to brushes, and rinses clean quickly. It can also be washed off a surface and will leave only a slight stain that can be flawlessly repainted. It is also relatively inexpensive.

In short, it is very satisfying to work with. And as everyone who paints knows, artists welcome obliging materials—too many materials are not.

Before getting down to cases and joining you in discussion and picture making, let's review the features of the medium we shall be working in.

Here's a summing up on opaques:

- It is transparent watercolor with white added.
- It dries quickly and is quite permanent.
- It allows you to change your mind and to paint over.
- It allows for dexterity of brush work and it will let the brush marks show if you wish it.
- It has the impact, solidarity, and vividness of oil, casein, and acrylic without their separate drawbacks and difficulties.
- It has one major difficulty in handling. The values and color intensity look slightly different when it is wet than when it dries. It takes experience and practice to learn how to compensate for this difference as you paint.

Now, let's take a look at some recommended brushes, papers and other paraphernalia and then we'll plunge in and paint!

Studio

Almost simultaneous with the artist's urge to paint comes the desire to have one's own studio. Some achieve this dream workshop in spectacular ways—converted barns or attics or outbuildings or lofts or rehabilitated factories. The very fortunate design their own buildings and have them constructed to their specifications. Some have north light—all have good light, plus ample space to work and to store materials, books, frames and all the other truck artists acquire over the years.

REFITTING "DRIFT" ►
In this picture I did at Mahone Bay, Nova Scotia, the emphasis is on wet-in-wet transparent wash.

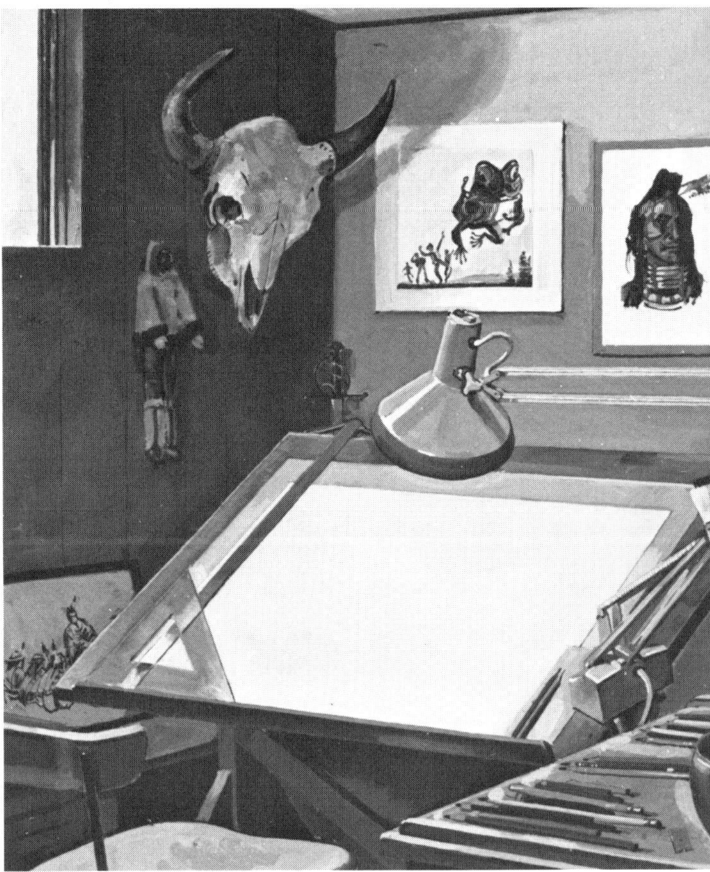

I have friends who have every imaginable kind of studio set-up. I've envied some of them, but I've also noted over the years that if you have too much room to start with, you will eventually fill it and wind up pressed for space.

Perhaps because I work out-of-doors much of the time I've never had the urge to have more than a comfortable quiet room to work in. I've seldom had a north light. All I seek is adequate light with no direct sun on my work. If I need to block out the sun in the morning in my present Nova Scotia studio I merely tack up a sheet of tracing paper until the glare passes.

Over the years I've made do with bedrooms, basements, and kitchen tables. My enthusiasm for what I was doing made up for my lack of a well-appointed formal studio. I was bolstered by the knowledge that the French master Chardin was

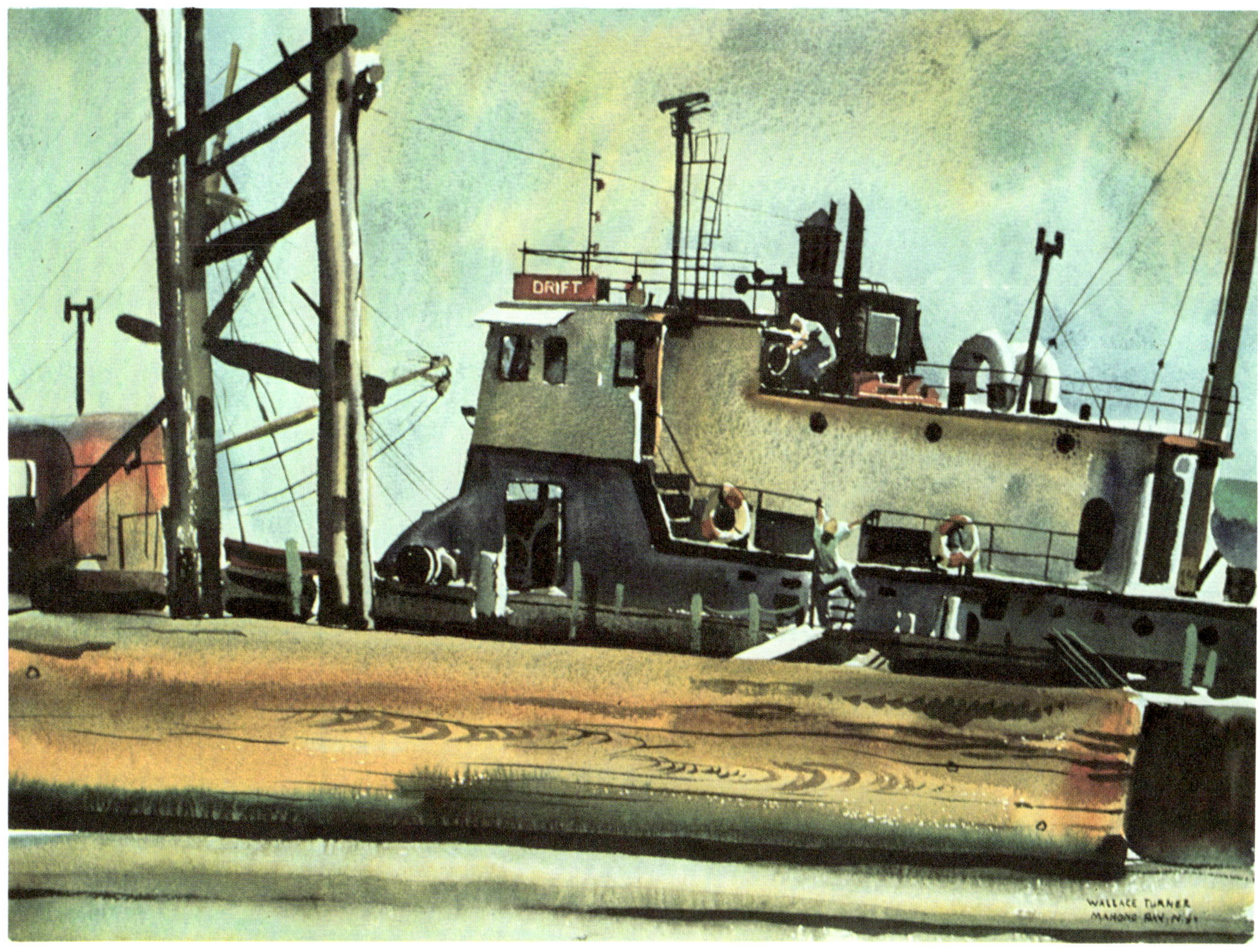

REFITTING "DRIFT"

also a kitchen table man. He even went so far as to paint what he saw in the kitchen: bread, crockery, vegetables, etc. Not only that, but he even used the scullery maids for models. That's what I call making the most of what happens to be at hand! I manage very well with a tilt-top drawing table, a taboret, and a clamp-on lamp that contains a combination of cool fluorescent and warm incandescent bulbs.

As to an easel, I'll leave that to you. There are endless varieties and prices. If you desire one, but are cramped for space, choose a folding type that can be easily stored.

Many of my fellow painters who like working out of doors as I do, use the folding easel that also holds a palette and paints and brushes. You can use it on location or as your indoor studio easel. Its ingenious design allows it to fold down so completely that you really wind up carrying away a simple paint box by a luggage handle. They're great, but expensive.

Palettes

I have found that after years of trying other things, my two favorite types of palettes for use with opaques are the porcelain butcher's tray which is sturdy and easily washed and the disposable paper type. This latter is especially practical on location where water supplies are either scarce or non-existent. I have been hostilely stared at in public parks for washing my palette at a fountain or in a stream. Disposable palettes avoid your being accused of not caring for the environment—unless you chuck them on the ground.

At home anything goes. Many artists use cracked or otherwise discarded kitchen china. This has the advantage of keeping the squeezed paint up on the rim and out of the mixture in the center.

There are commercial palettes with covers, designed to keep you from wasting unused paint. Remember that we're dealing with water base paint, so the retention of moisture is essential.

Continued on page 19

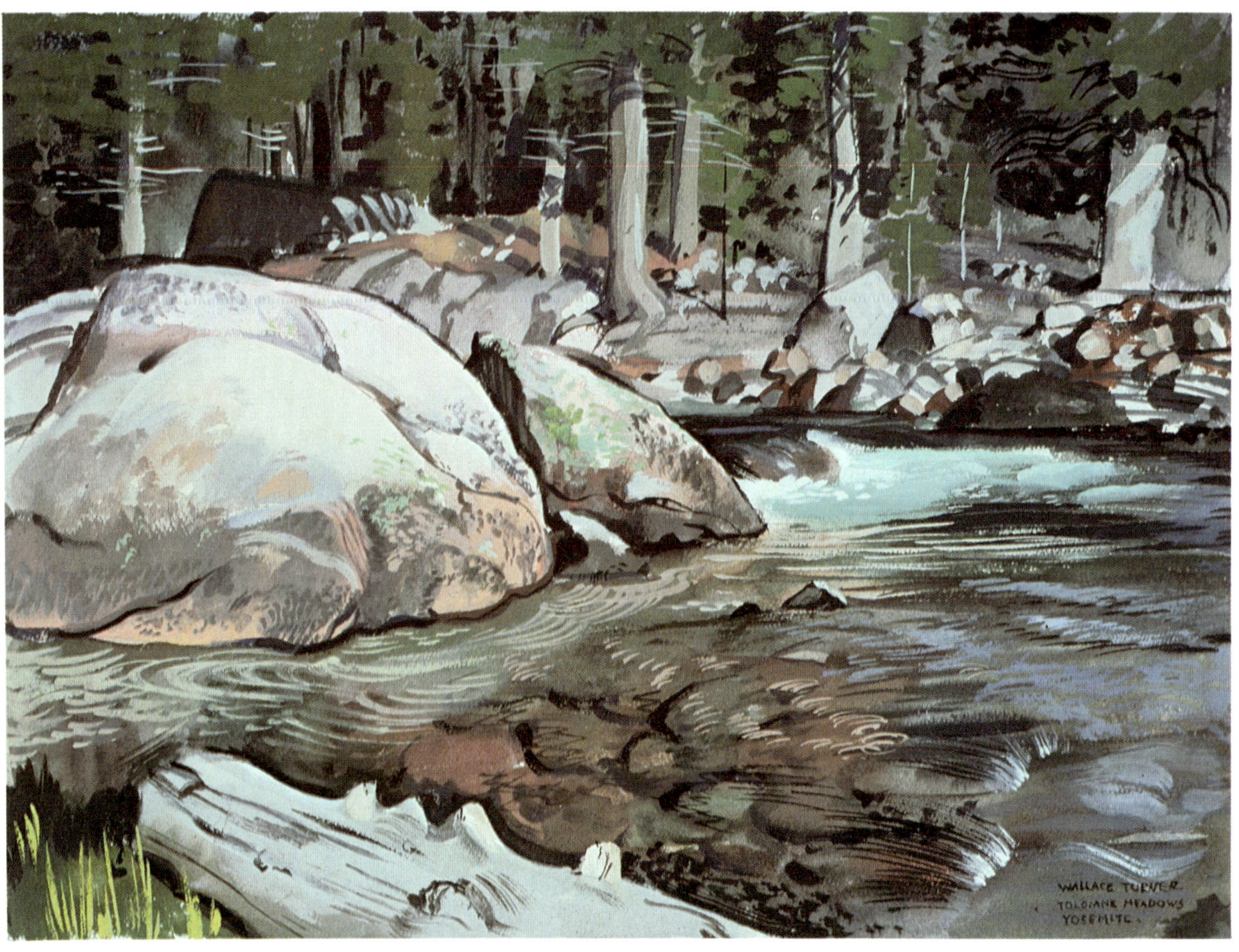

BOULDERS, YOSEMITE NATIONAL PARK, CALIFORNIA

While in Yosemite, my brother-in-law was anxious to show me a particularly beautiful waterfall to paint. On the way I spotted these massive boulders in their fine forms and simplicity; the waterfall was never painted. Boulders, large or small, like great mountains lend themselves very well to opaque watercolor. The steely gray granite, warm in the sunlight, cool in the shadow, can be reproduced quickly from Payne's gray, yellow ochre, and white. The russet tones of some rocks can be painted with various combinations of burnt sienna and cadmium reds. Almost every color is to be found in rock formations, and values, if accurately handled, give the boulders a feeling of weight and form. Edges are also important; the smooth worn surface of a boulder can be opposed by sharp jagged edges. Textures can also be used extensively, so in the painting of a little-noticed boulder we find form, value, color, and texture. Too, the painting of boulders can be a dress rehearsal for painting great mountains. The only difference is the size.

The overlapping tree in the foreground, painted over the boulder when it was dry, gives a feeling of depth to the boulder-strewn scene. In painting the branches, some curving brushwork was used in contrast to the weight of the boulders. The left profile of the foreground boulder was found to be rather interesting, so a halation of light pigment was used to define this profile.

The last step was to paint, with a variety of greens, the lichens which covered part of the boulders. This offered a use of textures painted with short individual strokes.

Putting your palette in a plastic bag containing a wet sponge helps for short periods.

But, in the end, your good judgment will teach you how much to squeeze at a time. Try to land somewhere between stingy and wasteful.

Accessory Equipment

I'll limit my advice here to the subject of outdoor painting. Experience has taught me the pitfalls of being in places away from home and art supply stores and even a water source. There is also the question of toting your supplies easily and safely—especially large pads or sheets of paper. The answer is to carry them in a rigid portfolio larger than the paper. Always bring extra sheets. Carry the rest of your material— pencils, paints, brushes, tape, razor blades, erasers, etc. in a single box.

I use a large coffee can with its own plastic lid for water. Unlike jars with screw-on tops, they never leak. Another fine container is a military canteen. These have the advantage of hooking on to a simple cartridge belt, so you can wear it instead of carrying it. Make sure you also get the cup that comes with it so you have something to pour the water into.

I include in my portfolio a thin sheet of plywood or masonite on which I clip or tape my paper.

A folding stool is a fine thing to bring along also since sitting on the ground can be uncomfortable.

Paper

Watercolor papers and illustration boards vary in weight, texture, size, color and price.

The paintings for this book were done on watercolor paper or medium illustration board with a kid finish. Although opaque watercolor adheres best to a porous surface such as paper or plaster, it can be used on practically any non-greasy surface. However, if cloth or canvas is used the surface must be sized or the paint will flake off when dried. Surfaces such as wood or masonite require coats of gesso sanded to whatever smoothness you desire.

In selecting paper you have the choice of a rough, medium or smooth surface. The rough surfaced paper will delay drying somewhat, giving the painter more time to work with the wet pigments. It will also give interesting surface textures. A smooth surfaced paper lends itself to more precise painting such as in illustration or advertising art.

With opaque watercolor the character of the paper has less effect on the finished painting than when painting with transparent watercolor, except when the opaque is applied as a thin wash. An advantage of a rough, heavier paper is that it resists wrinkling.

Although I prefer the rough surface and the luminosity of white paper, some artists choose less textured or tinted paper. If you are applying the paint heavily, the color of the paper is less important than if you are using thin washes where the color of the paper may show through or affect the luminosity of your colors.

For general painting and painting out-of-doors I prefer a rough paper such as Fabriano or Arches. Strathmore also offers a fine surface for opaque painting, especially their kid finish. Bristol board and other boards of this type are generally too glossy for opaque watercolors unless sized. There are many illustration boards on the market. It's advisable to avoid the very cheapest, however.

There are some watercolor papers that come in blocks or pads. Strathmore Alexis is one that beginners may wish to try.

The size of the paper selected depends on the individual preference and somewhat on the subject chosen. I usually use a 15 x 20 inch Fabriano when traveling. However, I also use Strathmore Alexis and other 22 x 30 inch medium rough or rough paper. The price of the larger and heavier paper may cause you to hesitate, but remember that if your results do not satisfy you, you can paint on the other side.

Try the different brands and surfaces and sizes until you find your favorites. To begin with you may select the less expensive paper, but remember that with paper, as with brushes, buy the best you can afford. In time you will be well repaid.

I would like to suggest that if you are going on a painting trip away from cities or to remote spots that you be certain to take plenty of paper as well as other supplies with you. When spending fourteen months in the South Pacific I ran out of paper. Surprisingly, I found a roll of excellent watercolor paper in Suva, Fiji. It wasn't until I put it to use on one of the distant islands that I discovered it was heavily mildewed, having been stored in a damp place for too long. The captain of our ship was good enough to bring me a new supply on his return from Australia.

On Mounting Paper

The usual method of mounting watercolor paper by soaking the paper and flattening it on plywood and holding the edges with gummed tape or tacks is effective, but it takes time and the stretching of the paper takes out the ridges in the paper, lessening its effectiveness as a "rough" paper. The textural qualities of the paper are diminished by this method.

Recently I have found that a most satisfactory substitute is the use of carpet tape which comes in rolls 2 inches wide. This tape is coated with adhesive on both sides and is used to anchor carpets to the floor. Cut off 5 or 6-inch lengths of tape, affix these strips along the sides of the plywood board and lay your paper on the board, pressing the edges of the paper firmly against the tape without wetting it. No need to soak the paper or to wet the tape as it is adhesive on both sides.

After completing your painting, the paper can be removed without difficulty from the tape and the board. I find this a fast method of mounting watercolor paper, and the surface of the paper is not altered in any way. Since this type of tape is not a normal art product you'll probably find it only at a carpet shop.

Illustration Board

Most grades of illustration board work well for opaque watercolor. Because of its semi-smooth character, this board will take anything from a sketchy treatment to finished detail. Illustration board is probably the most convenient surface to work on. It can be carried easily, seldom buckles or cracks, and you never have to worry about stretching it. However, some purists claim that unmounted paper is more receptive.

Arches Rough

The rough surface of Arches paper lends itself to a broad technique with jagged edges. Dry brush effects work well and add to the painting quality. Interesting contrasts can be obtained by combining a wet-in-wet against heavy opaque application of pigment.

Strathmore Alexis

This comes in blocks as well as single sheets. Due to its semi-rough texture, it has a delayed drying time. It will take broad brush handling as well as fine line treatment.

Fabriano (Medium-Rough-Smooth)

This heavy 100% cold pressed rag paper, made in Italy, is excellent for a broad treatment combined with a fine detailed handling. This paper is adaptable in the appropriate weight for even the most arduous demands, including surface scratching. It takes wet-in-wet washes and dry brush treatment well. It will not buckle or wrinkle. I find a 15 x 20 inch size convenient to work on. Its vertical use is good for portrait painting. Used horizontally, it is excellent for landscape work.

Brushes

Good brushes are imperative for good painting. They are expensive, but if selected carefully and given good care they will last. This is one item an artist should not skimp on. There is general agreement red sable brushes give the most satisfaction and are more durable, thus the most economical in spite of their high initial cost.

In looking through catalogs and in art stores you will find a bewildering display of brushes differing in quality (even among the red sables), sizes and manufacturer; each manufacturer has his own number system, so be alert as to this. Select the best you can afford. To begin with, you can do well with as few as four brushes, two round and two flat. In selecting your round brushes, be certain they point well, hold water well and have a springiness or resiliency—that they will spring back after being pressed to the paper when dry or wet. Some stores offer to let you test brushes in water.

Round Brushes

All artists differ widely in their choice of brushes—and so will you. The round brush I use the most is a Winsor & Newton Series E #9. I also use #6 of the same series. These brushes are of the finest quality red sable made from the tail of the Kolinsky, the Siberian mink. You need nothing smaller as these brushes are well tapered, enabling you to make very fine lines as well as broad brush strokes.

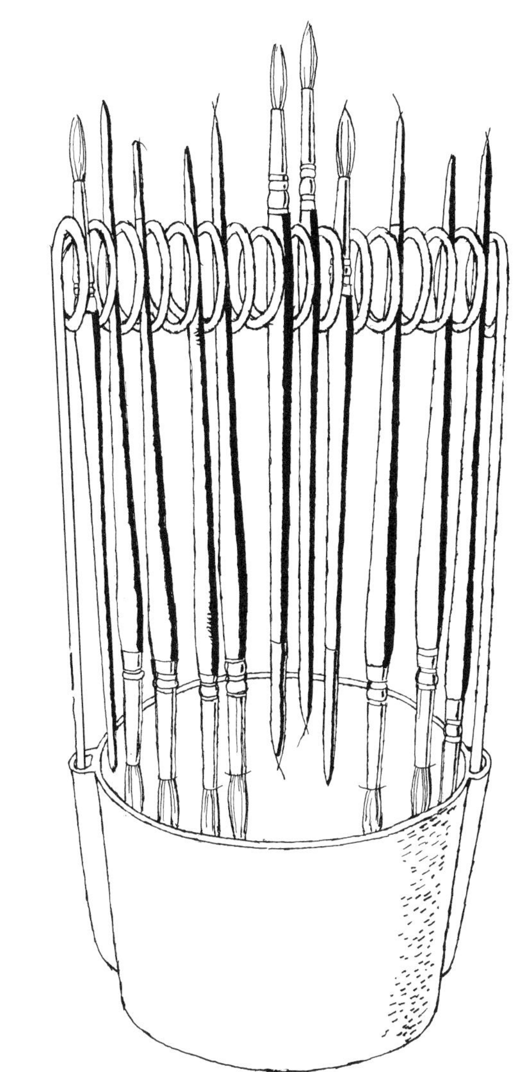

Flat Brushes

If you feel you cannot afford the red sable, economize in purchasing your flat brushes rather than your round brushes. Try sabeline or ox hair brushes. The general rule is for big areas to be painted with big brushes. My usual "workhorse" for opaque watercolor is the Grumbacher #14 flat 1½-inch Gainsborough 1217B, excellent for wetting the paper before painting and for laying in the background colors. The edge can be used for fine line effects. I also use the Delta #7 flat ½-inch brush. Recently I experimented with some flat oriental brushes. They hold water well, but lack the springy quality of a really good brush. However, they are inexpensive and worth a try. Keep your eyes open for new brushes on the market, adding to your collection according to your needs. Recently I found a Hanca Import from West Germany, a #16 flat ½-inch of "finest sabeline." I find this useful for laying in small areas.

Remember, start with a few large brushes of the best quality you can afford.

It is important to give your brushes the best of care, thereby adding to their longevity and quality of service. Wash them well during and after painting to keep the particles of pigment from settling in the ferrules, as this would impair the points and edges. Just rinse them well in clear water, shake but do not squeeze them, then gently bring your round brushes to a point. Roll them in a piece of plain heavy paper or place them in a brush tube, coffee can or jar, hair end up. Never allow your brushes to stand in water.

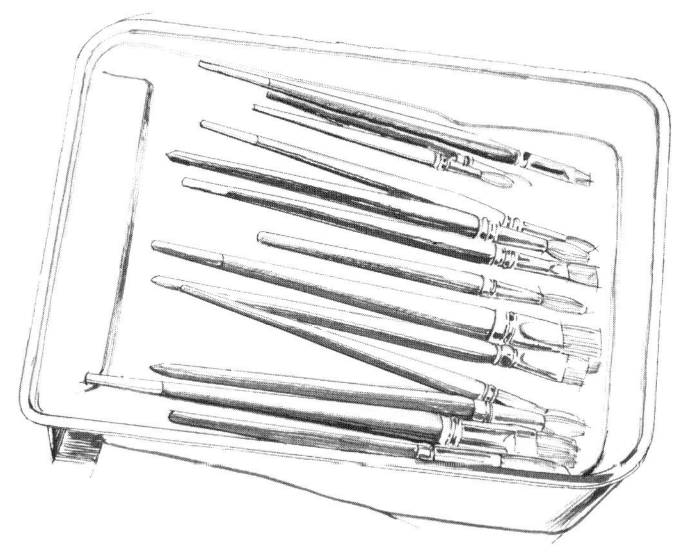

Some artists use an aluminum spiral wire brush holder about 4 inches in diameter, with a glass below it for water in which to wash their brushes. This will hold the usual number of brushes required for a painting, and they can be safely suspended in water when not in use.

I have found that the roller tray used by house painters is handy for keeping brushes in good condition. The brushes, lying on their sides, will keep their points and shapes. Water in the deep end of the tray is handy for rinsing the brushes not in use.

Another protective device shown here is a piece of corrugated wrapping cardboard which, when cut longer than your brushes, rolled around them and tied, will protect the points when the brushes are not in use or when carried on a painting trip.

Some years ago I purchased a stout plastic tube with a screw-on lid. It is over a foot long and will carry my favorite Winsor & Newton Series 7 #9 brush and a few other brushes. However, the tube is only 1 inch in diameter, so I wrap my flat brushes in the corrugated cardboard or heavy brown paper.

Keep your old brushes as they may be of use for some special effect or when experimenting with new techniques. Robert Fawcett, a leading illustrator, made periodic visits to his illustrator friends to inquire if they had any worn out brushes that they were about to throw away. He gladly took them, having a distinct liking for these tired oldtimers that others thought were ready only for the scrap heap.

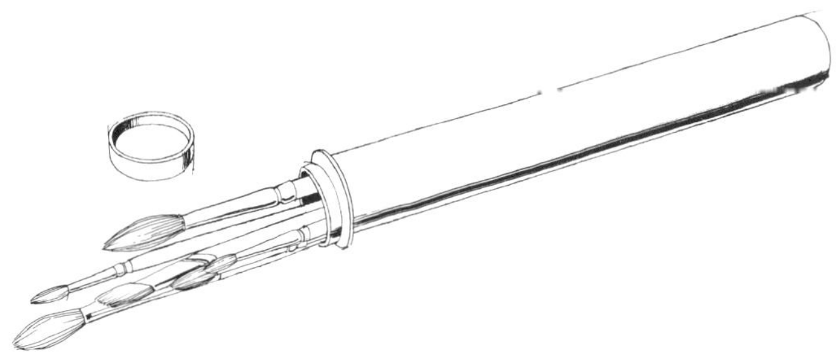

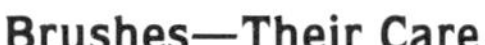

Brushes—Their Care

Some artists divide their brushes into three groups or more. The first group contains their best brushes, reserved only for transparent watercolor, and are not used for any other medium. The second group includes brushes for working with opaque watercolor. As stated previously, the heavier opaque pigment will settle in the ferrule of the brush, and to avoid damaging the pointing qualities, these brushes require special washing care. In the third group, no less important, are the brushes used in ink renderings or color dyes. In working with ink lines, a fine point is necessary, so the best sable brushes are used. As ingredients from the ink settle in the ferrule of the brush, in spite of careful washing, the hairs have a tendency to become brittle and break. Brushes used with these mediums tend to have the shortest lives.

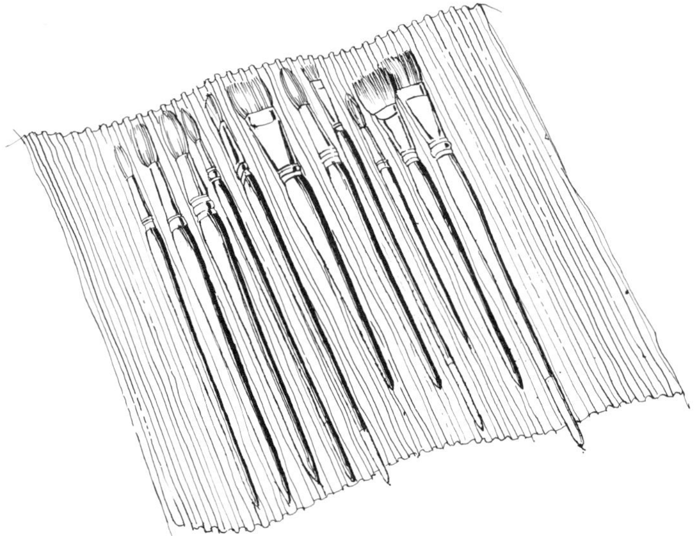

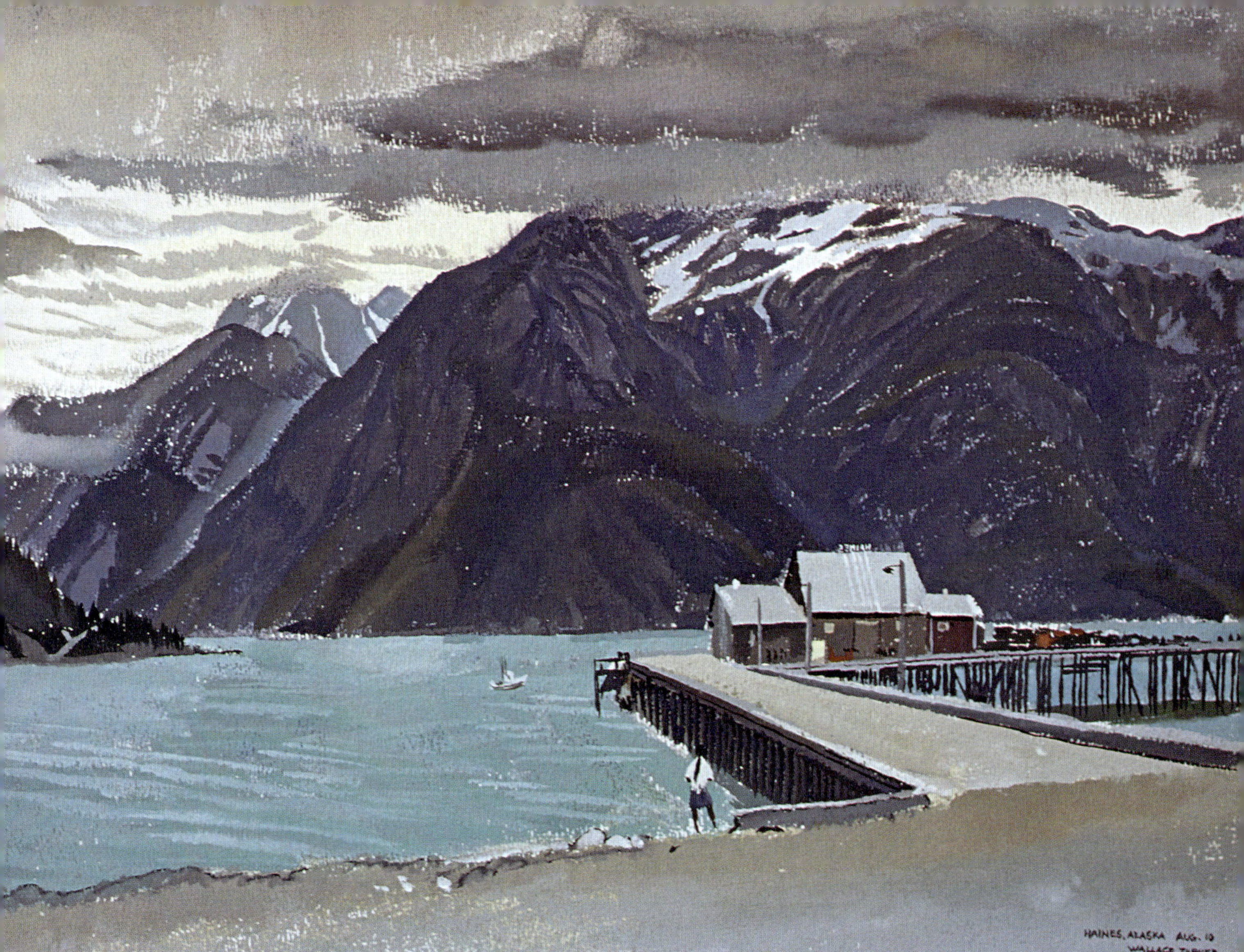

HAINES, ALASKA

CHAPTER 2

Color

Color is important to most artists and is important to the effectiveness of most paintings.

An in-depth study of color can be quite technical and deal with scientific aspects of light and how we see. However, for most of us this is not essential. But, it is important to have an understanding of its properties of color and how they work. These properties are: hue, the name of the color; value, the lightness or darkness of a color; and intensity, the strength or tinting power of a color. It is also necessary to know the effects of these factors on a painting and on the viewer.

Colors have a psychological as well as an aesthetic effect. An artist is often attracted to a subject because of its color rather than its subject matter or composition. Color is important in everyday life; to a great extent it is the color that influences the selection of our clothes, and we give it great consideration in choosing a car, or painting our house.

Every artist also needs to be aware of the interaction of color, the effect one color has on another, and the interdependence of colors. Some people have a natural sensitivity to color, while others de-

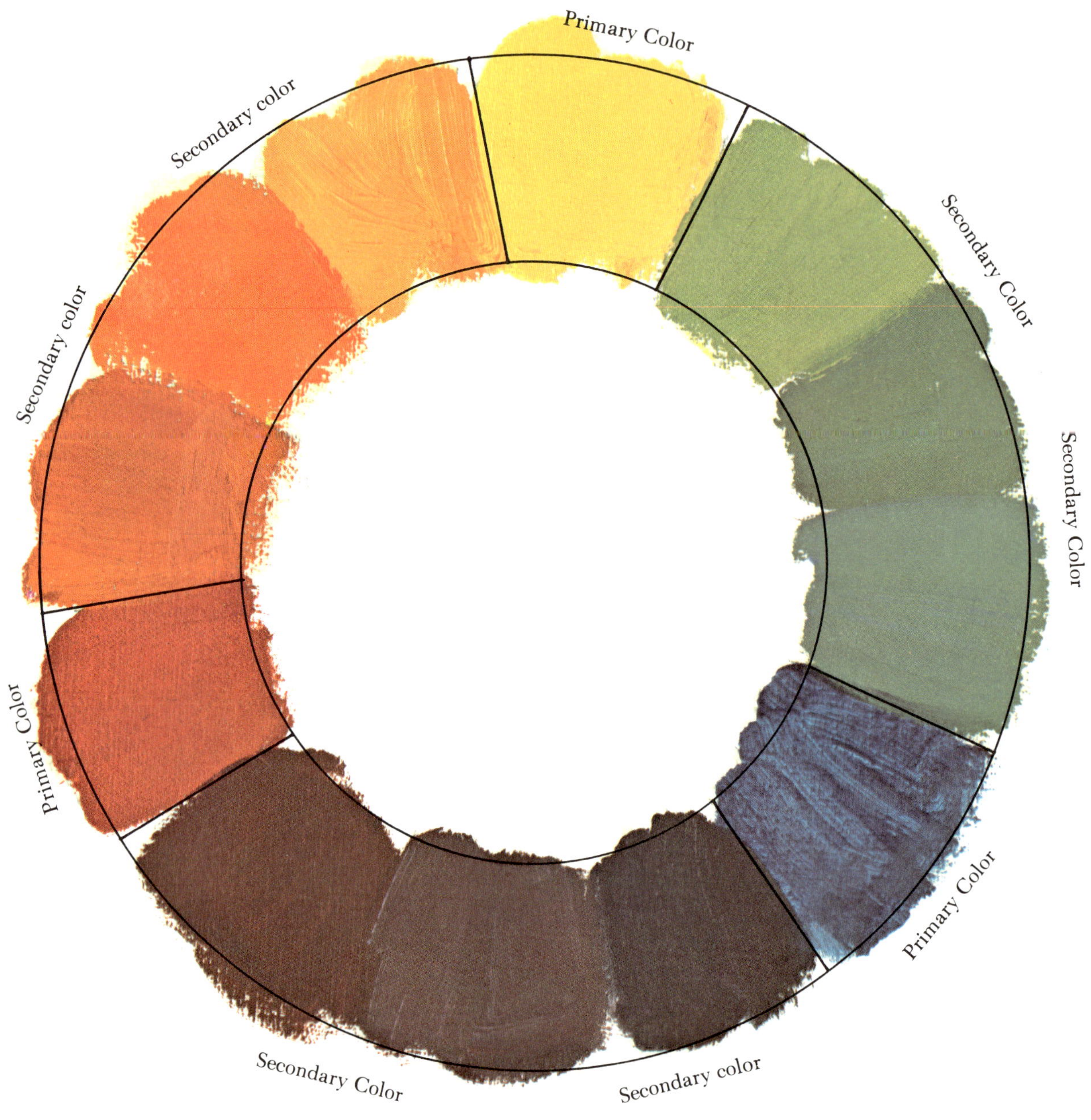

velop a sensitivity through study and observation. Some of us learn to see color better by the study of the color wheel and charts of color mixes. Some artists find it helpful to make their own chart of color mixes which are used to approximate colors seen in nature.

I find it more meaningful to work directly from nature, mixing the colors as they appear to me, and applying the hues to paper. Sometimes I mix the colors on my palette, but often the mixing is done directly on the painting surface.

The greatest influence on color in painting by any group of painters was undoubtedly that of the French Impressionists. They brought air and atmosphere into painting, following the lead of Turner and Constable. They showed us that a painting made out-of-doors will lose much of its sunny effect when the picture is brought indoors to a darker area. To avoid this loss of light, the sunny areas should be strengthened by warmer and brighter colors and, in contrast, more cool colors used in the shadows. When colors are exaggerated in this manner, the brilliance of a sunny painting is more likely to survive the transition from the outside to indoors.

The brilliant and atmospheric vibration practiced by some Impressionists was brought about by laying one pure color next to another pure color of the same value. From a distance the eye mixes the two colors, thus producing one color. This method of painting is referred to as "Pointillism" or "Luminism" which, besides bringing life into the painting, eliminates a certain grayness that is produced when complementary colors are mixed together. This painting discovery caused a great sensation when introduced in the nineteenth century and has had a lasting effect.

Color awareness is sometimes changed by a painter's experience. Travel brought about a startling transformation in the color outlook of Sir Frank Brangwyn on his first trip to the Middle East. His expression of color changed from the cool grays of England to the vivid hues he found in the Middle East.

Another outstanding artist who underwent a complete change of palette as the result of a trip was Eugene Delacroix. His journey to Morocco resulted in a change to brilliant colors and picturesque settings which set off a new wave of romanticism.

Terms Used in Describing Color

Primary colors are red, yellow, and blue.

Secondary colors are made by mixing two primary colors.

Complementary colors are opposite one another on the color wheel.

Tint is a gradation of a color made by diluting with water in opaque painting or by adding white to lessen its intensity. It is usually a more delicate or pale color of less saturation and less intensity than the color at its maximum strength. It may have only a slight coloration. Adding white also makes the color look cooler than the pure color.

Shade is a gradation of a color made by adding black or the color's complement to decrease its brightness, darkening its value. This also creates grays of different shades, depending on the amount of black added. Adding black also makes the color look warmer.

Hue

The hue of a color is the name of the color, such as red, yellow, blue, or any gradation of a color such as red-orange, red-violet, or yellow-orange.

The related or harmonious hues are close together, next to one another on the color wheel, each containing some of the color next to it. Hues more separated are less related. Those opposite one another on the color wheel have nothing in common.

As shown, the hues on the left-hand side of the color wheel are warm colors, while those on the right-hand side are cool. Generally, a hue can be warmed by the addition of yellow and cooled by the addition of blue. If you wish to create a feeling of a hot day or bright sunlight, you would tend to use a predominance of warm hues. For a cooler feeling you would use more cool hues. You will want both warm and cool hues in the same painting, but one or the other should dominate.

By using complementary colors you create a strong contrast which will help sharpen your shadows or emphasize a shape. It is usually best to keep your strongest contrasts near your picture's center of interest.

Muted or subtle hues lie between the two extremes of warm and cool colors. They tend to be more neutral, neither warm nor cool. Observe the hues around you in nature, buildings, clothing, and cars. Notice how the hues reflect the temperature of the season or the day—warm hues for the sunlight and its reflections; cool hues for the water, shadows and deep recesses of the woods; neutral hues between or mixed in.

You will learn much more from observing your surroundings and from experimenting by mixing hues than you will learn from merely studying the color wheel or color charts. Make it a practice to study the subject you have chosen to paint for its hues, its values, and intensity, both when planning and evaluating your painting.

Intensity

Intensity of a color refers to the power or strength of that color. The greatest intensity of a color is as it comes from the tube. Mixing a color with white lessens the intensity. When mixed with its complement, the intensity of a color is also lessened. Adding another color, such as red to yellow, intensifies the yellow, but it is no longer a pure yellow; a different hue has been created.

Many factors can influence the intensity of a color; it may depend on a choice of subject, the purpose of the painting, the mood or emotional impact you wish to create, or upon your own reaction to color, or the degree of excitement you feel. As an example, strong reds can suggest strong emotions, while a soft green or yellow may have a relaxing or calming effect, suggesting peace with one's surroundings. Deep blues and violets suggest a more somber mood, sometimes threatening and mysterious. Large areas of gray express a feeling of dullness, of lack of spirit. You may have noticed that colors of low intensity are usually chosen for such places as hospitals where a relaxed, calm, and peaceful atmosphere is desired. Color intensity varies in different lights and in different seasons. The view from my window (pages 29-32) gives evidence of the change of the intensity of the colors in nature over a period of but a few days. The effect of light and shadow on the intensity of colors can be seen in the illustrations on this page.

Depending on its neighbor, the intensity of a color can heighten, diminish, or remain the same. Therefore, it is to your advantage to experiment in placing colors side-by-side to determine their interaction, just as you are encouraged to experiment with mixing colors, observing and studying your results and keeping your charts for reference, remembering what colors were used to obtain your results. Using colored paper in place of paint is a quick and an effective way to study color relationships.

Some people have a highly developed sensitivity to color intensity as well as to color value. As with the choice of subject matter or the "style" in which one paints, the intensity of colors used is a highly individual matter, as personal as one's handwriting. When you use intense colors in your paintings, vary the size of the areas of intensity, for two areas of equal intensity have a tendency to minimize the desired impact.

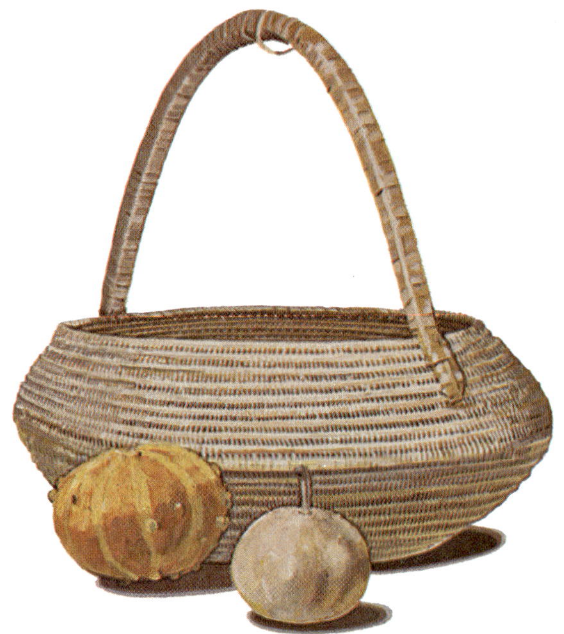

Basket with gourds in light

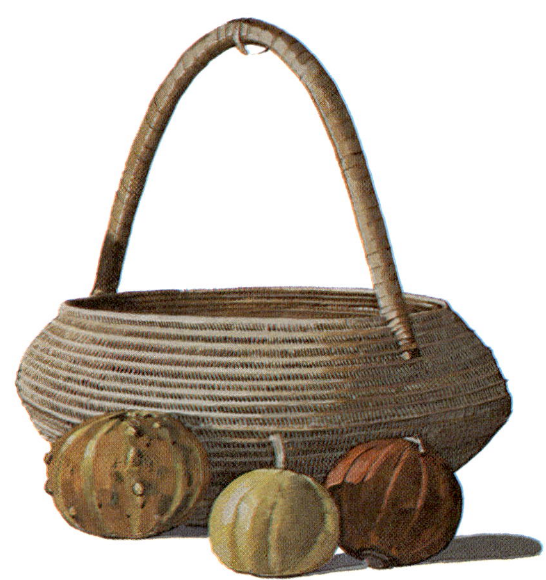

Basket with gourds showing local color

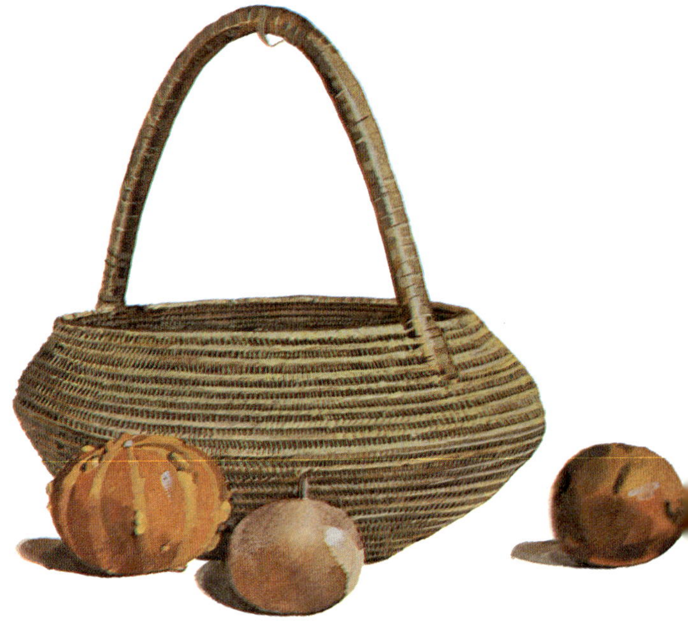

Basket with gourds in low-key lighting

Value

Value refers to the degree of lightness or darkness of a color. Most artists consider value as the most important of the three main factors of color. The visual impression of the darkness or lightness, as well as the warmth or coolness of a color, depends largely on the colors next to it.

The top panel at the right shows the gradation from black to light gray. The three panels below have the same value but are different in hues. Notice how the values of a panel of color ranging from a light to the maximum intensity of that color match the values of the black and gray panel above. The matching of values can be better seen by squinting your eyes and moving quickly from the color panel to the black and gray panel. You see the red and blue panels match the gray/black panel more closely than the yellow panel.

In painting from life or nature, the ability to interpret the hues and values of the subject to the hues and values in your picture is important. Your painting will take on solidity and will progress more quickly after developing this ability.

Mixing Colors

In order to insure a clean color, it is necessary to have one of the two pigments used be in a larger quantity than the other; if two pigments are used in equal amounts, the result will be muddy. The results of the mixture of two pigments, one dominating the other, are shown in the swatches.

A. Many values of gray can be mixed from black and white. Fine grays can also be mixed from colors, but the grays mixed from black and white pigments are considered by many to be the only truly neutral grays.

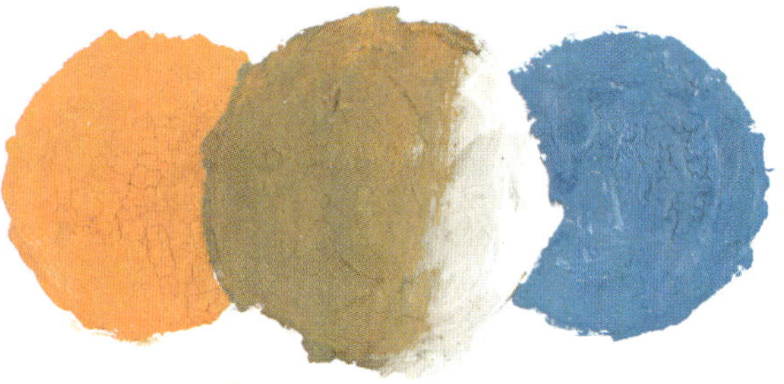

B. Cadmium orange is mixed with cerulean blue with cadmium orange dominating this combination, resulting in a warm ochre.

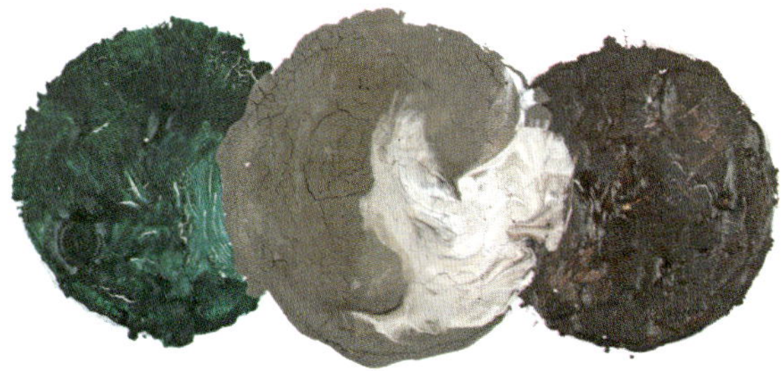

C. This is a combination of viridian green and burnt sienna, both full strength from the tube with white added. The burnt sienna dominates the mix with the result in the center showing a decidedly warm neutral.

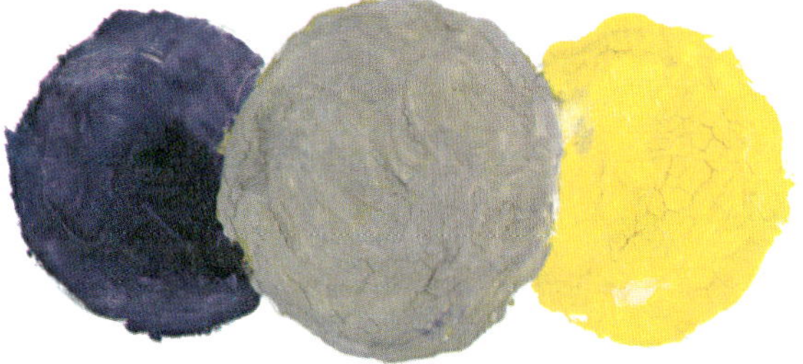

D. Mauve and its complement cadmium yellow pale were selected. A cool purplish gray is the result from this combination.
Try this exercise and discover the great number of colors you can create by the mixture of just two colors.

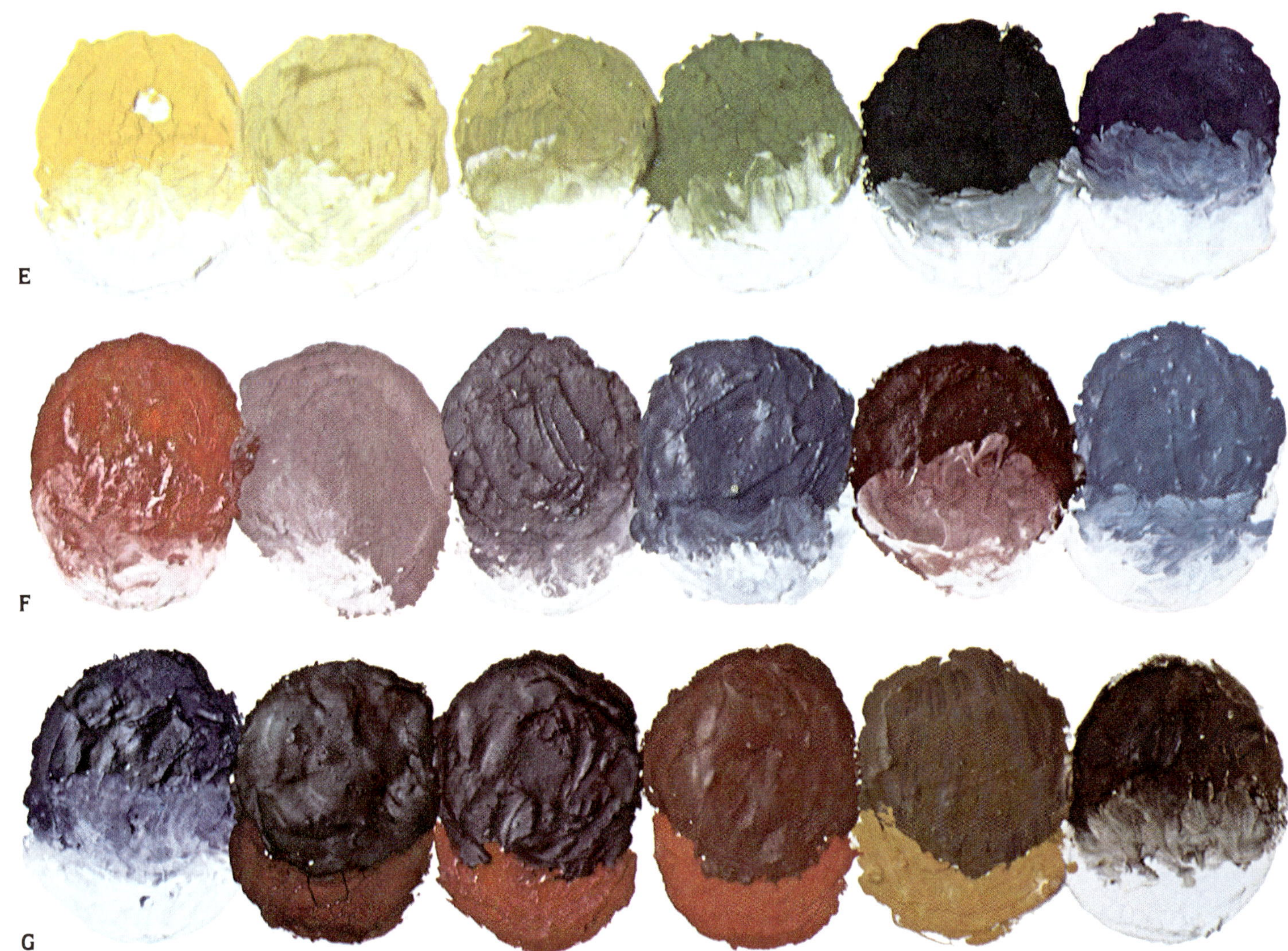

E. By mixing different amounts of two colors together, in this case lemon yellow and ultramarine blue with a bit of white added, we have four different hues and values. The three lighter swatches to the right of the lemon yellow show the lemon yellow predominating. The results are three different shades of a yellow-greenish hue. The swatch of color to the left of the ultramarine blue is a blueish-green, with the blue predominating.

F. Here we see the results of mixing vermilion with cerulean blue. Both of these colors are of full strength with a bit of white added. Notice how the dominance of a color can decidedly influence the mixture. The muted hues between the vermilion and cerulean blue clearly show this influence. The two swatches to the right of the vermilion, with vermilion the dominant color, are of a warm hue though of the purplish family. The next swatch, fourth from the left, though made of the same two colors, with the cerulean blue dominating, shows a decided cool cast. In contrast, the color next to vermilion has a warm brown reddish hue.

G. Violet thalo purple, shown in the first swatch on the left is the basic color for all the swatches in this row, showing various hues that can be obtained from mixing different colors with the same basic hue.

The colors at the bottom of the next four swatches came directly from the tube with no white added. The colors at the top of each of these four swatches are the result of each color mixed with the violet. Alizarin crimson mixed with violet results in a warm dark earth color. Vermilion mixed with violet gives a similar dark earth color, but a slightly warmer hue. Cadmium orange added to the violet produces an intense red-orange similar to Venetian or Indian red. Cadmium yellow mixed with violet brings a decided change of hue, a rich warm hue of the ochre family. In the last swatch, raw sienna added to violet creates a deep warm earth color.

View from window of my home in Wolfville, Nova Scotia.

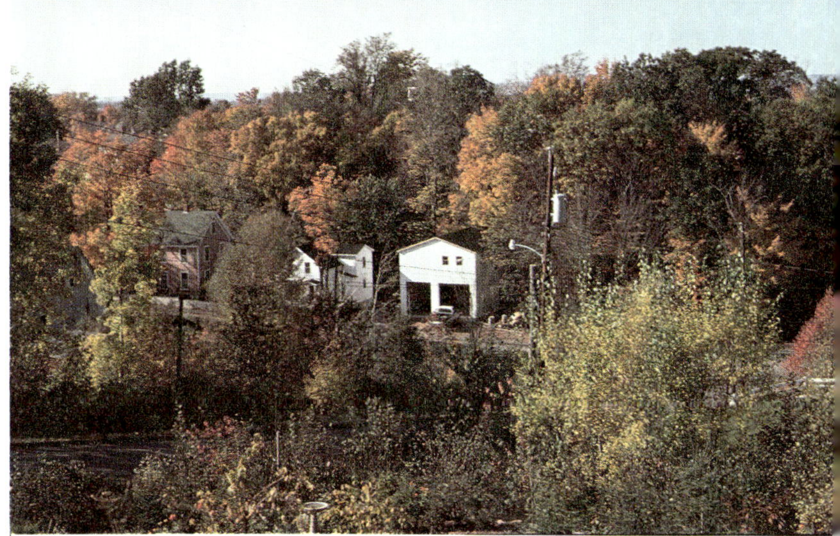

Color in Nature

It is not necessary to travel great distances to find paintable subjects. Subject matter close at hand has inspired painters for centuries. Camille Pissarro comes to mind, looking out from his upper story window onto the busy streets of Paris in the 1880's; or, Paul Cézanne painting his Provencal countryside over and over again; or Constable's masterpieces of Salisbury Cathedral painted from the adjacent marshy fields, as well as from the streets of this historical city.

On a bright October morning I looked out of the living-room window of my hillside home in Nova Scotia at an inspirational and challenging subject —nature in a blazing array of autumn hues. To capture the impact of these brilliant colors of nature on paper, a high-keyed palette would be demanded (cadmium yellows, cadmium orange, cadmium red light—all used at their maximum strength right from the tube).

The color photograph shown at the top of this page is the view I saw. However, photography seldom reproduces the true colors in nature and sometimes tends to flatten heights that in nature appear commanding and impressive.

The small illustrations, painted directly from nature, show more color and value contrasts than appear in the photograph.

1. Greater detail in the shapes and color patterns of the trees is seen in this rendering of a selected area of the same view as the photograph. The form and color of the trees to the left of the pink house are also shown in more detail. The tree form in yellow ochre is emphazised by the tree rendered in burnt orange, while above the roof of the house and to the right is a vivid yellow-green tree which offers a bright cool contrast.

2. This panel is from the center of the view. The tree in front of the white house is painted with a warm yellow ochre greenish combination. Cool hues reflected from the sky call for white, ultramarine blue, and yellow ochre applied with short, squarish strokes to simulate leaf forms. I wanted to capture the impact of the brilliant hues of nature by painting the trees as color shapes, not as a collection of leaves. Strong darks helped to bring the foreground forward, while neutral greens in back of the house receded. The general rule that dark values and warm hues advance while light and cool values and hues recede applies here.

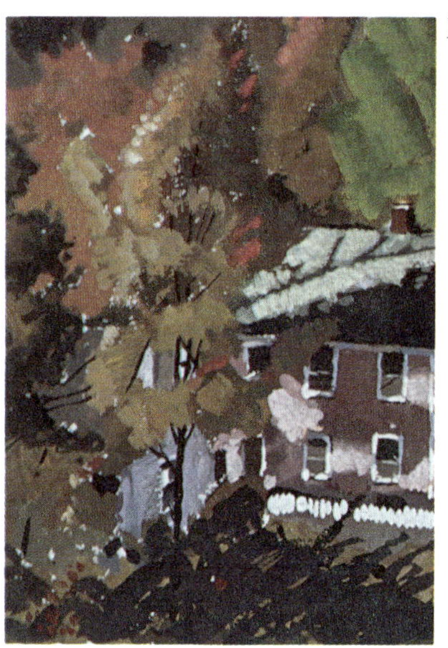

1.

Selected areas from same view.

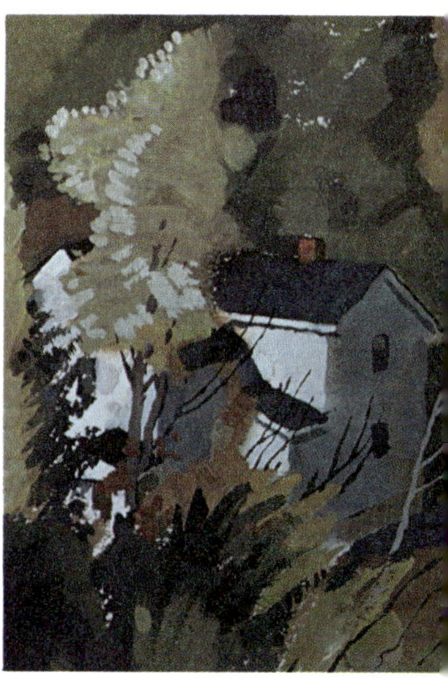

2.

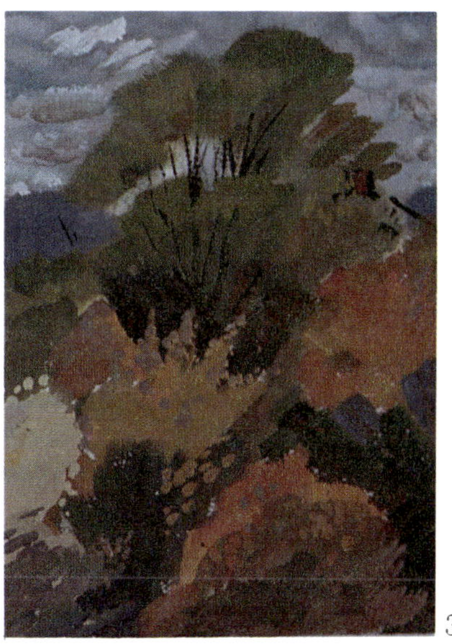

3.

3. This small section of the landscape has a surprising array of colors. The tree forms in their autumnal hues were selected from the upper right of the composition. Below the cloud forms a variety of hues are again evident in the tree foliage, painted in mass with a high-keyed palette.

For this composition, the buildings and trees of varied shapes and contours were sketched in with a 4B charcoal pencil, starting from the horizon, working back to front and downward to the house that appears in the middle distance.

Following the loosely indicated and quickly rendered charcoal sketch, the entire surface of the paper was dampened and, selecting the largest brushes, the painting began. Beginning with the vast expanse of sky, which at that time was clear of clouds, a mixture of ultramarine blue, cerulean blue, and yellow ochre was swept across the paper. This blueish hue was lightened as it approached the horizon line; the long sweeps of the brush moving quickly across the paper from left to right. At times I held the paper upside down to insure that the darkest value of this blue remained at the top of the paper.

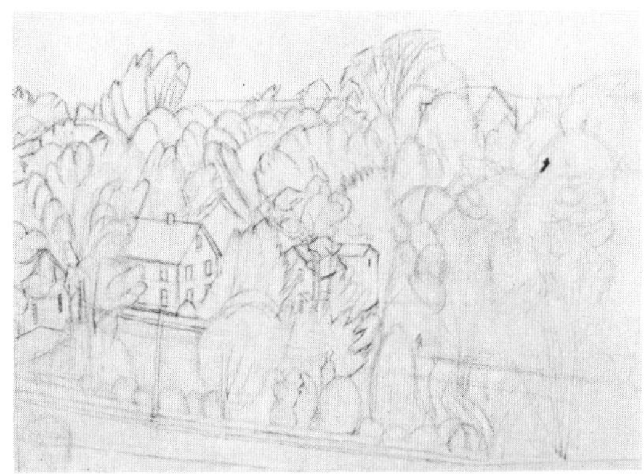

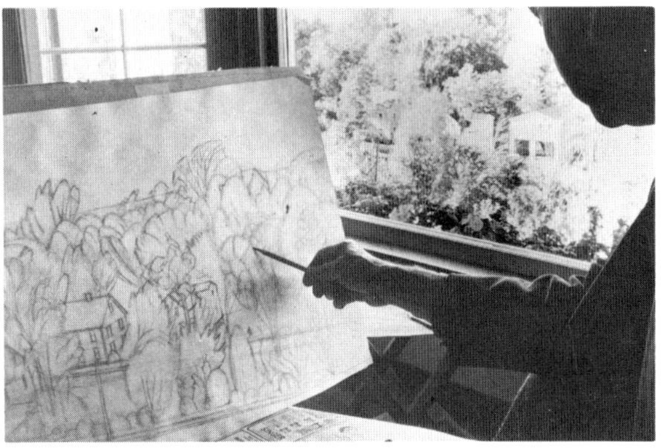

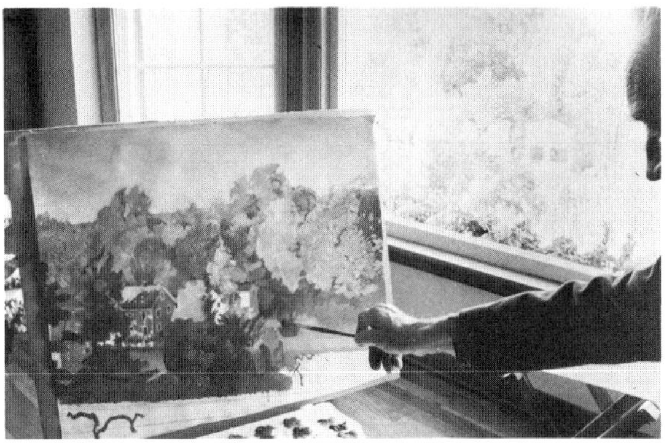

Again starting at the horizon line, the tree shapes were added, using mainly hues of high-key yellows and greens (lemon yellow, cadmium yellow, cadmium orange, viridian green and Winsor emerald green). Contrasting cool colors (ultramarine blue and thalo violet) were added to the various greens to form the cool shadow areas. Payne's gray and ivory black were included in the palette, but little was used. Although a small amount of white was mixed with some of the colors for the trees, most of the hues were taken at maximum intensity directly from the tube.

Working for a vibrant effect, many colors were applied without mixing, while others were loosely mixed directly on the paper. The opaque pigment was painted quite heavily with little suggestion of the transparent wet-in-wet technique.

The sunny area of the green roof of the pink house with the picket fence in the middle distance was rendered with a mixture of Winsor emerald green with cadmium yellow and white; the shadow area of the roof was painted with viridian green, Payne's gray, and burnt umber; the shadows on the pink house called for alizarin crimson, yellow ochre, and white; the sunny light spots on the house were mainly white with a touch of vermilion. In order to keep the tree shapes from blending into a flat mass, a soft irregular outline of blueish green was brushed in to partially separate the tree shapes. This cool hue also offered some contrast from the warm hillside colors.

4. The center area of the composition is shown here. Against the white pigment of the house, the muted dark tones (burnt umber, Hooker's green, raw sienna, ultramarine blue) of the surrounding trees advance, so that the foreground area now seems quite close. This points up the center of interest, the white house, which is further emphasized by the dark hues around it.

5. Looking at a section of the hillside on the center right of the composition, a variety of hues and shapes is again seen. The color range of this panel goes from an intense yellow-green on the right through a cadmium yellow and cadmium orange to a muted green on the left side of the panel.

First the general shape and hue of the trees were painted in mass; then the shadow side, using contrasting warm and cool colors and values. To suggest the leafy character, a more intense and lighter value of the warm side of the tree foliage was mixed right on the paper, then painted with short strokes into the light side, following the tree shapes, generally applying heavy pigment.

Panels 6 and 7 were painted a few days after the completion of the painting, showing the sharply advanced autumn colors, the hues quite radically changed, the intensity increased to the peak. The slender tree in front of the white house has changed from a yellow ochre to a bright cadmium red light with cadmium orange highlights direct from the tube. This display of color is highlighted by the background tone of muted greens and burnt umber.

Panel 7 is taken from the horizon right-hand area of the painting, again showing the change of hues in the advancement of autumn a few days later. In comparing these hues of the same trees with the completed painting, the increase of intensity of color is again apparent. The completed painting shows these trees as having a warm green color, while the same trees in this panel have assumed a brilliant cadmium orange with areas of vermilion and burnt sienna. The sky and clouds have also changed. As they approach the horizon they become a solid mass, and the violet color deepened. These changes are a challenge to the painter for he must keep up with and adapt to the rapid changes of nature.

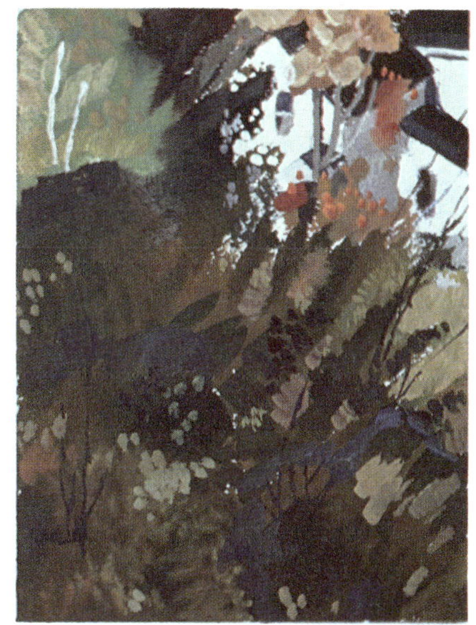

4.

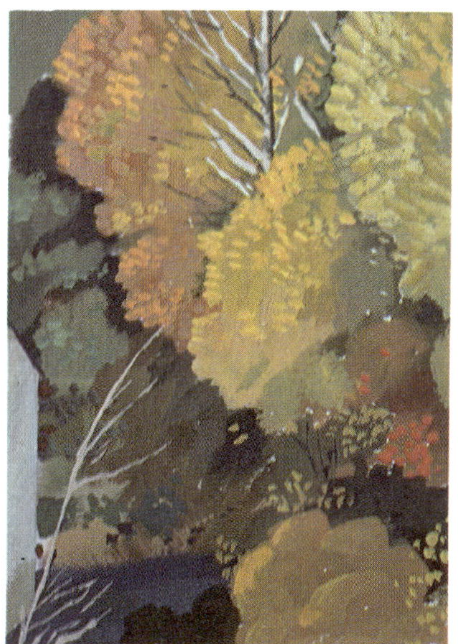

5.

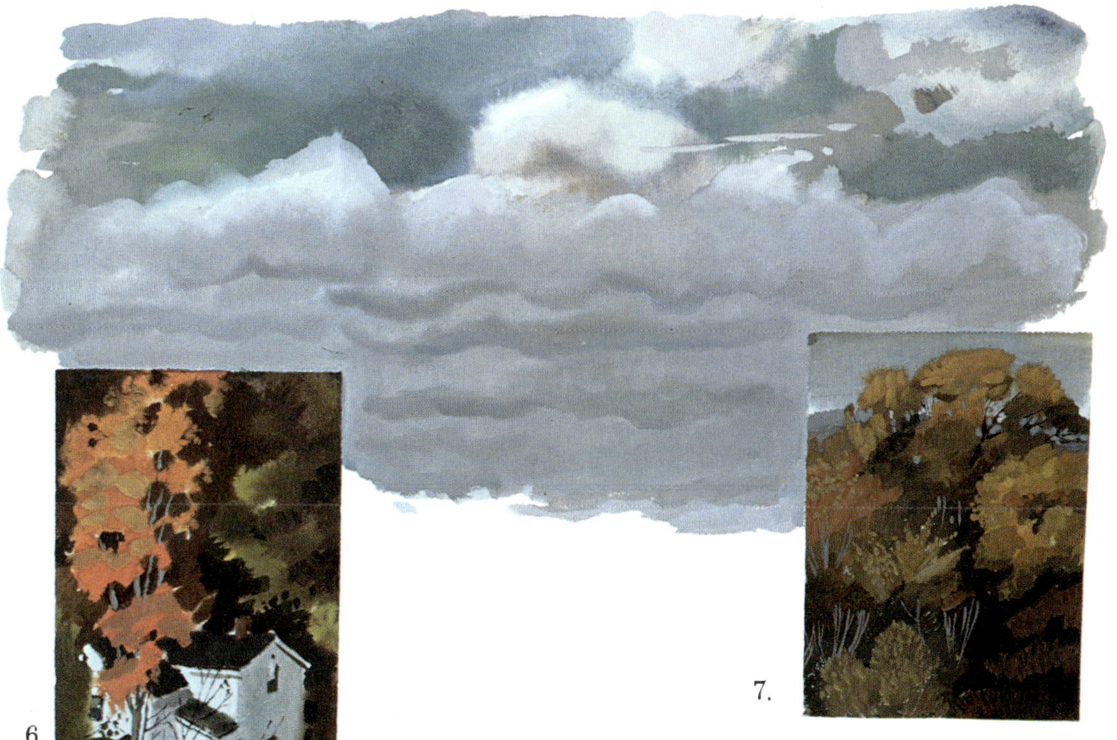

6.

7.

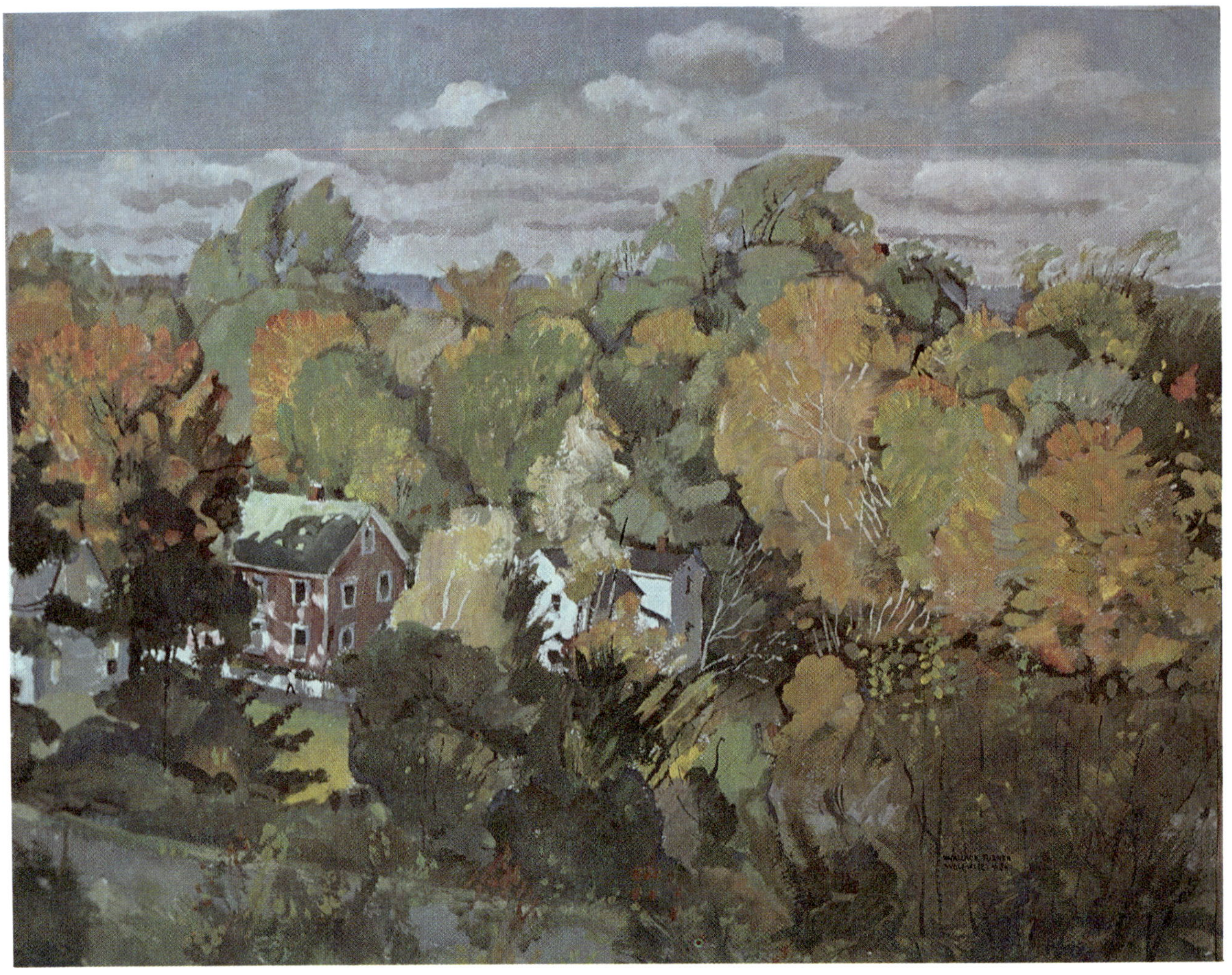

PAINTING FROM MY WINDOW Wolfville, Nova Scotia 18 x 23½ inches

The morning I completed this painting, the sky had changed drastically—and for the better. Instead of the previous flat expanse, floating clouds filled the sky, stretching across the full length of the horizon. Here the advantage of painting in opaque came to the fore. I could paint in the clouds. Starting with the horizon and working upwards, I brushed on a thin tone of ultramarine blue, yellow ochre, thalo violet, and white, using a large round brush. The upper layer of clouds were more definite in shape, showing greater value contrast. As they approached the horizon, the clouds tended to merge into a cool gray. The underneath shadow side of these clouds called for Payne's gray, thalo violet, and white.

Leaving the sky and now concentrating on the tangled and confused mass in the foreground, a variety of greens were used to relieve this relatively uninteresting area. To the greens (viridian, Hooker's green, olive and permanent green) warmer colors, yellow ochre, burnt sienna and burnt umber were added.

If not finished in one sitting, it is important to paint on a subject under the same light conditions on another day. This is especially important in landscape painting when light conditions change so rapidly, demanding that you paint rapidly as well. The sun's rays are more colorful in the morning or late afternoon and the least colorful at and near noon. So, as in photography, avoid the midday hours for richer colors.

CHAPTER 3

Applying Paint and Techniques

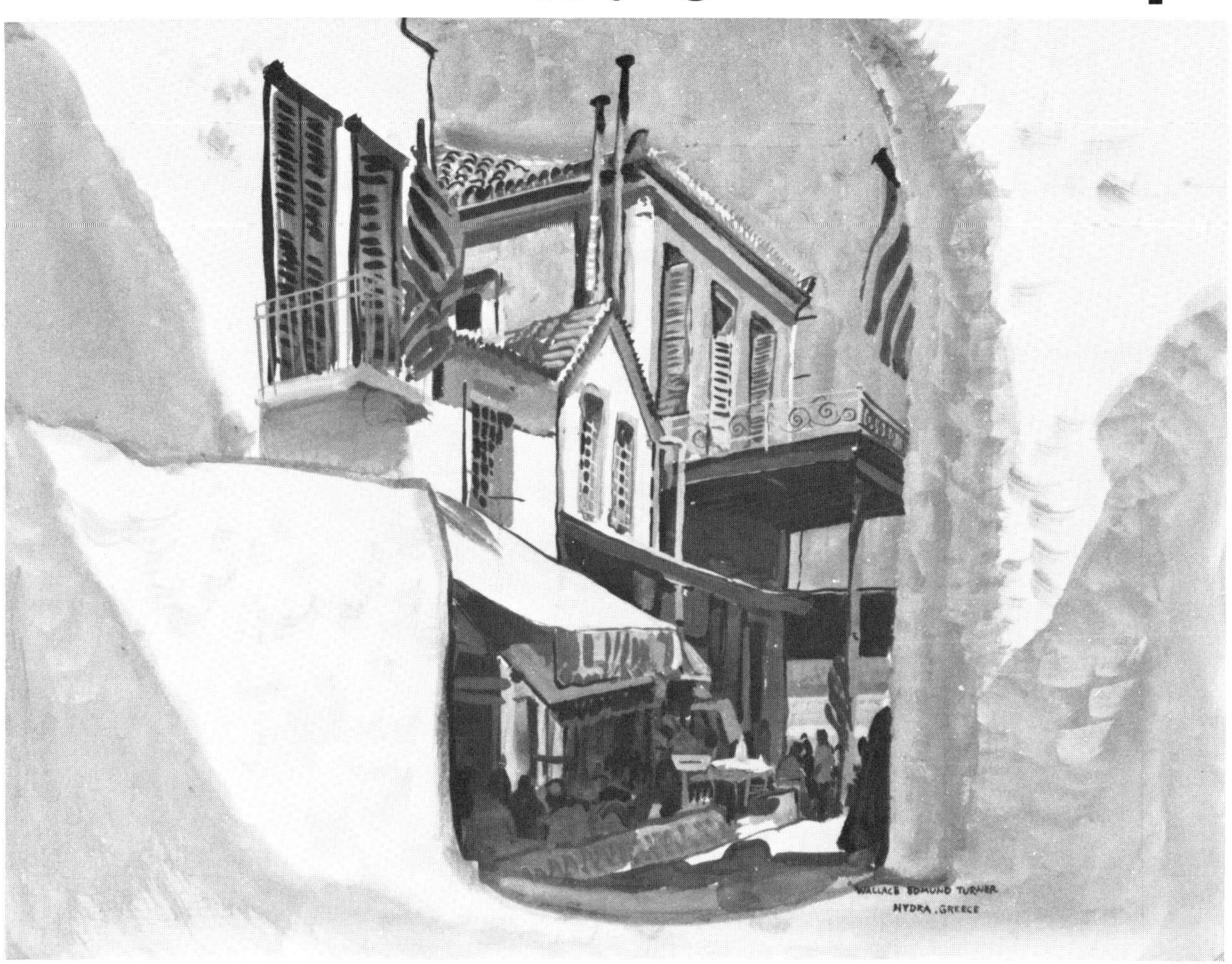

TAVERNA (Restaurant), HYDRA, GREECE
15 x 20 inches
The stone buildings of the Greek islands, covered with white-washed stucco, offer an example of the intense light so common in this area. The white paper serves as the highest light forming the walls, awnings, and buildings. These focus the attention on an enclosed area. The texture of the walls was suggested by using a flat spread brush directly on the white surface.

Although you may wish to diagnose and to try the techniques of others, you should always aim toward developing your own, ones that best suit and satisfy your ideas and your feelings. Experiment with brush strokes; use different sizes and shapes of brushes and different weights and textures of paper and other surfaces. Try the dry brush technique on dry paper. You do that by almost exhausting the supply of paint on your brush then barely skimming the surface of the paper with your strokes. Use different amounts of water in the wet-in-wet technique. This is where you first wet the paper with clear water. Then when you apply thin paint it spreads out and becomes soft at the edges. "Accidents" (unplanned effects) often bring exciting and successful results.

Learn to control your tools. Make them do what you want them to do. Try different ways of holding your brush, both for comfort and for the different effects a varying grip will produce.

In general, hold your hand so that it does not come in contact with the surface on which you are painting to avoid soiling it or smudging your paint. I find it helpful to use my little finger as a prop, being certain the surface beneath it is dry. Some artists use a homemade "bridge," which is a slat of wood with a small block fixed to both ends. You merely rest your fist on it while you work.

Your experimenting should be tried before attempting a finished painting or while painting the same subject in different ways. The manner or style you work in is up to you—abstract, semi-abstract or realistic. You may wish to give only an impression, a suggestion of your subject leaving something to the viewer's imagination and leaving exactness to the camera. Or you may wish to paint in minute detail.

Experiment with thin and heavy washes as many opaque watercolor paintings are a combination of the two. This gives contrast to the separate qualities of transparency and opacity. It will also allow you to discover opaque's ability to cover, and to allow you to make changes.

When you wish to capture a moving object such as cloud patterns, a thin wash of opaque color will grasp the subject quicker and more forcibly than the use of heavily pigmented opaque. Where light strikes clouds, a heavier pigment can be used.

There is a school of opaque painting that uses heavy pigment exclusively with very little blending of edges. The modeling of a form is done by individual brush strokes of variable colors and values. This type of painting can be found in poster art.

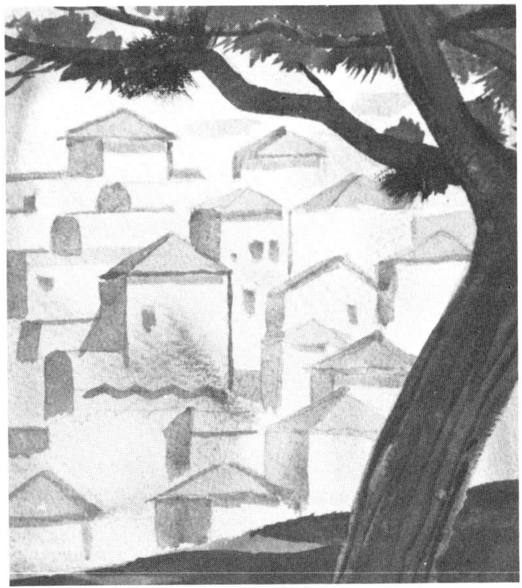

Rather than comment further on techniques abstractly, I prefer to refer you to my step-by-step explanations in developing the paintings shown throughout the book.

Again I urge you to learn to see, to feel, to relax, and enjoy what you are doing and have the courage to experiment.

Techniques are secondary to creativity. Therefore, do not let concern for or mastery of techniques take over and restrain your impulse to create. No one can say what you do or the way you do it is wrong if it is satisfying to you and if it fills a need. Your technique and your evaluation will develop and change as you paint more and more. The important thing is to paint at every opportunity you have.

A Repertoire of Techniques

A technique is usually established as a result of an accumulation of assembled methods that have proven their worth as a result of practice and usage. Opaque watercolor is a versatile medium that can be used in many ways from a wet-in-wet transparent watercolor technique to a heavy impasto, similar in some ways to oil painting. When you use lots of water with opaques, the white surface of the paper comes through the color, giving highlight areas. With the impasto or heavy pigment method, the value of the pigment itself must give the highest light. The white paper surface ceases to be a factor.

There are also intermediate stages where opaque white may be used in some areas. However, I have found that when pigment is applied extensively to one area, it makes for a more consistent painting if everything is done opaquely.

A. **Wet-in-wet technique with line.** A wet-in-wet technique with line is used here to depict a group of buildings on a hillside on the island of Hydra in Greece. These stone buildings were mostly white, but there were some pastel shades, too. The building area was wet first, then cool colors were flowed into the wet surface. A gray tone was then used with a pointed brush to add a line to accentuate the form of the buildings. A few shadow sides were then painted in. The tree was added in the foreground to give depth to the painting.

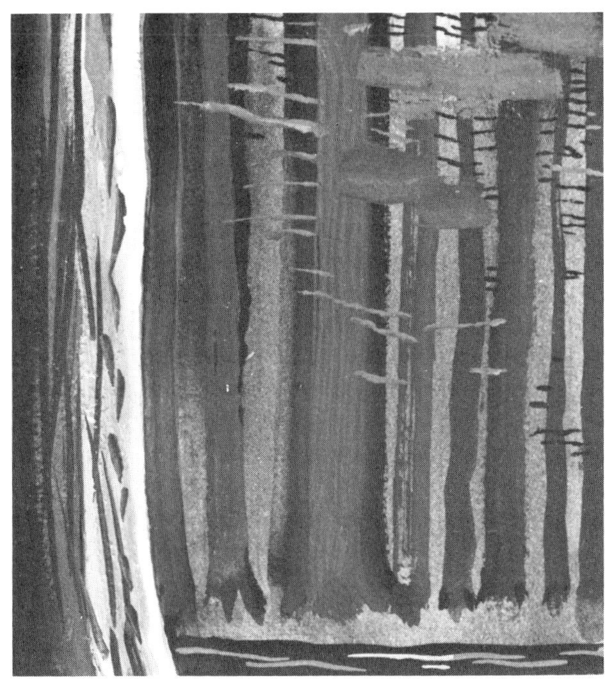

B. **Wet-in-wet with opaque: vertical forms.** The painting of a forest bordering the Merced River in the valley of Yosemite National Park in California was done by combining wet-in-wet with some solid pigment application. The forest across the river was mainly in shadow. The whole paper was wet first, then, using a flat brush, the straight tree trunks were struck into the medium cool wash. A variety of related colors were used for these trunks—blues, blue-violets, and burnt umber. To suggest a root system at the base of the tree trunks, pressure was applied to the brush, spreading it at the base. Following the broad handling of the trees, a pointed brush, charged with a dark tone, was used in painting some branches which ran horizontally from the vertical trunks. With these dark branches a light tone was mixed and was used to paint contrasting branches. A few flat horizontal strokes from a brush loaded with a heavy neutral green were finally applied to depict foliage. For contrast, a tree trunk in sunlight was added, painted mainly in warm colors and using heavy opaque pigment for the highlights.

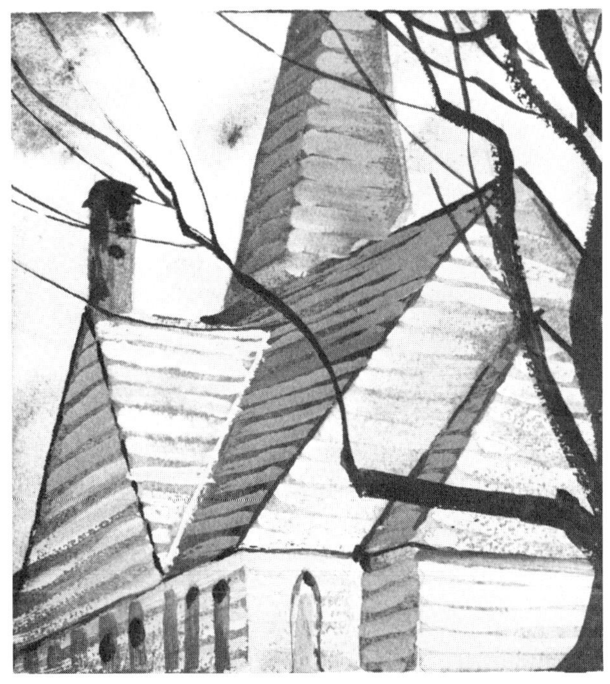

C. **Wet-in-wet combined with horizontal opaque strokes.** This old church in Pound Ridge, New York was painted with a combination of wet-in-wet transparent watercolor for the sky, while the building was painted in heavy opaque pigment. The clapboard siding of the building and the horizontal character of the roof suggested using a flat brush and heavy opaque. Related colors were mixed and, using a flat brush, horizontal strokes were painted in following the form of the building. This flat horizontal stroke treatment goes a long way to explain the complex form comprising the old church. Finally, mixing a dark value and using a dry brush treatment, a tree with branches was painted in the right foreground.

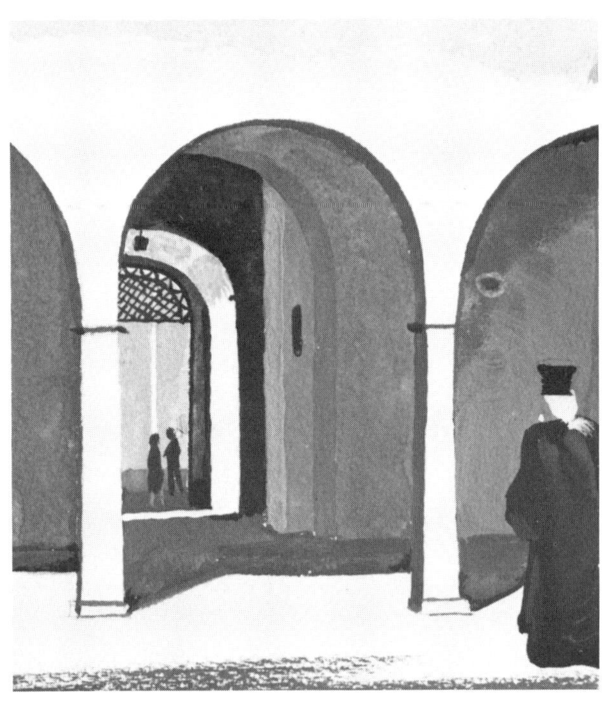

D. **Maximum use of light by using white paper with opaque.** In painting the inside courtyard of a church in Hydra, Greece, the white surface of the paper was left intact for the arches and stone floor. The walls inside the arches were painted with heavy opaque, as was the Greek priest in the foreground. This combination of white paper and heavy opaque color offers a textural contrast to the painting and helps interpret the blazing white light of the Greek islands.

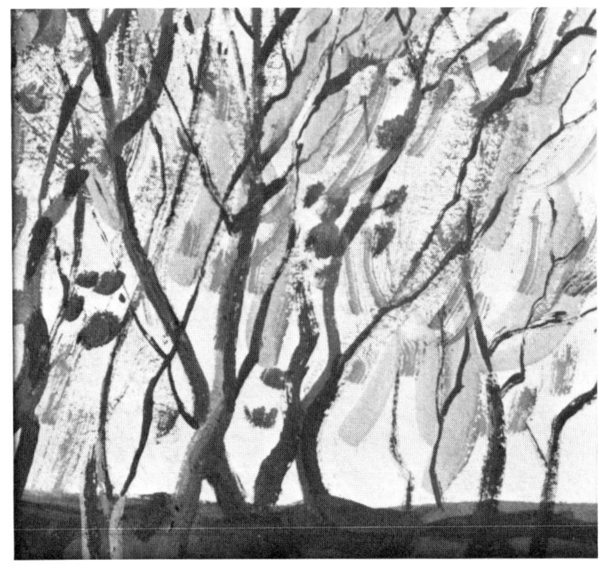

E. **Flat brush bearing two colors or more for one stroke.** In painting the branches of a tree, it is advisable to get the general effect rather than attempt a labored painting of every branch. To show this branch effect, a neutral gray-blue opaque tone was applied. Following this application, two mounds of gray pigment were mixed on the palette, one hue being warm, the other cool. Then by picking up some of the warm gray on one half of a flat brush, and with the other half picking up the cool gray, strokes were painted over the neutral background color following generally the direction of the branches. Thus a mixed tone was achieved by using one brush loaded with two colors. This formed a lively background for the detailed branches. This loose mixture will add variety and life to practically any subject, whether it be landscape, still life or figures, but it does require practice.

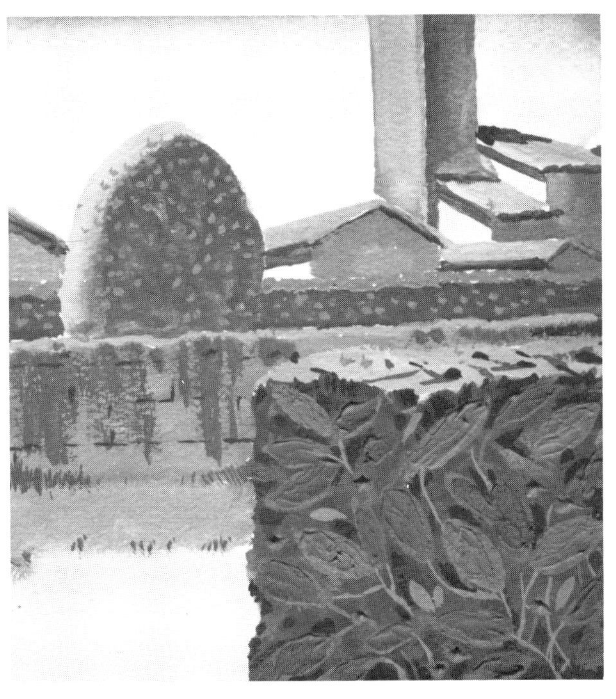

F. **Wet-in-wet with heavy opaque applied with palette knife.** Here we are searching for textural contrast as well as form in this painting of a hedge, walls, and medieval towers in Fiesole outside Florence, Italy. The ever-blue Italian sky was painted wet-in-wet; the buildings, background, hedge and walls were painted with medium opaque pigment. In contrast to this, the foreground leaves were painted with very heavy pigment applied with a palette knife, thus assuring textural contrast and giving a suggestion of another dimension.

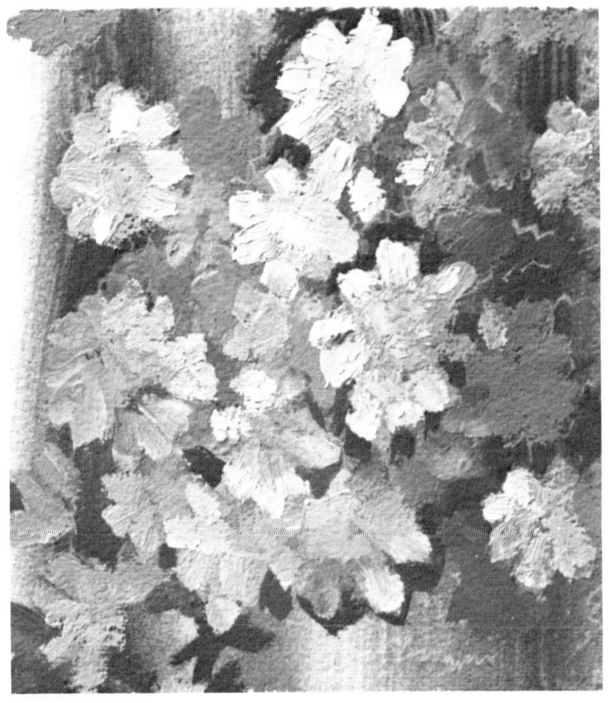

G. **Using rosette forms and heavy opaque.** To show clumps of foliage without carefully painting each leaf, various values and colors of related color were mixed on the palette, using heavy opaque pigment. These hues are loosely mixed and, with a flat brush, were applied heavily, approximating the structure of the foliage. Variety in values gives prominence to some clusters of leaves while others remain in the background.

Description of Basic Techniques in the Use of Opaque Watercolor

Flat Wash

To paint this example of a flat wash in opaque watercolor, the borders were protected by a strip of masking tape. The rectangle was then wet with clear water. Using a large brush, Arbee #12, the color was quickly flowed in. Without going over it, it was allowed to dry.

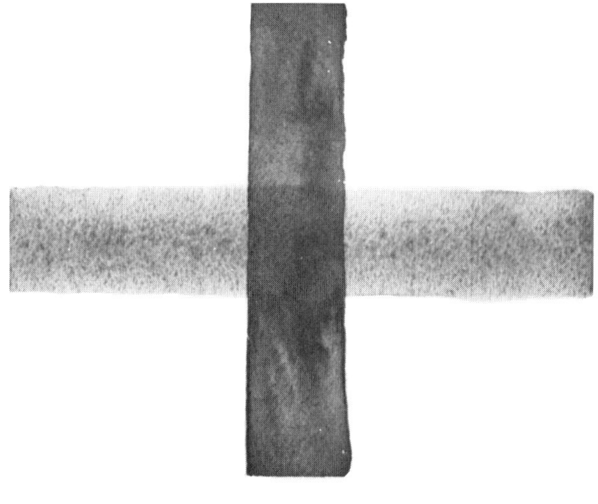

One Flat Wash Over Another

The first color was laid in a vertical stroke. When completely dry, a stroke of another color and value was run horizontally across the vertical stroke. Where the two strokes intersected a third color is dimly seen as though through a haze. This is referred to as "glazing."

Graded Wash

Starting with a thoroughly wet surface a light value of color was rapidly applied. Using a large brush, the movement was from left to right. The value of the opaque used was deepened while moving toward the bottom of the panel. The paper was kept at an angle to insure that the darkest value be maintained at the bottom. Never go back over it.

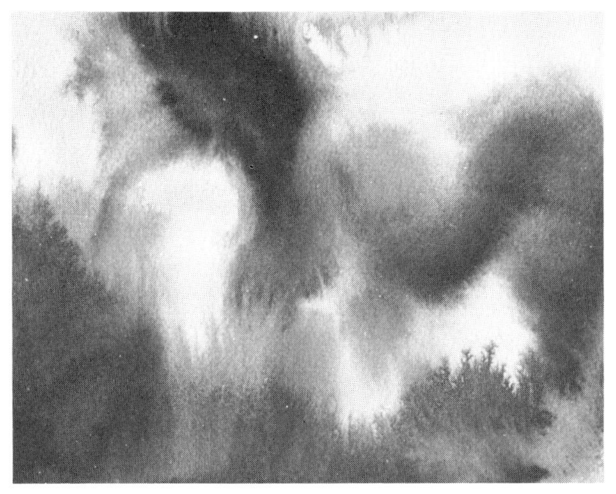

Irregular Wash

Many stunning effects can be made by dropping color into a previously well-wetted panel. The color is allowed to drop onto the wet surface, falling where it may. If you tip the board new shapes, soft edges, and dramatic movements of color will occur. An irregular wash such as this shows the value of happy accidents. I find this technique unsurpassed for striking cloud formations, old walls, and reflections on water. The effects of true wet-in-wet technique are difficult to attain by conventional painting.

Flat Granulated Color

Some colors carry more sediment than others, and when the wash is dry they create a texture. Viridian green, burnt sienna, cerulean blue, ultramarine blue, yellow ochre, and raw sienna are some of the colors that have a heavy sediment and produce a granular effect.

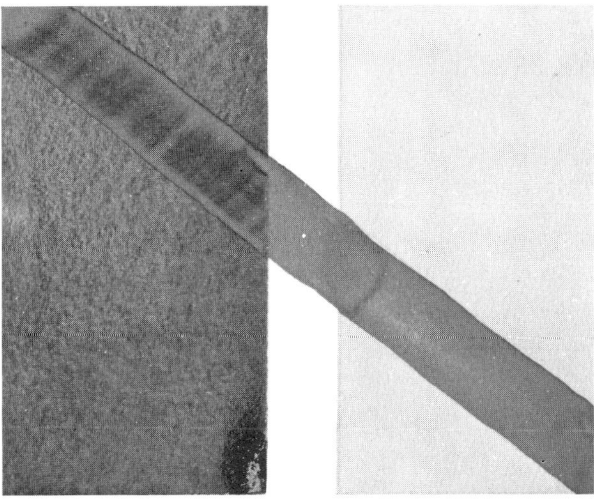

Superimposed Color

Here the covering power of colors is shown. A strip of cadmium red was painted over a panel of viridian green and a panel of yellow ochre. It can be seen that the green bled through the red, but over the yellow ochre the red covered well. Experiment to discover for yourself those colors that cover well and those that don't.

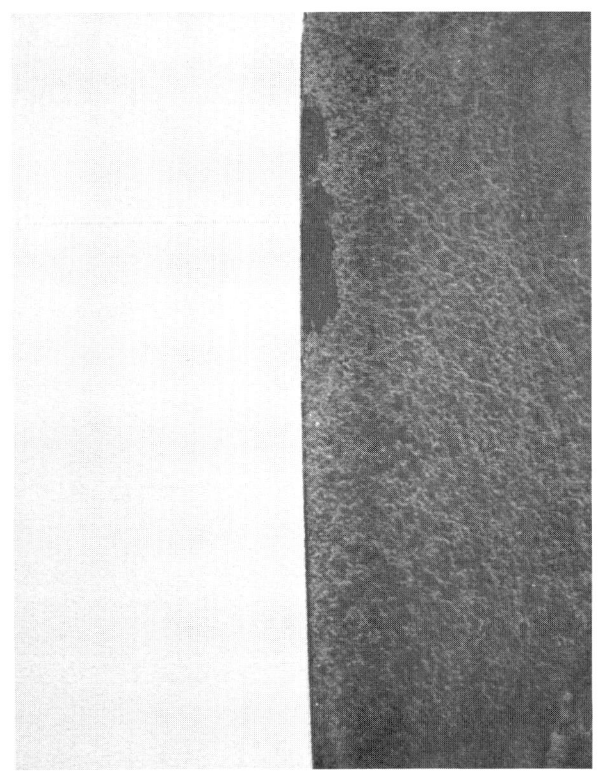

Side-By-Side Flat Colors

The color on the left was floated into a wet surface and allowed to dry before the second was applied. I was careful not to pull in the color from the first wash.

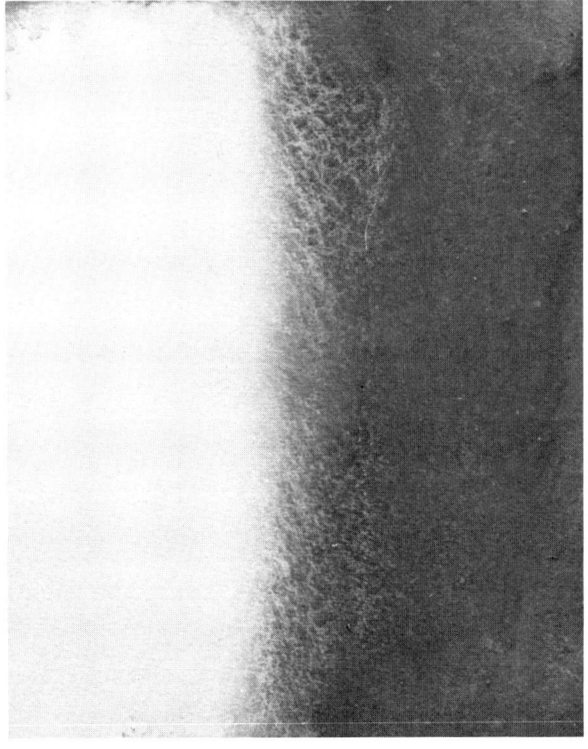

Blended Colors

The two colors were fused while both were wet. One panel was laid in with the next panel painted directly next to it so that the colors blend. One must work quickly and NEVER GO BACK over. The wetness of the paper must be observed closely as success here depends on the relative wetness or dryness of the paper. In all experiments it is essential that BRUSHES BE KEPT CLEAN.

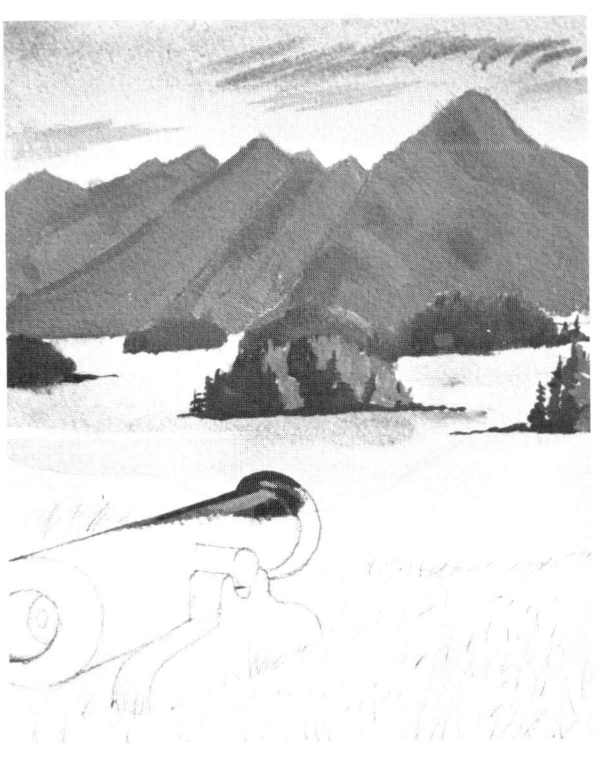

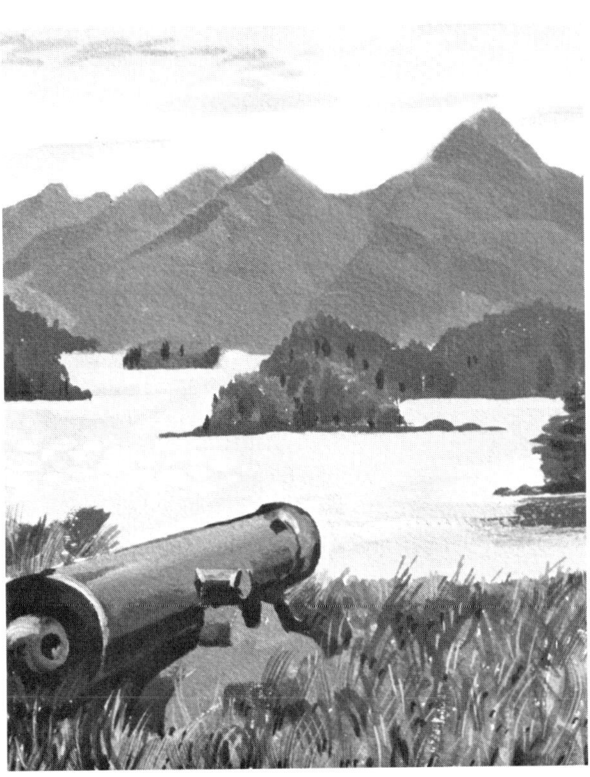

Working Back to Front

Working "back to front" pertains primarily to landscape painting. It means to paint first the areas that are farthest away, such as the horizon or objects that comprise the background. This method is helpful because the value contrast is greater in the foreground than in the background. It is therefore easier to judge the background values. Also, the darks in the foreground are usually much darker than background values and are more difficult to pin-point. Less boldness is required in striking the background values than the dark contrasting values of the foreground.

In the accompanying sketch, painted at Sitka Harbor, Alaska, I started with the sky value followed by the range of mountains across the water. The contrast between value was increased step-by-step in painting the islands "back to front." The greatest value contrast is in the cannon in the foreground.

Dry Brush Techniques

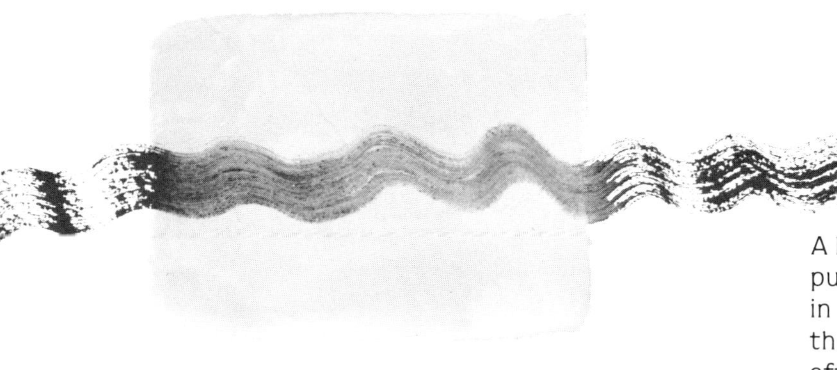

A large flat brush, Delta #7, loaded with color was pulled across a damp area into dry paper. The paint in the dampened area immediately spread out to the width of the brush or beyond, giving a linear effect with a great deal of sparkle.

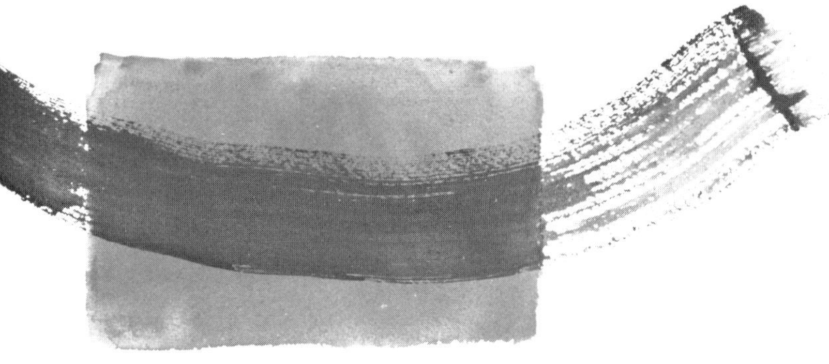

Here a similar dry brush technique is shown using a Gainsborough Flat #14.

Sweeps are made with the same brush on a dry surface, turning the brush on its edge as it is pulled through the stroke.

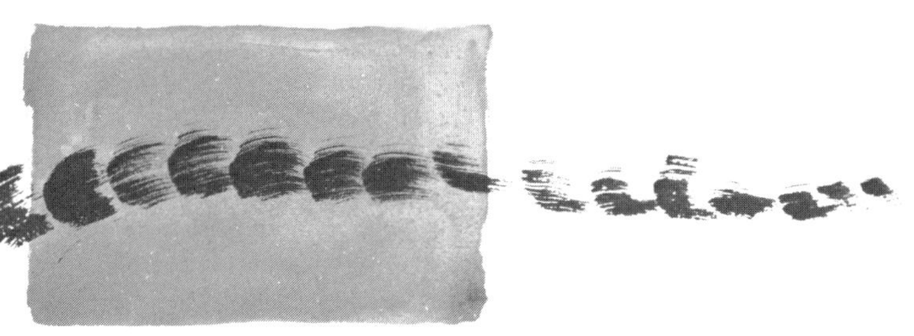

On a dry surface the bristles of a round Arbee #12 brush were spread slightly. Using a touching then lifting type of stroke, the brush was carried across the paper, giving the effect of representing the tracks of an animal.

WET-IN-WET

After the entire picture area was dampened with a sponge, the mountain shape was painted into the wet sky. A brush loaded with opaque white with a touch of yellow ochre was floated in to form cloud effects against the mountain. By tipping the paper, the rundown of the pigment emphasized the mistiness of the scene.

Simple value patterns are shown here. Wet-in-wet allows the pigments to diffuse. You must work rapidly to attain the desired soft and the lost and found edges.

White mixed with a bit of ultramarine blue was painted at the base of the mountain to suggest the water, bringing us to the foreground; a "back to front" technique. See completed painting on page 47.

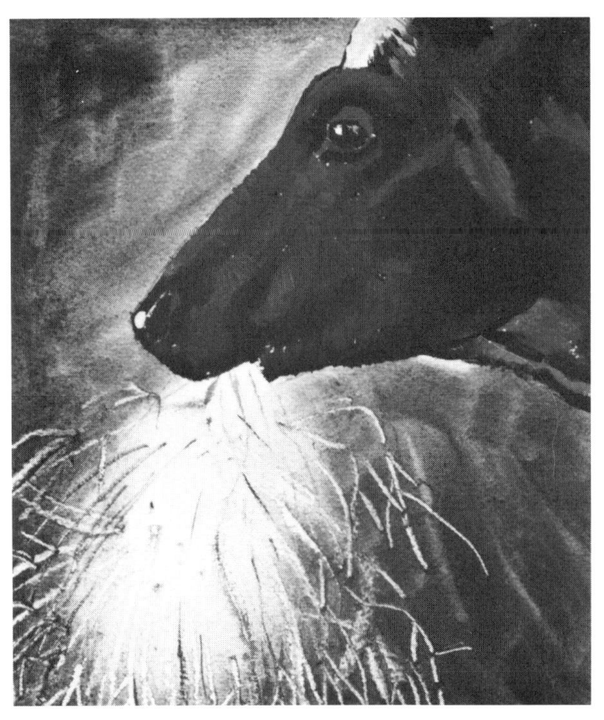

Scraping

In watercolor painting, whether working in transparent or opaque, it is easier to scrape out a thin line from a damp surface than to attempt to paint around it. Scraping is effective in depicting thin branches, grass, straw, ships' riggings—practically any situation where a thin line or edge is desired. Many a glittering star has been nicked out of a dark sky by the edge of a razor blade or a knife point. For demonstrating this technique, I chose for my subject Lady Wellington, a fine Holstein cow on the Conrad dairy farm.

For the large mass of fodder, clear water was shaken from a large brush used to blot out much of the pigment which had been applied, leaving a large soft-edged yellowish blot. To give the effect of the light-colored wisps of hay, a Paasche swivel knife was used to scrape through the dark pigments of the background. This scraping technique can also be used on a dry surface, but the line you get will be more ragged.

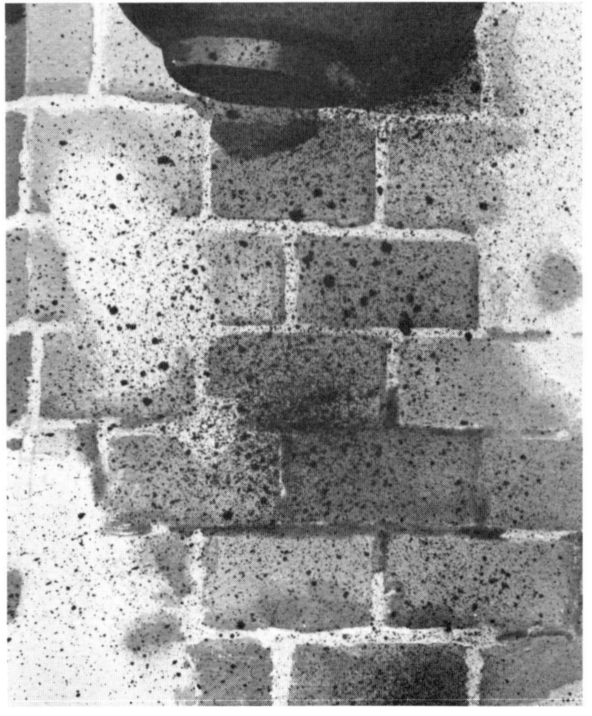

Spatter

Spatter, the technique achieved by the use of a pigment-loaded toothbrush and knife blade, is a substitute for an airbrush. The results shown by the toothbrush-knife blade technique have much more character than the work of its mechanical counterpart, the airbrush. The size and shape of the dots can be varied by merely using more or less pressure on the knife blade.

A razor blade will also do, but a knife is my favorite. For large spatter spots, the knife blade is pressed deeper into the toothbrush and, for a blurry effect, spray is directed onto a surface that is quite wet. Spatter is an excellent technique to convey a feeling of antiquity to old walls, stone, brickwork, old wood, sea spray, sleet and rust.

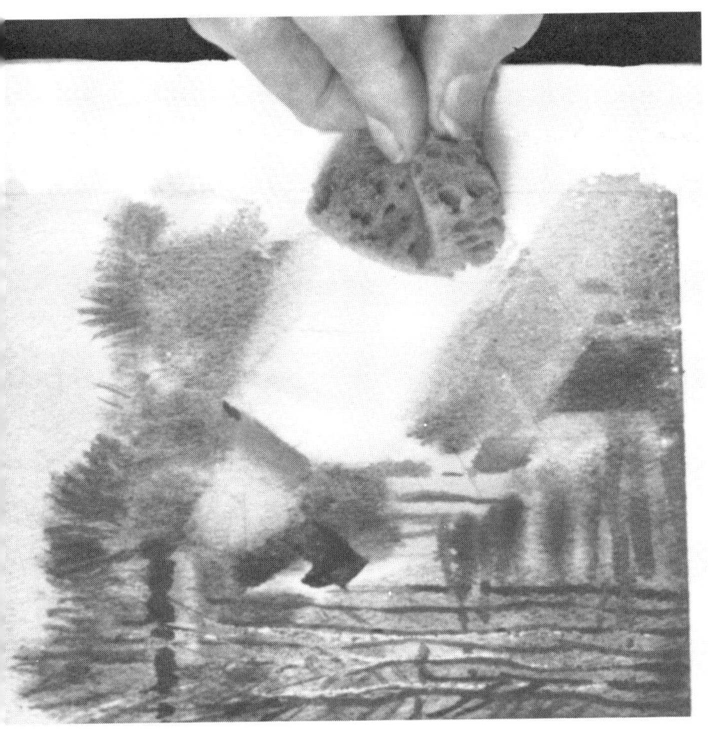

Wiping Out

"Wiping out" is a method of regaining the almost white of the paper. It is most successful when the surface of the paper is still wet. With clean water on a big brush squeezed dry, boldly run the brush through the area you wish to lighten. For best results, this may have to be repeated. This technique is desirable where soft edges are wanted.

Sponges, tissue, or a soft cloth also serve.

Wiping out areas is effective in working with cloud masses, reflections on water, and in rendering hair in a portrait. It's a way of producing natural looking highlights.

A word of caution in using this technique. You must lift out or blot out with care as excessive scrubbing will ruin the surface of the paper and the freshness of your painting will be lost.

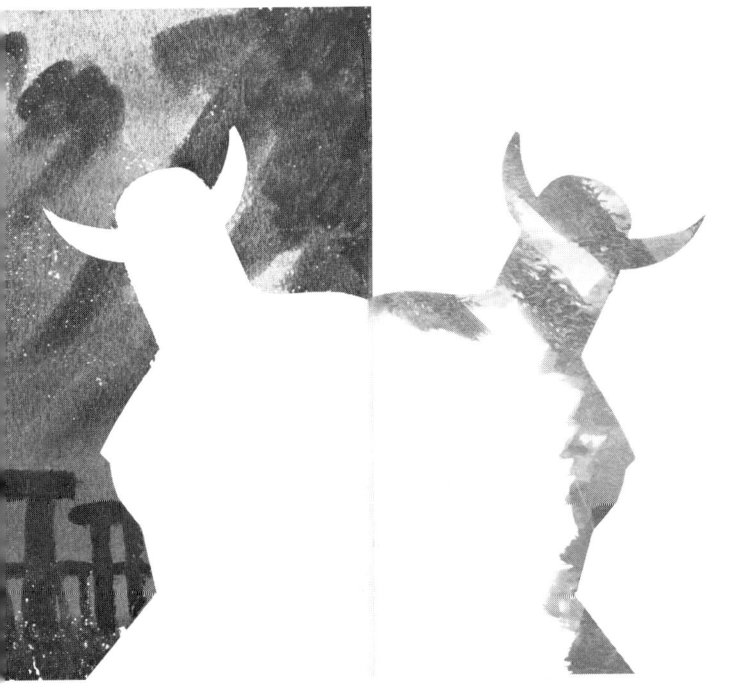

Masking

By masking you protect the white surface of your paper to preserve it for future development. Frisket paper which is a thin transparent material with adhesive on one side is commonly used. Here I made my own frisket. On a sheet of transparent layout tissue I laid a thin coat of rubber cement. Another thin coat of rubber cement was applied to the surface of the drawing. After both surfaces had dried completely, the tissue was laid on the drawing. Then, using a sharp swivel knife, I cut the outline of the figure through the tissue, leaving the drawing of the horned figure completely covered and shielded.

Washes can now be laid over the entire area of the painting. When these washes are dry, just remove the paper, rub away the rubber cement, and the white surface is there, ready for further development.

Cropping

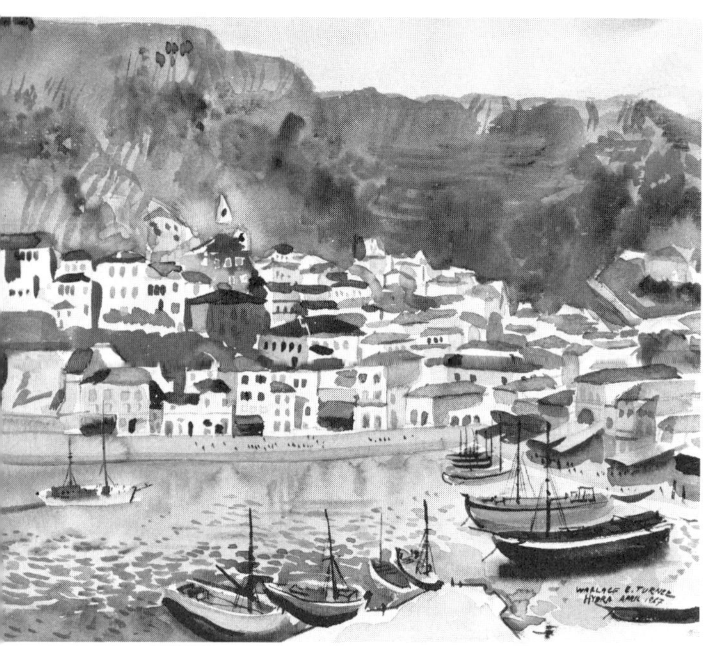

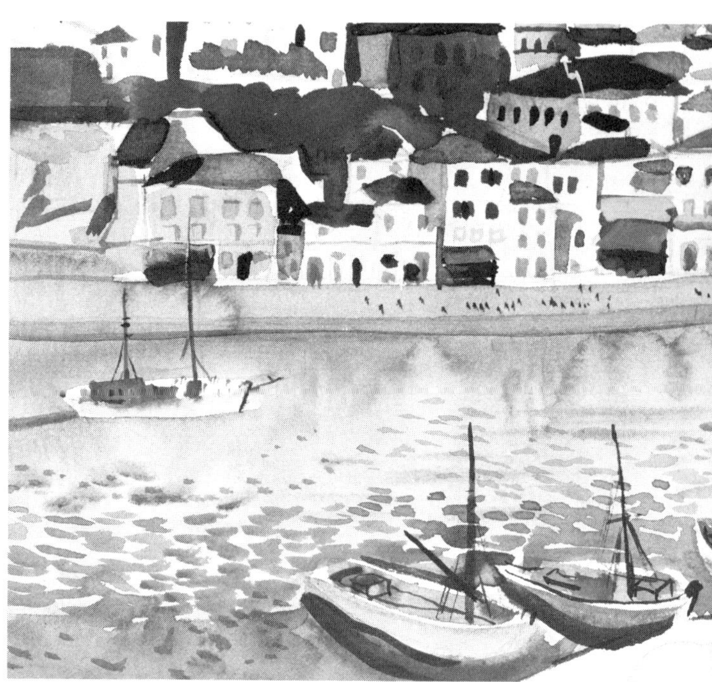

HYDRA HARBOR, GREECE

15 x 20 inches

Evidently I was dazzled by the Greek sunlight and intense color of the harbor front when I sketched this scene. I overlooked the fact a picture should have a center of interest. After completing the painting and evaluating it, I decided to lay it aside for future consideration. A year later I still liked the foreground. Could I do anything to salvage at least a part of the painting? I thought of how photographers "crop" their negatives, so I placed wide strips of paper around areas of the painting until I found a better composition. With its widely scattered interest from buildings to shipping, I found that judicious cropping could concentrate the viewer's interest and bring some order out of confusion.

Cropping, as shown here, eliminated the busy hillside with the many buildings competing for attention against the harbor and boats. This cropping also did away with the contrast caused by the dark rows of windows and white paper. Attention was then focused on the yacht gliding into the harbor, which became the center of interest. The yacht's wake shows its movement and motion, and also helps to bring the eye into the picture. Instead of various competing facets of the former composition, there is now mainly one dominant feature. This improved composition gave me a desire to use the cropped area as the subject for a new painting. The cropped area could be cut out and framed as a small painting. A second area might be cropped at the lower right side. A few preliminary sketches would have helped in composing this picture.

Tips on Painting

When working outdoors one of the most important things to do is to make yourself comfortable. I prefer sitting on a stool and holding my drawing board upright or flat on my knees with my palette on another stool beside me. If you're lucky, nature will provide you with a stump or a rock. Some painters prefer to place their drawing boards flat on the ground and kneel or sit for fear the paint will run. I find I can pick up any unwanted run with my brush. Sometimes these unexpected runs enhance the work.

Keep your paper in the shade as much as possible, as this will keep the values in your painting more constant. Remember that your colors may

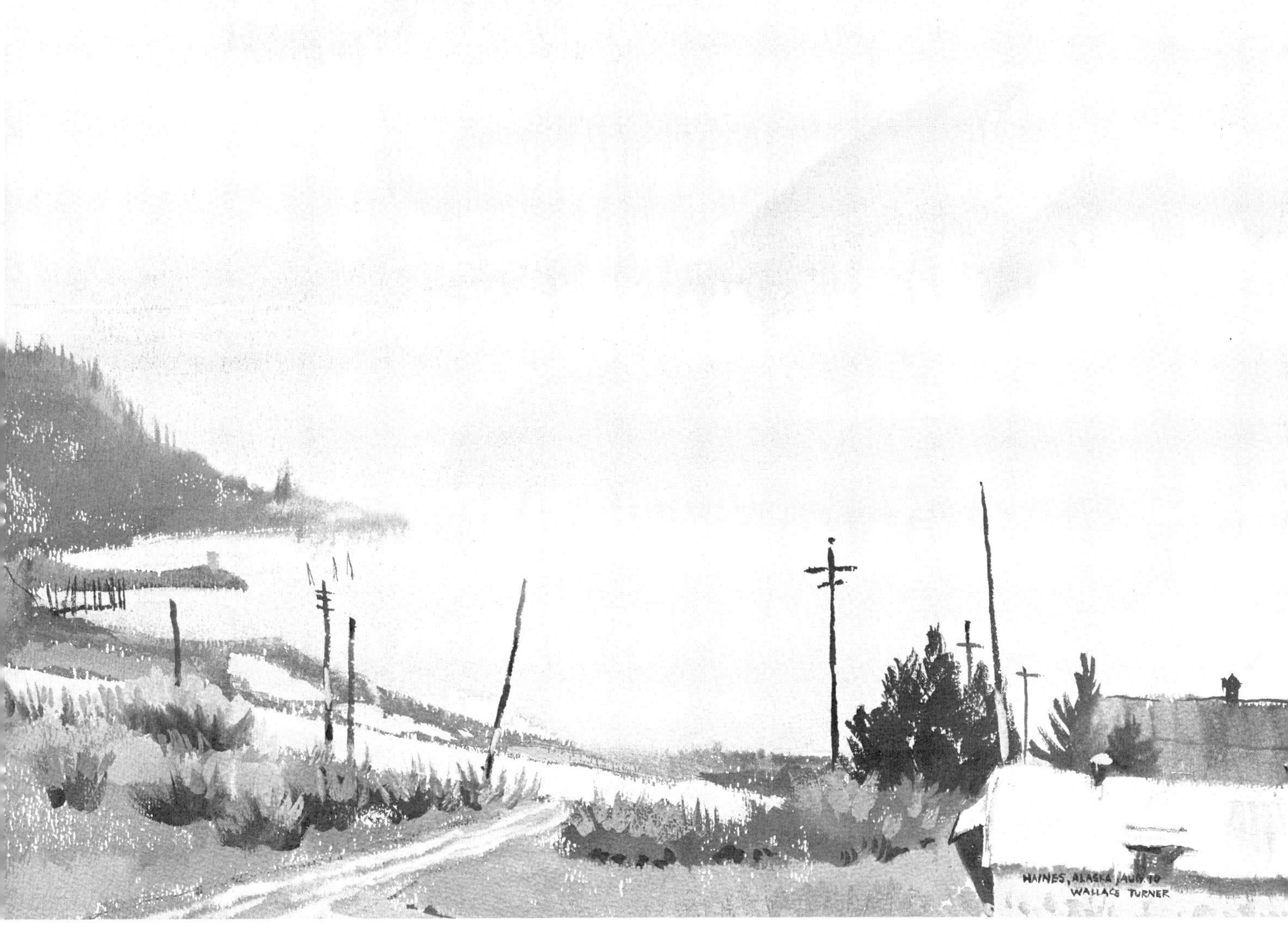

RAIN AND FOG, HAINES, ALASKA
15 x 20 inches.

Here is an example of wet-in-wet opaque painting. The weather in Alaska in the summer is something less than constant. A heavy rain turned to drizzle, then to fog accompanied by a dramatic change in light. I had taken shelter beneath a leaky roof of an abandoned barracks. The light changes were intriguing, and I set up my painting gear quickly. Working rapidly to catch the ethereal beauty of the scene, I painted wet-in-wet on Fabriano, using Designers gouache colors. The sky and water were considered as one plane, painted with yellow ochre and ultramarine blue. Rapidly the mountain shape was flowed into the wet sky. It is a challenge to capture the spontaneous, misty quality of fog. Yellow greens and purple masses of wild flowers brighten the foreground.

change, so compensate for that.

I usually start my palette with lemon yellow in the upper left hand corner, then continuing with the warm colors from left to right and the cool colors starting from the lemon yellow downward on the left side of the palette. I squeeze the white out in a larger quantity on the right side of the palette.

Some artists never use the same palette. This is because your palette depends somewhat on the colors most prominent in your chosen subject. As an example, if I am painting a desert scene in which there is seemingly no green, I still place greens on my palette, as green mixed with burnt umber might give the desert color desired. The same can be said in the painting of skies. Red, yellow, and green will prove useful in varying the blues. I'll touch on this later when I discuss skies.

Before applying the paint, I wet the entire paper using the 1 ½-inch wide flat brush. Usually, but not always, I start with the sky, having first mixed two or three mounds of color that approximate its colors and their values. I mix two cool colors and one warm. If the sky is a cool blue I use ultramarine blue with white and a touch of alizarin crimson. For a warm blue I mix ultramarine blue with viridian green or cerulean blue. For yet another warm color I mix ultramarine blue with white and yellow ochre.

Be sure to mix enough paint to cover the area, as it can be disasterous to run out of a mixture in the middle of painting the sky.

Before applying the paint you may need to quickly wet the sky area again with clean water using your widest brush. Starting at the top of your paper, lay in your sky colors in very thin washes, using the wet-in-wet technique. Work as rapidly as possible before the paper dries. The thicker pigment is reserved for light values to be painted later as the painting develops. Throughout your whole painting the first lay-in of color should be thin washes.

As you go along, heavier pigment may be used to strengthen and enhance the color and to make any changes considered necessary. A brush loaded with opaque watercolor will help define the drawing of forms such as buildings, trees, and other objects. Also, one of the values of opaque watercolor is the active brush work that gives virility to your painting. But, too heavy an application of opaque pigment might result in the pigment cracking or flaking off.

When you have finished your painting, stand off to evaluate it, or put it on the ground and view it from above. Don't expect 100% success the first time or the fiftieth time you paint.

Try putting your paintings aside for awhile, and later give them a second evaluation to study your progress. It's a good idea to date them. Don't be too hasty in discarding the ones that don't immediately please you. Painters, like composers, sometimes throw away work of value.

The important thing is to paint frequently and enjoy it. Don't wait to find the time, take the time. The more you paint the more stimulated you will be, and the more satisfaction you will gain from your progress.

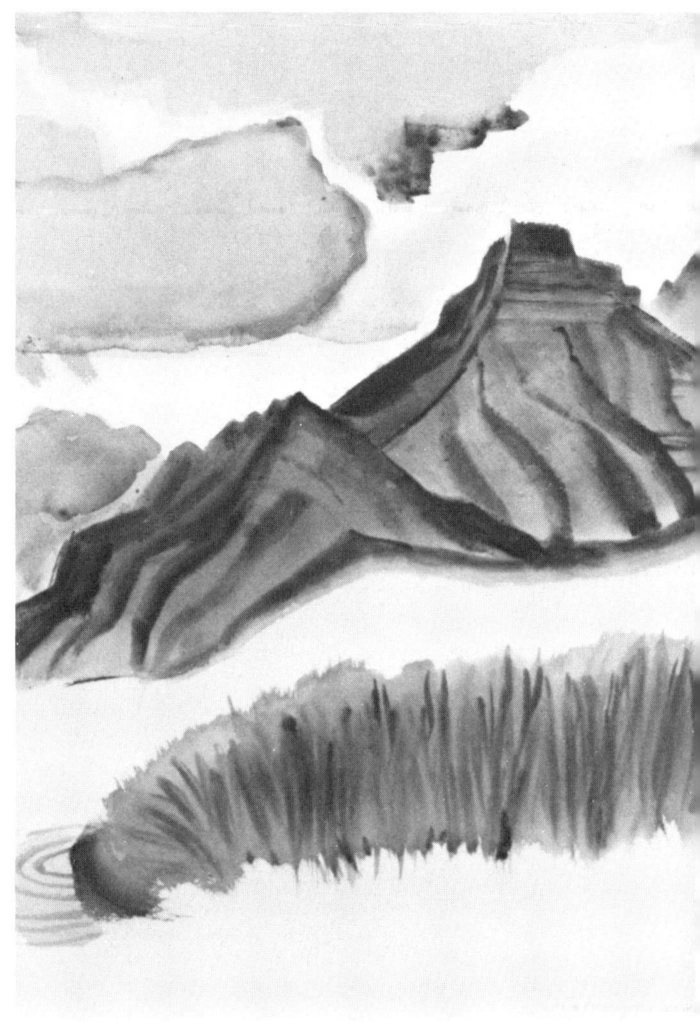

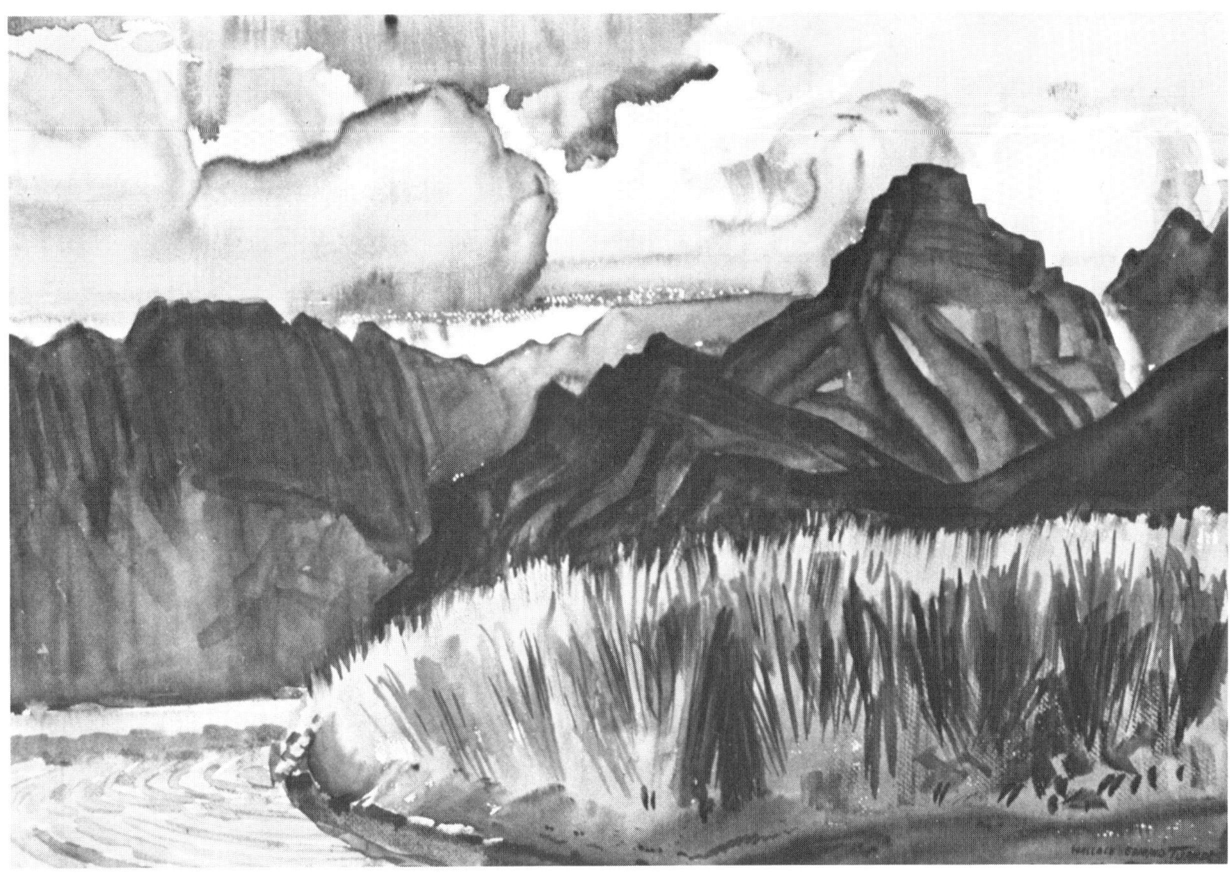

STORM OVER OAHU
19 x 25 inches.

In Hawaii, the great cube-shaped mountains, and the vivid light-green of the sugar cane fields with dramatic storm-clouds forming overhead make an irresistible appeal to the painter, even though he may have to dash for shelter to avoid a rain squall.

Here Arches watercolor paper with a combination of Winsor & Newton transparent and Designers Colors were used. Clear water was washed over the sky area, leaving the white surface of the paper for the lightest sky areas as no white opaque was used here. Using a large red sable brush #12, color consisting of yellow ochre with a touch of indigo blue was dropped onto the wet surface, forming the cloud shapes. These shapes were left mainly untouched except for adding indigo blue to the edges to suggest the turbulence and coming storm.

Tipping the paper gave the clouds a downward thrust. The angular shapes of the clouds are repeated in the inverted shapes of the mountains below, creating a sense of unity to the composition. The sugar cane field in the foreground was painted first in a general tone of lemon yellow with cadmium yellow light. Using a pointed brush and starting the sweep from the bottom up to give the effect of the sugar cane stalks, darker strokes of Hooker's green and burnt umber were brushed into the yellow area while this tone was still damp. The lighter color of the sugar cane field is in contrast to the mountains and ominous clouds above.

This detail shows the method used to establish the background pine trees.

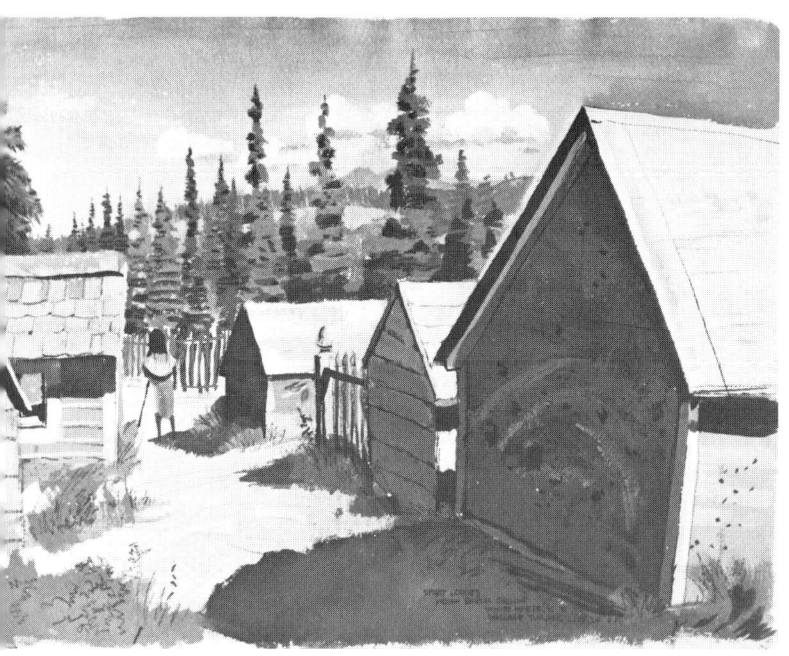

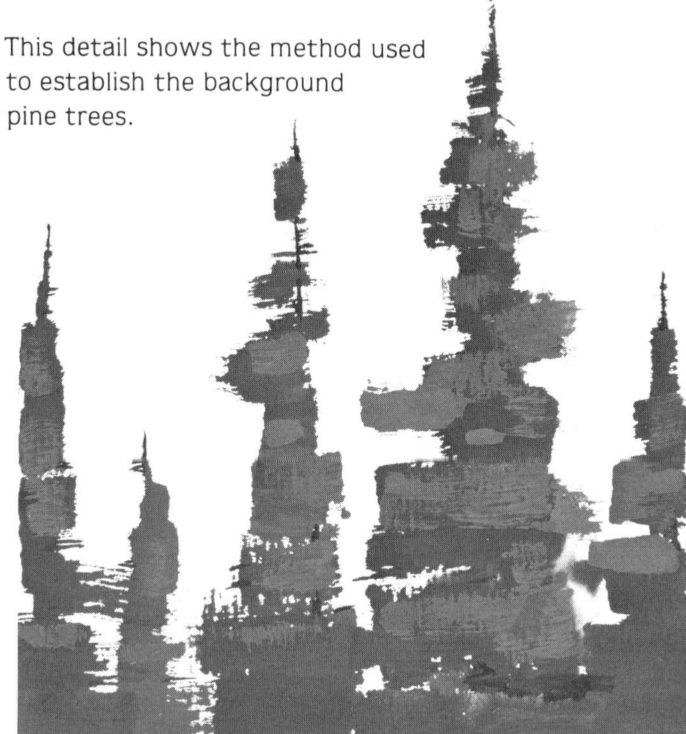

SPIRIT LODGES, WHITEHORSE, YUKON TERRITORY
15 x 20 inches.

Textures are rampant in this opaque painting of an Indian burial ground found just outside of Whitehorse. Fairly heavy opaque was used on Fabriano. The final touches are strokes made with a black Prismacolor pencil, using the point or chisel edge mainly on the trees in the background. The textures shown on the sides of the lodges were mostly dry brush in technique, ranging from spread brush to dragging a heavily loaded brush across a partially wet surface. I've often thought this subject would have made an impressive picture with the spirit lodges deep in snow. I'd like to go back sometime and see.

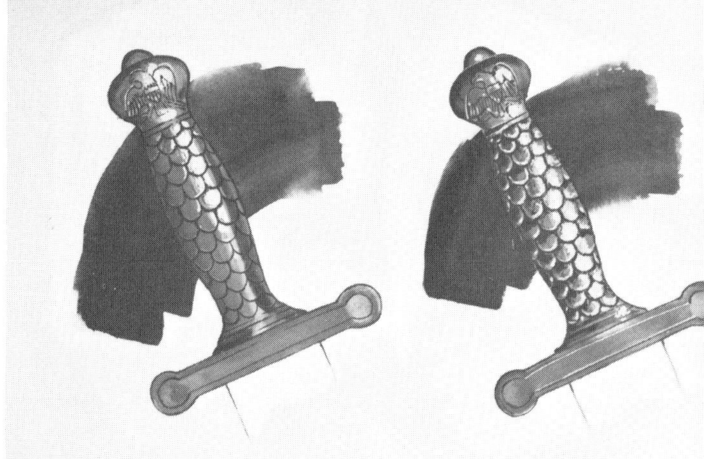

Working Back to Front

"Back to front" painting is sometimes effective in painting still life objects, as well as landscapes. The Roman sword hilts shown here are an example. Roughly three values were used. A general tone of middle value came first. The colors consisted of Hooker's green, burnt sienna, yellow ochre. The scales were built up by using gesso in order to capture their high-key value. The gesso was laid on with a palette knife, much as a bricklayer works with a trowel. After the gesso was perfectly dry, white was mixed with lemon yellow and applied to the built-up scales. This procedure is shown partially completed at the left, and in its completed form at the right, with added black outlines of the scales.

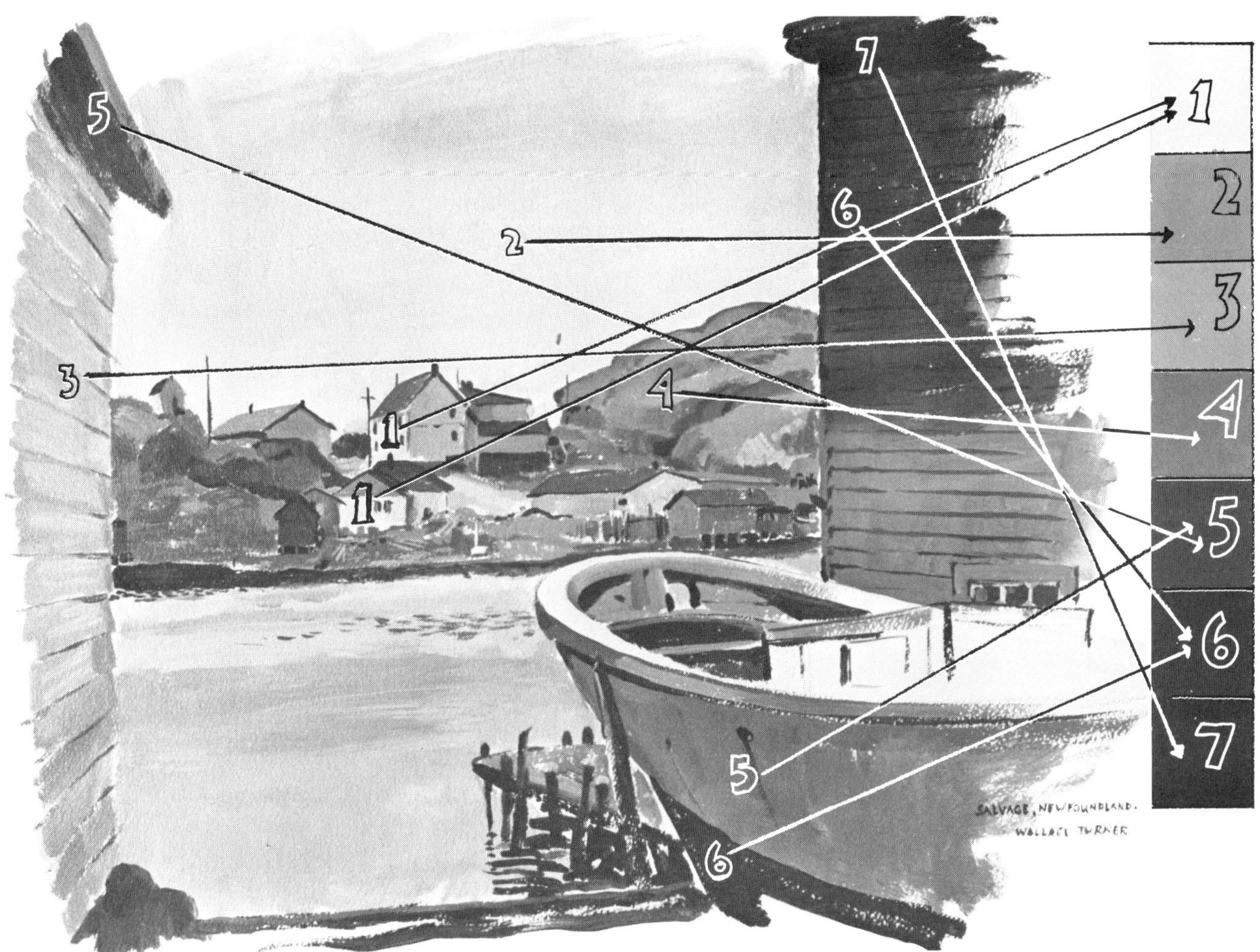

CHAPTER 4

Values & Edges

One of the most important considerations in painting in any medium is the control of values. As mentioned earlier, value means the lightness or darkness of a shape or a color. Basically, there are two reasons for different values.

First you have the local color of an object or, in simpler terms, its natural color. The red of an apple, the color of a house, etc., all have value as one of the distinguishing characteristics that help us to identify its unique quality. Another element and the most important one that affects the value is the degree of light and shadow under which the object is seen.

One other factor that has an effect on the value of an object is the atmosphere under which it is seen. The farther objects are away from you the less distinct will be their value differences and contrasts. In other words, the values of objects seen in the distance tend to blend together.

Values vary a great deal, all the way from pure white to black. Usually we think of values in terms of gray but, as you know, values are always present in all colors. Achieving convincing values and establishing a believable overall value relationship in your picture is extremely important for every painter.

I have already cautioned you about one of the few difficulties inherent in opaque painting. That is, the values change slightly from the wet state to the dry. Usually the values of opaque appear a little darker when dry. (Transparent watercolor, on the other hand, often appears lighter after it is dry.) With a little experience you will learn to compensate for the value difference, and in most cases it probably won't affect your painting much. It is, however, a factor to be considered.

If it is necessary to match a painted value exactly, it is a good idea to paint a swatch of your new mixture of color along the edge of a piece of scrap paper. When it is dry compare it with the value in your picture you wish to match.

As you paint from nature, remember it is not possible to match in paint the colors and values our eyes can see. Nature's spectrum is far greater than our palette. The best we can do is to try to establish a convincing relationship of color and values to suggest the range of what we see.

One helpful way to judge values of an object is to squint at it so you are not confused by details and subtle variation. Looking through half-closed eyes will allow you to determine just how light or dark or bright an object is.

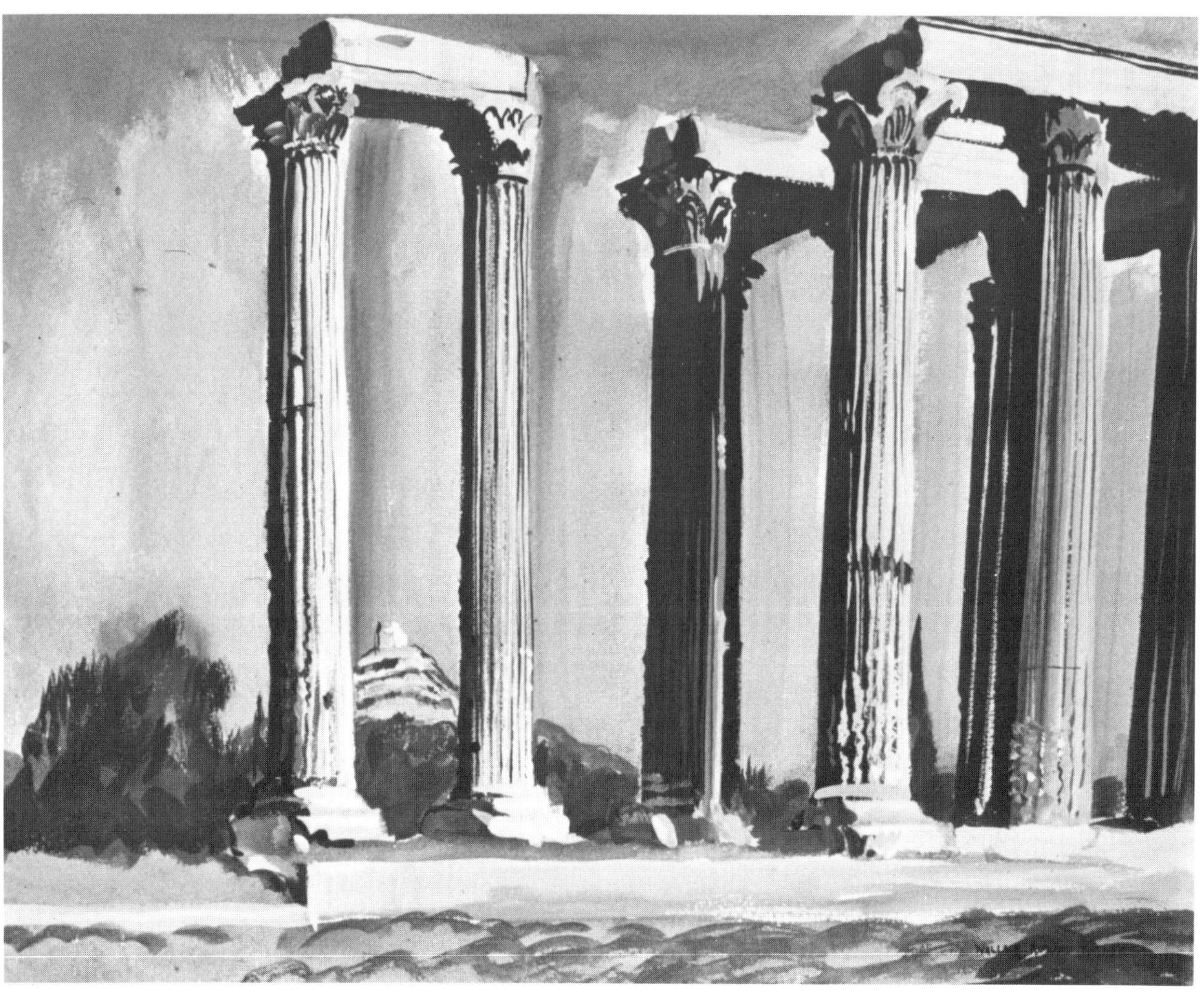

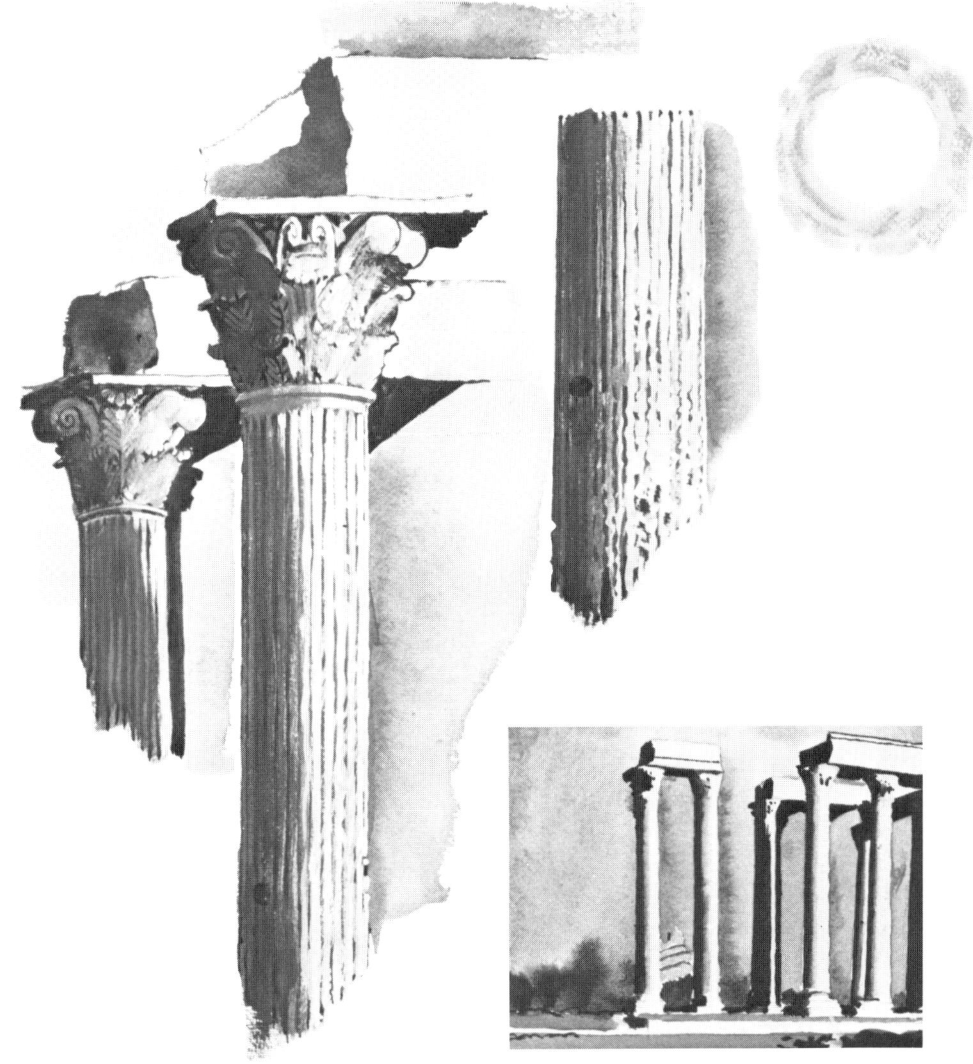

Light and Shadow

The Temple of Zeus, built in 530 B.C., was considered one of the most majestic temples in Greece. Even today the few remaining upright columns make an impressive sight with broken drums and other fragments of columns strewn on the ground around their base.

The sunlight striking the columns from the upper right hand side is most important as the light and shadow pattern firmly establishes the forms of these great columns. The light also brings out the fluting of parallel grooves incised in the columns. The light and dark shadow pattern is more important than the muted and subtle color of the painting. The sky tone was washed in first, wet-in-wet, leaving the white paper for the light side of the columns. Where the sky tone bordered a light side of a column, a darker tone was allowed to settle along the column's edge to emphasize the light marble. Some of the columns are in deep shadow. It was hoped that these dark shapes would push those columns in light out into the sunlight.

Again we have a basic range of three values: the highest key is the sunlit part of the columns; the middle value, the sky; the darkest values, the shadows of the columns and the background. The pigment used in painting the shadow areas was quite thin, giving the dark areas a transparent effect. It was anticipated at this stage that the light areas would be painted with heavy pigment and, like the intense light on the columns, the heavy pigment would tend to soften the details and some edges of the fluting and carving of the capitals. As it was necessary to show some sharp edges in the fluting, a brush with a good point was used to paint these grooves in the marble columns. Near the bottom of the columns a wiggly type of stroke was used to represent the damaged parts despoiled by man.

The character of the columns in the light was painted by using a fully-loaded brush of white mixed with a touch of yellow ochre, or viridian green, or burnt sienna. These colors vary as all the marble of the columns did not seem to be the same color. This pigment was laid on using a partial dry brush technique to show the ravages of time.

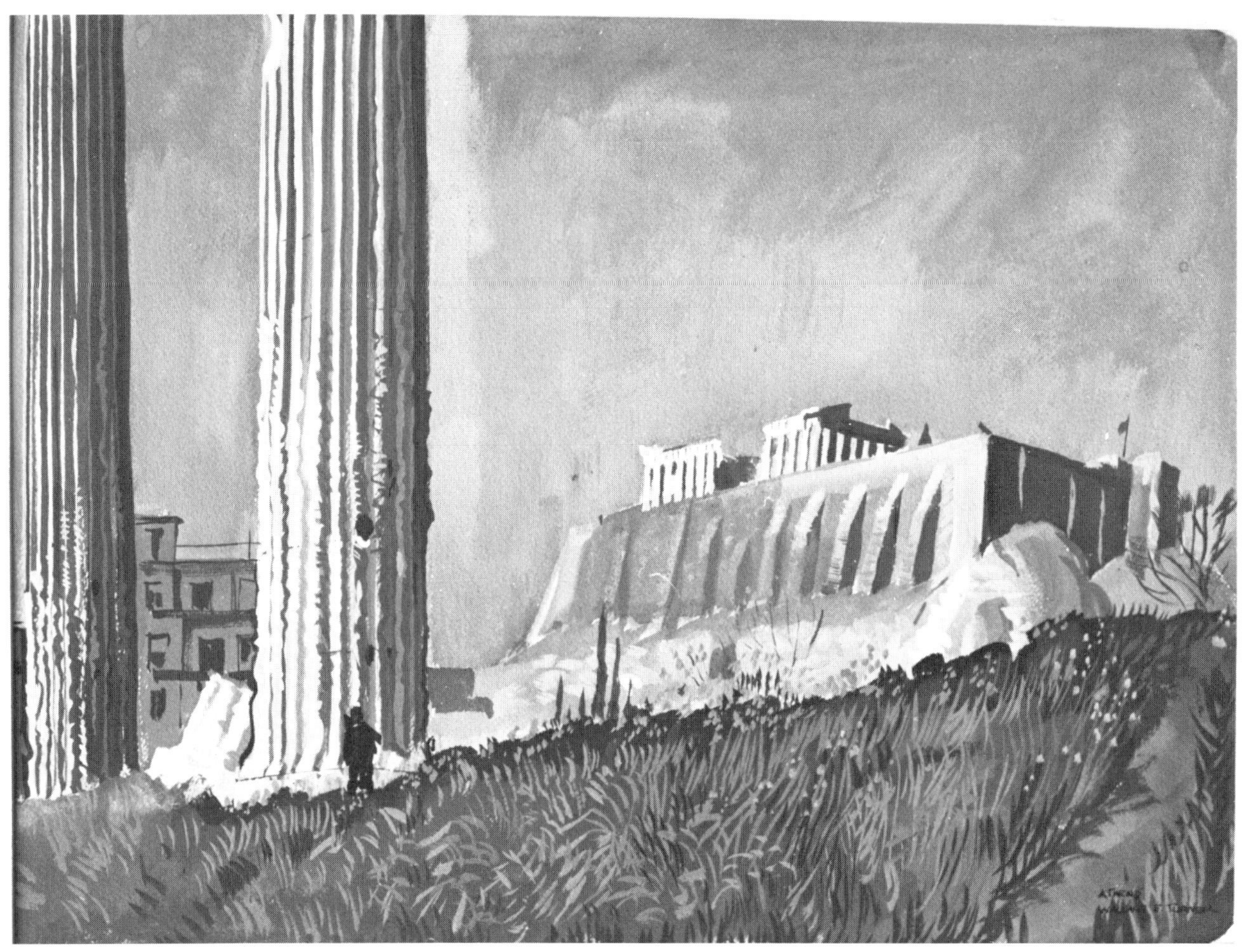

Lost and Found Edges

Sometimes artists refer to edges as "lost and found" or "soft and hard." A soft or lost edge is achieved by painting two areas of similar value next to each other.

There is little contrast in these values. Instead, the edges are soft, indistinct, losing any line of separation, and losing contrast.

There are many ways to paint a lost edge: painting a lighter tone along the edge of the shape, adding clean water to weaken the value of a mass or shape, using the wet-in-wet technique to create blended masses and hazy edges.

In direct contrast is the hard or found edge which gives character and authority to what would otherwise be a flat composition. The hard edge has a higher contrast of light and dark, as on the shadow side of the columns in the foreground against the lighter sky area. Another found edge is seen at the top right edge of the Acropolis. Careful planning of a variety of soft and hard, lost and found edges will give your painting greater strength and character.

Many examples of lost and found edges are to be found in the painting of The Temple of Zeus.

Providing closeups of the main units in the painting, a sharp division of light and dark values is shown on the column on the left. The function of the value of the sky is evident here as it makes prominent the light on the column.

You should show no hesitancy when painting edges in a sketch such as this. Use a pointed brush loaded with a high-keyed pigment and go over your drawing of the fluting rather recklessly. In a few minutes you can age a marble column 2000 years. If your brush strokes vary in width, so much the better. Sable brushes #3 and #9 were used to produce these effects.

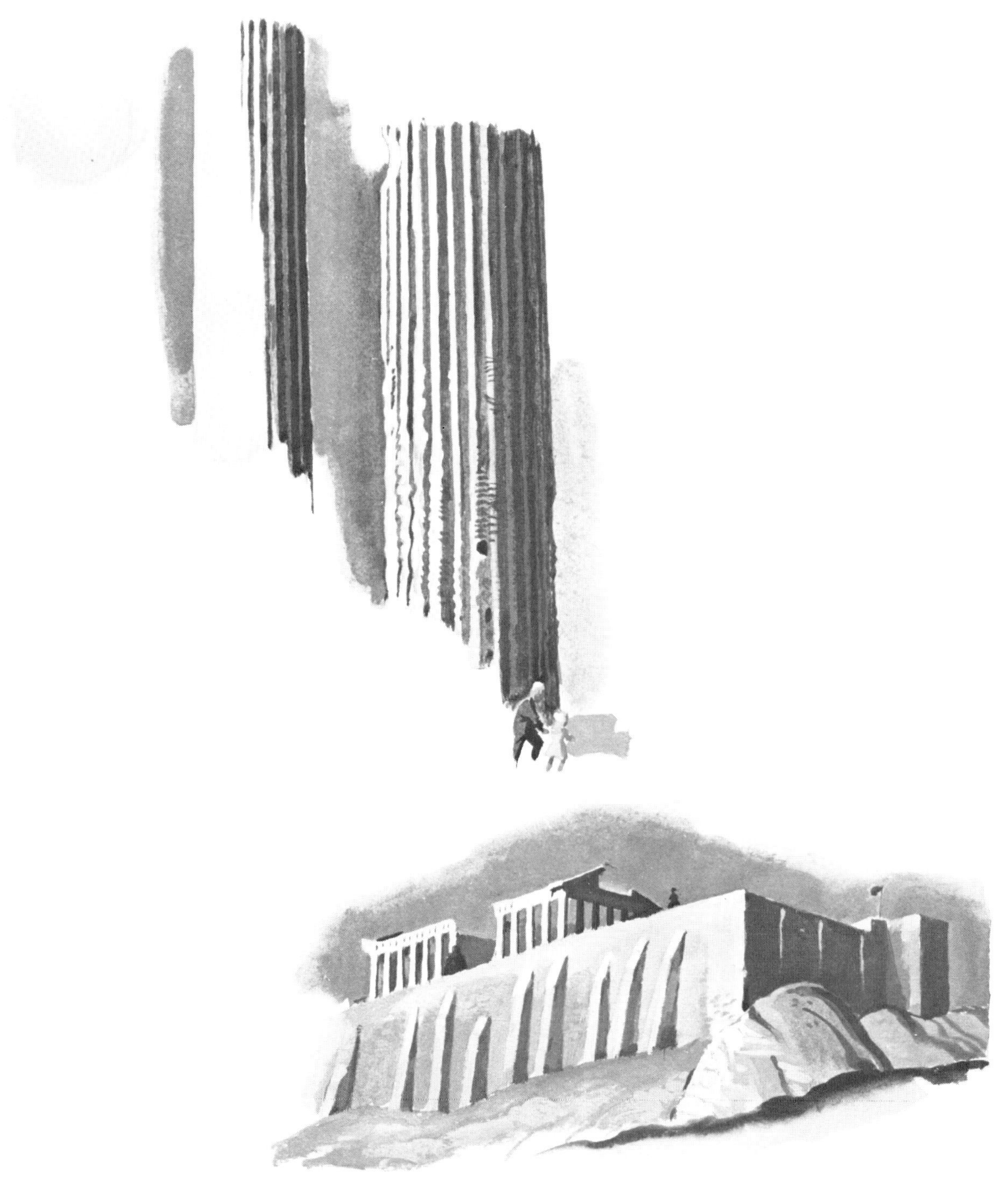

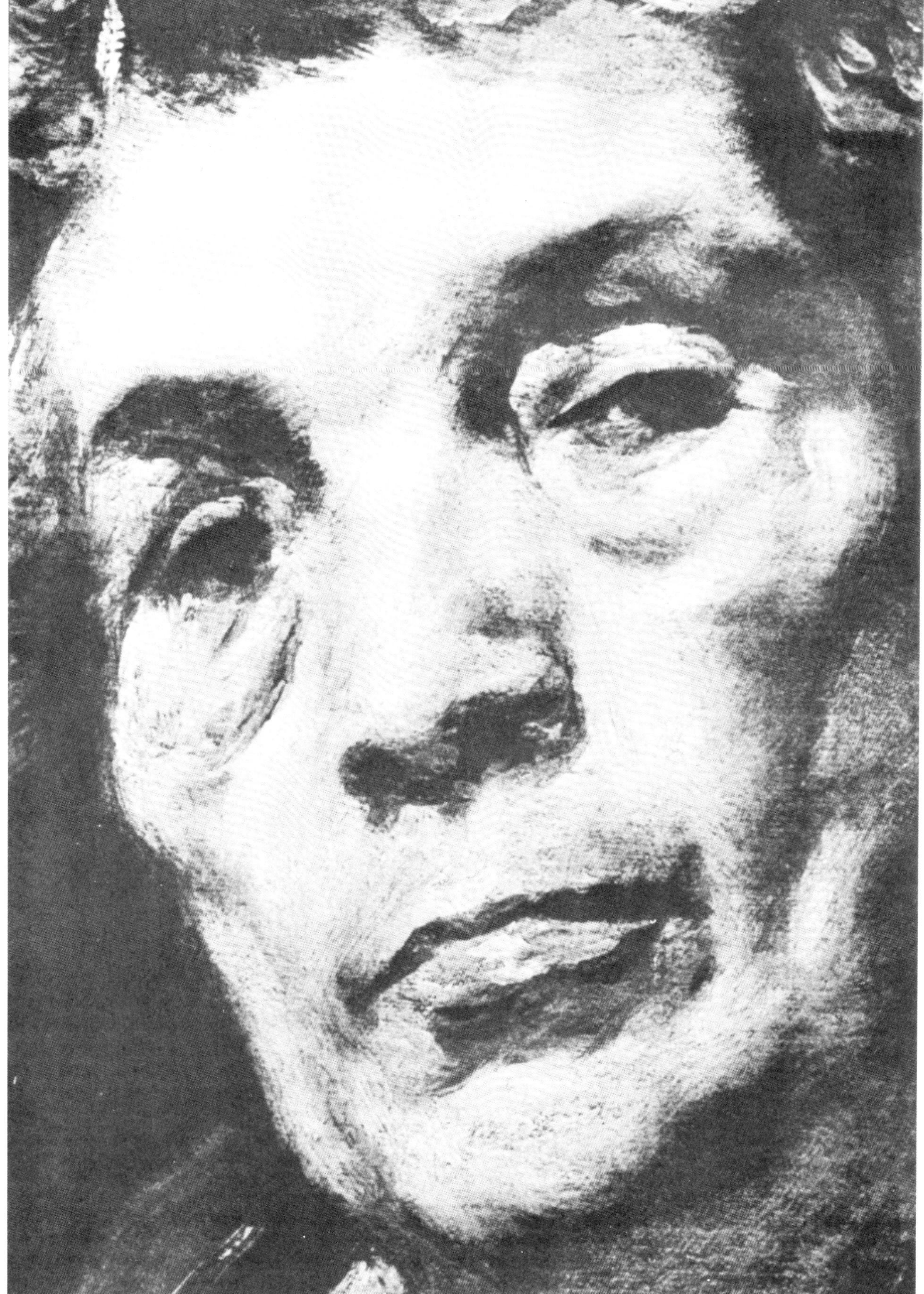

Detail of ESOPE
Diego Velazquez

PRADO MUSEUM, MADRID

This great 17th century Spanish master was a virtuoso at controlling edges. A study of this detail will show beautiful examples of many of the types of edges we have discussed.

CHAPTER 5

Composition

The composition of a painting is usually the result of a painter's sensitivity to the elements of design, whether it be intuitive or developed through experience and training. The development of a composition is, like the use of color, a highly individual matter, reflecting how a person sees and how he feels. It involves his emotion as well as his intellect.

The importance of good composition cannot be overstressed, for a reaction to it can be the deciding factor in acceptance or rejection of a painting —even though the color and its rendering are of superior quality.

Every composition requires an individual evaluation. Although there are no set rules for composing, there are some basic elements of design that you should be aware of when selecting and studying a subject. It's often color that first attracts. But you must train your eye also to look further for shapes and values—for lines that give rhythmical movement; lead the eye to the focal point of interest, and to spaces between shapes. Look for relationships in these elements—balance, variety of space, size and shape and a feeling of unity.

The key to your composition will be partially established by the subject matter. Almost instinctively you'll choose a center of interest. Various methods can direct attention, to lead the eye to where you wish it to look first.

Line is an important element of design. Curved or straight lines lead your eye to the center of interest. Avoid lines that point to the corners or borders of your picture. Devices often used to keep the eye from straying out of the picture, or turning it back toward the focal point, are fences, roads railroad tracks or a curved tree branch. In an abstract composition, where it is not necessary to be literal, you can bend and turn elements at will.

To unify your composition, overlap the main objects, thus avoiding "pockets" which tend to localize the viewer's attention. This will concentrate attention on the focal point and avoid scattered interest. Your composition will also be helped by "drawing through" as if the objects were of transparent material, so that all objects are in correct spacial relationship, space being another important element of design.

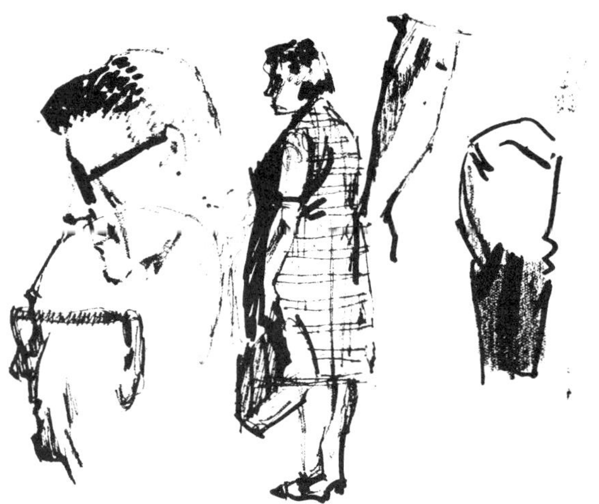

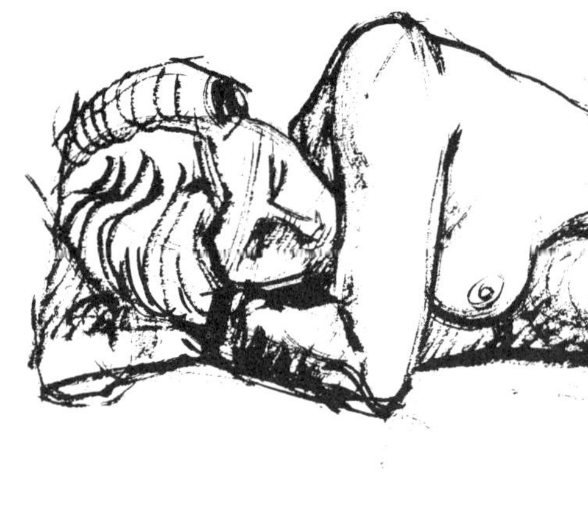

The small sketches shown here are beyond the thumbnail stage. It is neither necessary to carry the sketches this far, nor to show recognizable subject matter. Abstract shapes serve just as well at this stage.

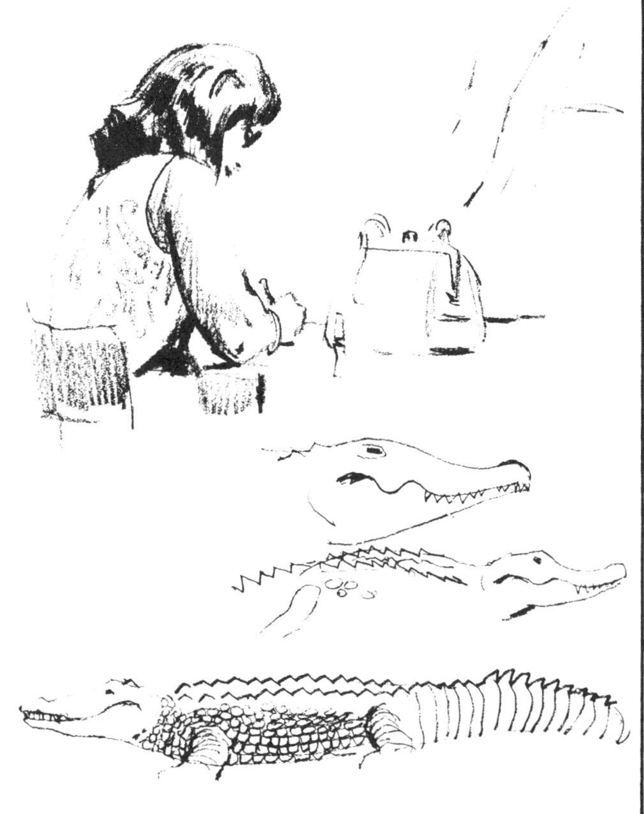

These principles apply to still life as well as to landscape. In figure or portrait painting the compositional problems are simpler, as the figure is the center of interest and the picture is self-contained.

When developing a composition, your mind must be kept open and flexible. If you are having problems in developing a composition that satisfies you, you may be helped by experimenting with just shapes and values. One of my instructors at the Art Institute of Chicago gave us "loosening up" exercises by having us work for several lessons with brush and India ink. With eyes closed we dabbled an ink-laden brush on our paper in several different areas. Then we selected one of the masses of shapes, covered it with tissue paper and, with a soft pencil, followed the basic forms of the dabbles, drawing more definite rhythmical lines and abstract shapes, intuitively or consciously applying the elements of good design. We then developed our design in two or three values, later adding one color. This exercise, stressing just shape and value, relaxed us and helped us to see to observe, to select. It helped to build confidence and freedom of movement.

One of the most widely used methods to help germinate a compositional idea is "doodling"—quick scribbles that, when observed upside-down, often jolt a dormant idea into something tangible and active.

Another helpful method is the making of small quick sketches, such as you would do in your pocket

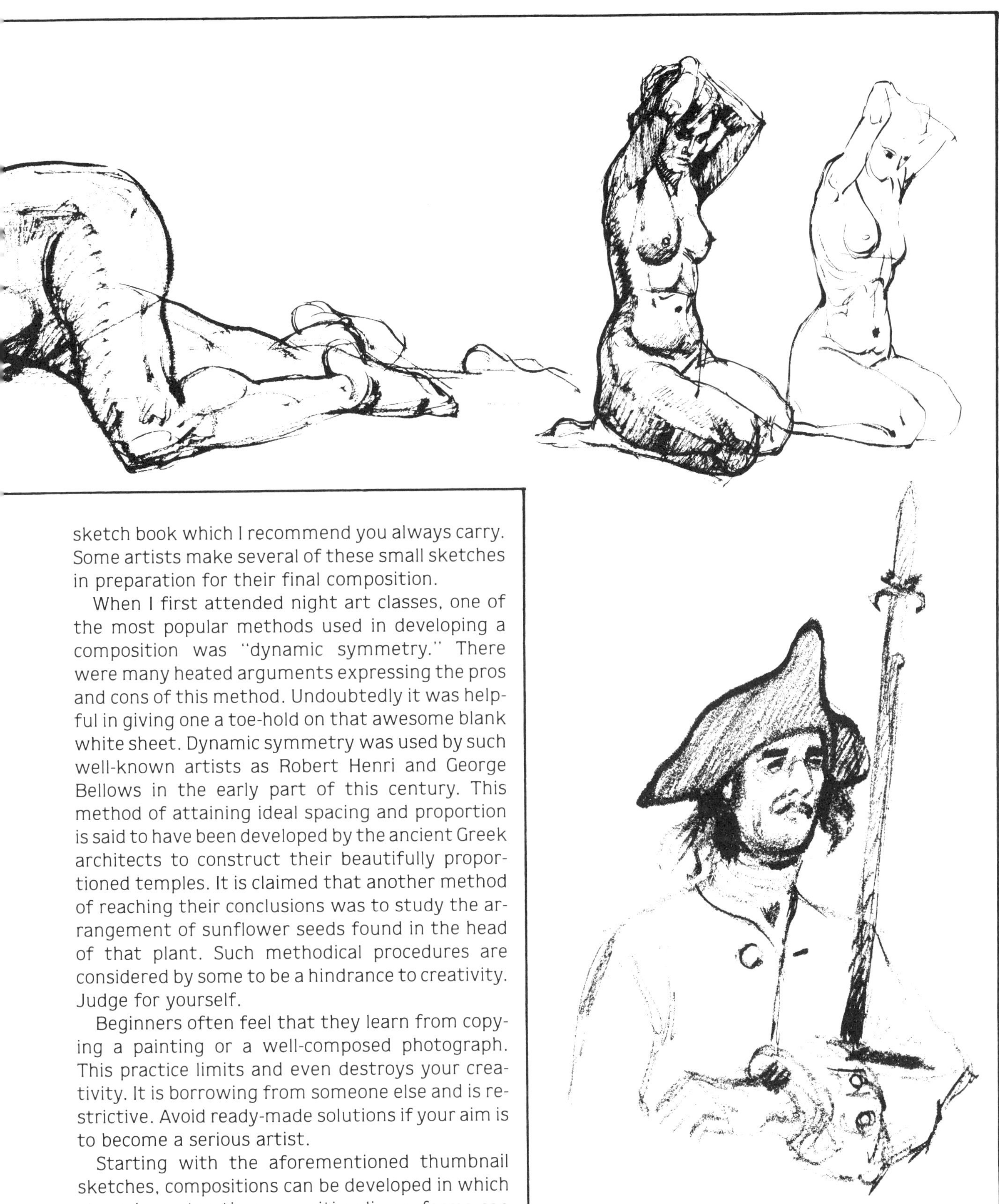

sketch book which I recommend you always carry. Some artists make several of these small sketches in preparation for their final composition.

When I first attended night art classes, one of the most popular methods used in developing a composition was "dynamic symmetry." There were many heated arguments expressing the pros and cons of this method. Undoubtedly it was helpful in giving one a toe-hold on that awesome blank white sheet. Dynamic symmetry was used by such well-known artists as Robert Henri and George Bellows in the early part of this century. This method of attaining ideal spacing and proportion is said to have been developed by the ancient Greek architects to construct their beautifully proportioned temples. It is claimed that another method of reaching their conclusions was to study the arrangement of sunflower seeds found in the head of that plant. Such methodical procedures are considered by some to be a hindrance to creativity. Judge for yourself.

Beginners often feel that they learn from copying a painting or a well-composed photograph. This practice limits and even destroys your creativity. It is borrowing from someone else and is restrictive. Avoid ready-made solutions if your aim is to become a serious artist.

Starting with the aforementioned thumbnail sketches, compositions can be developed in which strongly contrasting or exciting linear forms can dominate. These will serve as the nuclei of ideas that can lead by stages to viable compositions.

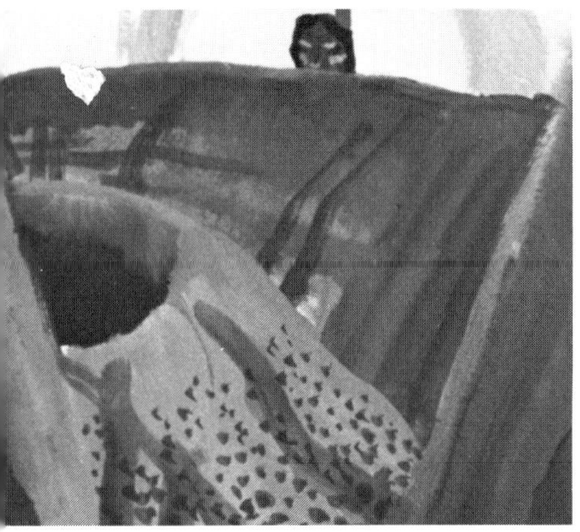
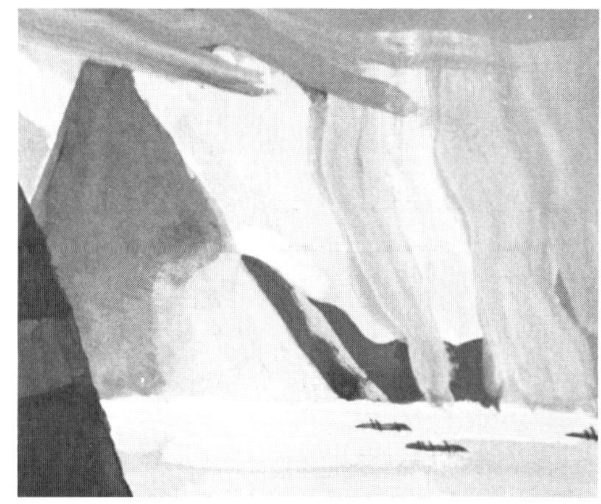
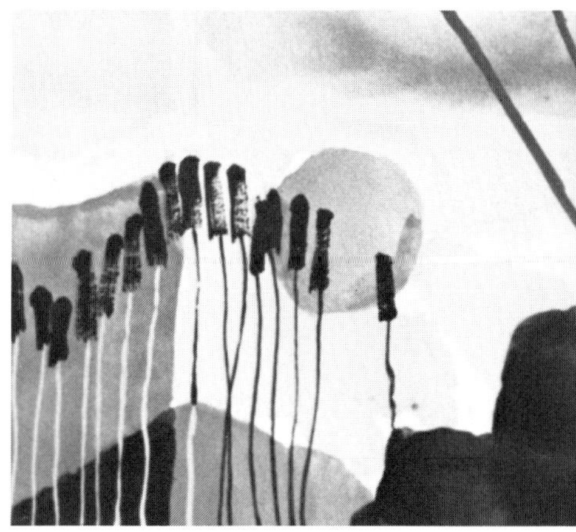
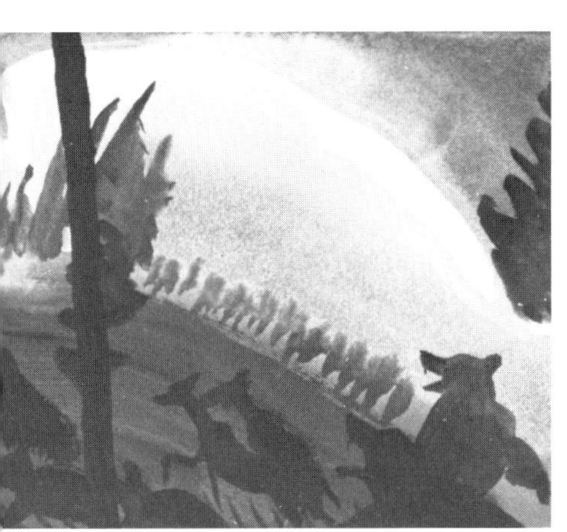
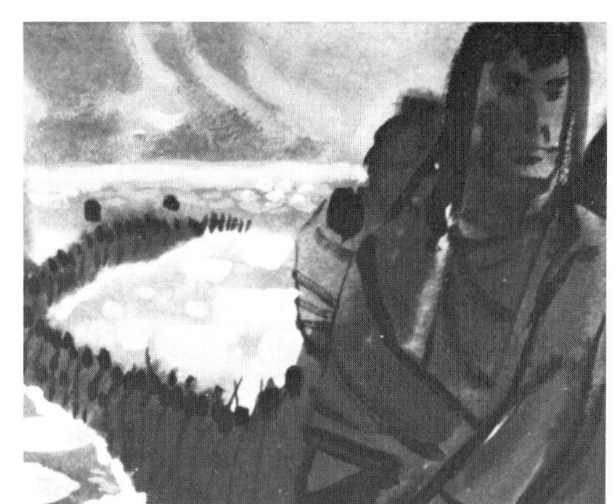
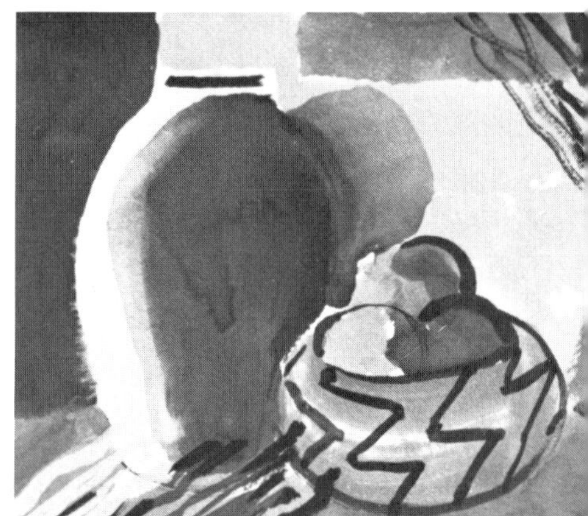

Move right in with powerful darks. Quickly establish patterns, shapes, and values. Don't hesitate to turn the paper around. If it doesn't jell quickly, scrap it and try another approach. Some prefer to search for compositional answers by arranging colored paper cut into various shapes. You might find that satisfying.

One of the main things to seek in these "instant" compositions is the division of space. Does the space between shapes (negative space) leave interesting patterns? If not, would overlapping the objects help? Is the skyline below or above the center of the paper to give variety to the spacing? Do the perpendicular lines form varied spaces? Have needed objects been added to fill an otherwise too empty space?

In many abstract designs, division of space is almost entirely dependent on geometric shapes, often the same shape repeated in varied sizes and positions. Shapes and spaces work together in organizing your composition and adding visual appeal.

These sketches illustrate a variety of spacing problems. Always study your spacing in relation to the other elements, selecting from your quick sketches the one that seems to offer the best possibilities. Solving the compositional problems in these six sketches allowed me to proceed directly into finished paintings. I needed only to scale each to my working size—and plunge into the painting.

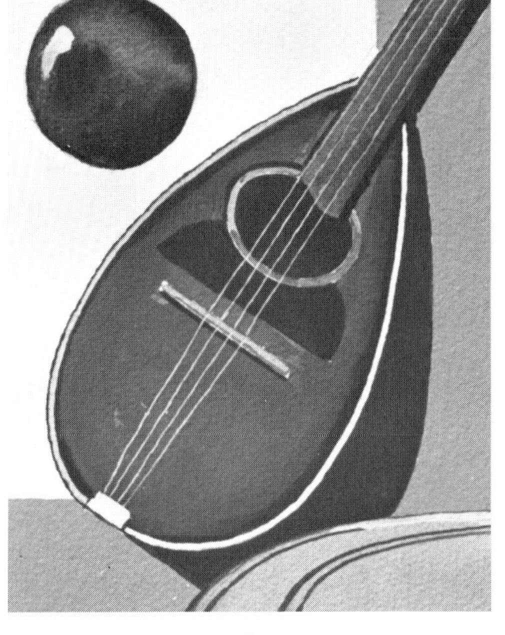

1

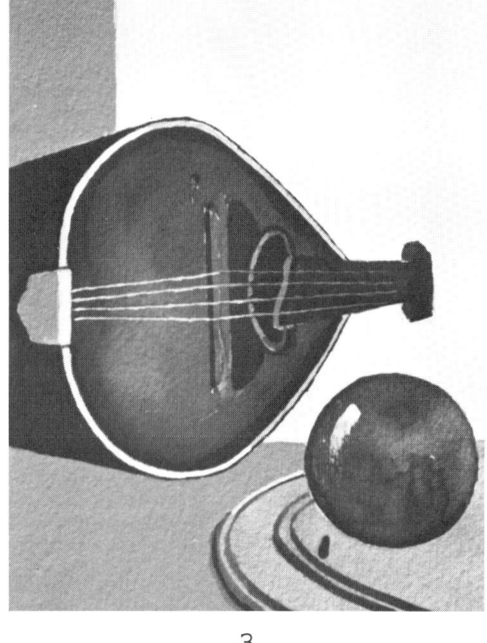

3

2

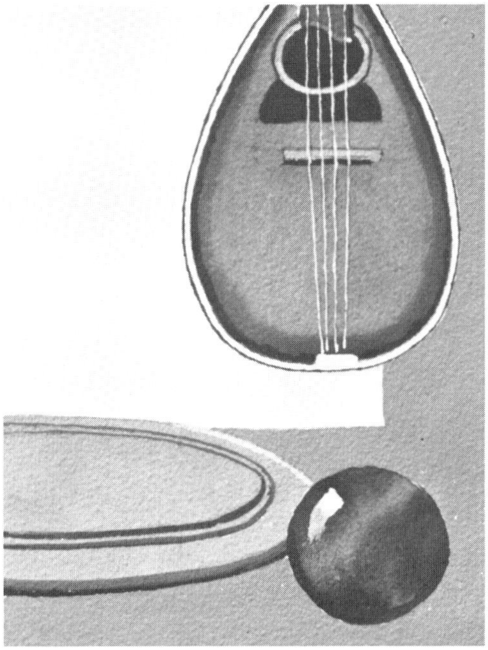

4

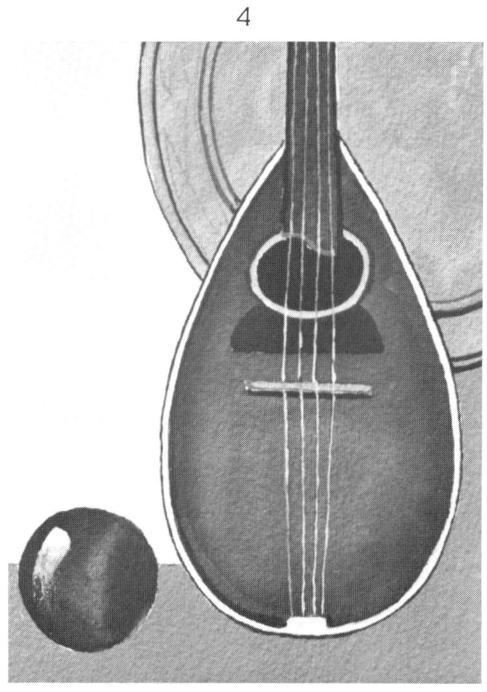

In these four compositions, three objects—a mandolin, a glass ball and a cutting board—were composed in a non-ordinary way. Instead of having atmospheric depth, they are painted as silhouettes, without cast shadows and without such subtleties as lost and found edges. The elimination of depth and edges allows the painter to stress arrangement of shapes and spaces. And the restriction to four hues with the neutral white further simplifies the task. Emphasis is on design only. Balance, movement of lines, variety and proportion of size and space and their relationships is what was sought exclusively.

1. The position of the mandolin creates a strong diagonal movement. A slight overlapping in the foreground gives unity. The glass ball fills an otherwise empty space and adds variety.

2. The supine position of the mandolin expresses a more relaxed mood. Here the movement takes the eye from the mandolin across the axis of the instrument to the glass ball.

3. The suspended mandolin with its perpendicular strings produces a different accent of design.

4. The lower and perpendicular position of the mandolin suggests a stability that is not found in the other compositions.

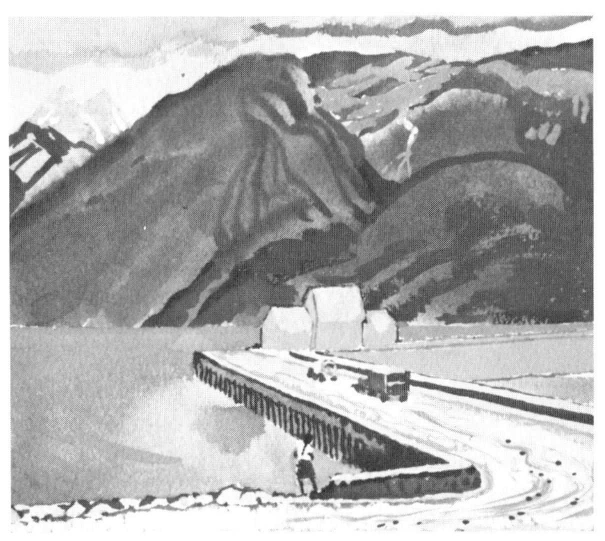

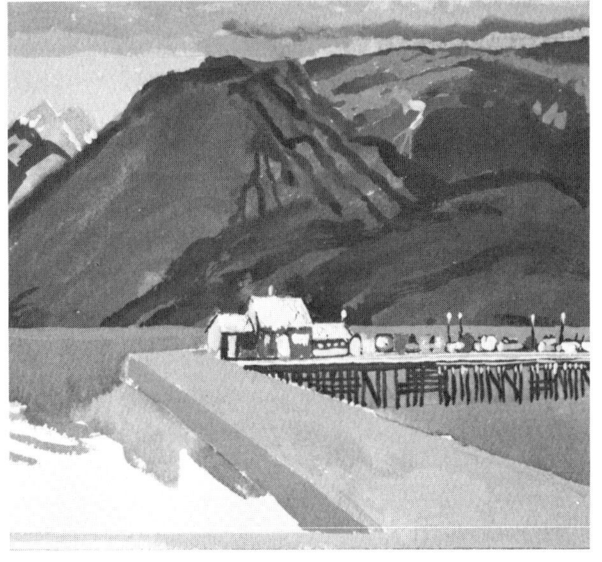

Directing the Eye

Whether a painting is low or high-key, quiescent or full of movement and visual excitement, it should have a center of interest: a focal point on which the eye comes to rest. The viewer's eye should be led to this point without encountering obstacles. To illustrate this, two sketches from Ellis Sound, Haines, Alaska, are shown.

In the upper illustration, high-key values have been used in contrast to the darker surrounding values to lead the eye along the wharf to the buildings in the middle distance. These high-key values, with some texture and the two cars, are utilized to lead the eye to the center of interest. The buildings and wharf leading to the right are painted in muted tones to emphasize the high-key tones.

In the lower sketch, the wharf in the foreground leading to the buildings in the middle distance is painted in a muted tone while the wharf leading to the right is of high-key, hence it directs the eye out of the picture. This is to be avoided.

These two sketches illustrate how high-key values as well as lines can direct the eye into or out of a composition.

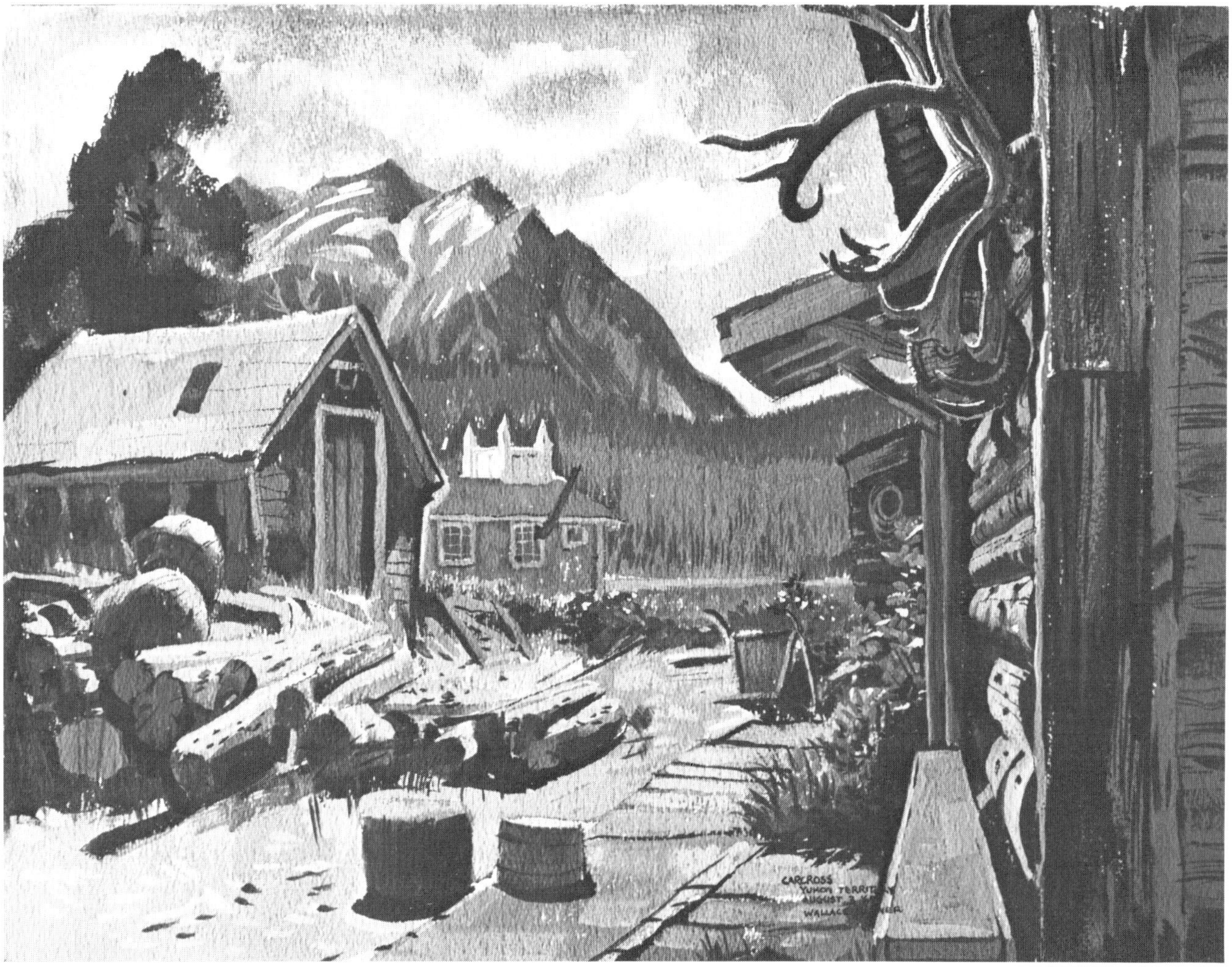

TRAPPER'S CABIN, CARCROSS, YUKON TERRITORY

This composition is full of strong directional lines that direct the observer's attention to the center of interest—in this case, the small structure in the middle distance. Notice the lines of the mountains which tend to lead the eye upward are stopped by the placement and values of the clouds. Needless to say, everything at the scene was not exactly in the indicated positions. Some adjustments were necessary to make the composition work right. One of the great advantages the artist has over the photographer is that he can shift things around to satisfy pictorial needs.

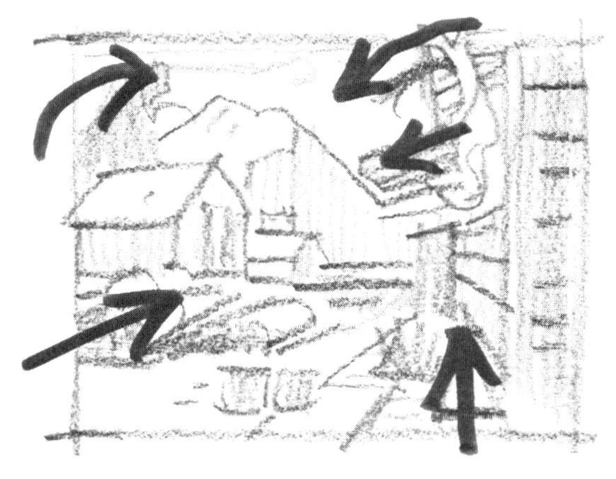

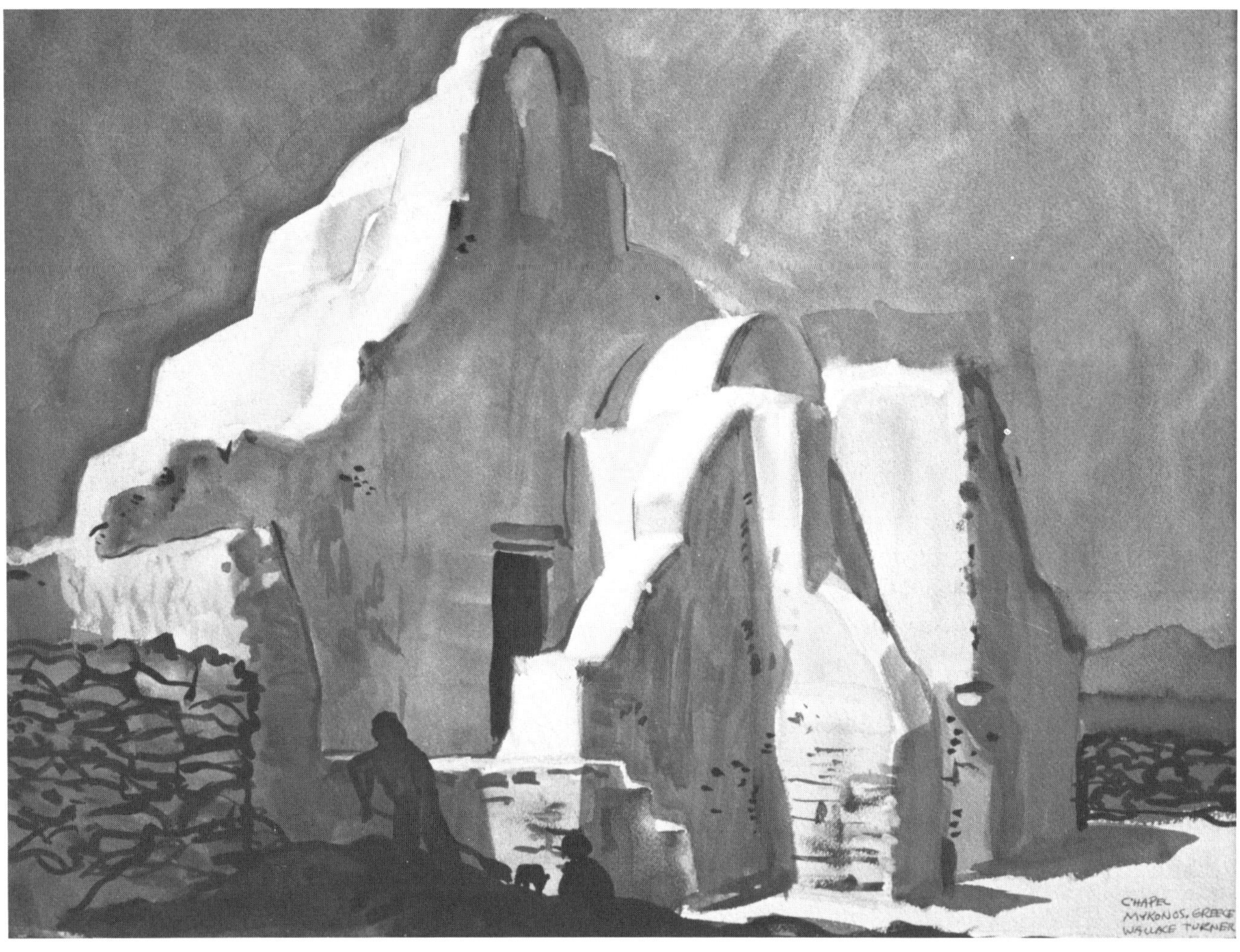

MYKONOS CHAPEL

This painting can be roughly summed up in three values: the white building areas in sunlight, the reflected light in the shadows, and the sky. While painting, I kept these three values in mind, reminding myself the sky was several shades darker than the light areas of the chapel. The subject was painted "back to front", that is, I started with the sky. As this was to be a rather solid painting, the sky was painted wet-in-wet. While this surface was still damp it was reinforced with heavier opaque, especially along the left-hand steps of the chapel. A variety of blue hues were used here, noting that the value of the sky lightened as it moved toward the right. Originally I left the white of the paper for the light areas of the chapel, but as the paper proved to be of a slightly yellowish tint, pure permanent white was brushed over it. To the white was added just a touch—very little—ultramarine blue.

As a composition, the picture, like the building itself, is designed more or less like a pyramid. It starts at the ground level with a strong base and everything leads upward to the peak. The contrasting color and darker value of the sky stop the movement at the center of interest, the curved, recessed opening for the bell. I also tried to emphasize the paint handling quality in the sky to add interest and to serve as a relief against the stark shapes of the structure.

Notice how everything in the picture, including the figures and the background scenery, is kept subordinate to the building. Compare the compositional problem here to the approach taken with the trapper's cabin shown previously.

Diluted wash of ultramarine blue and cerulean blue flooded onto the wet surface of the paper.

A heavier wash of opaque blues was then brushed in. This wet-in-wet technique works admirably for the initial assault.

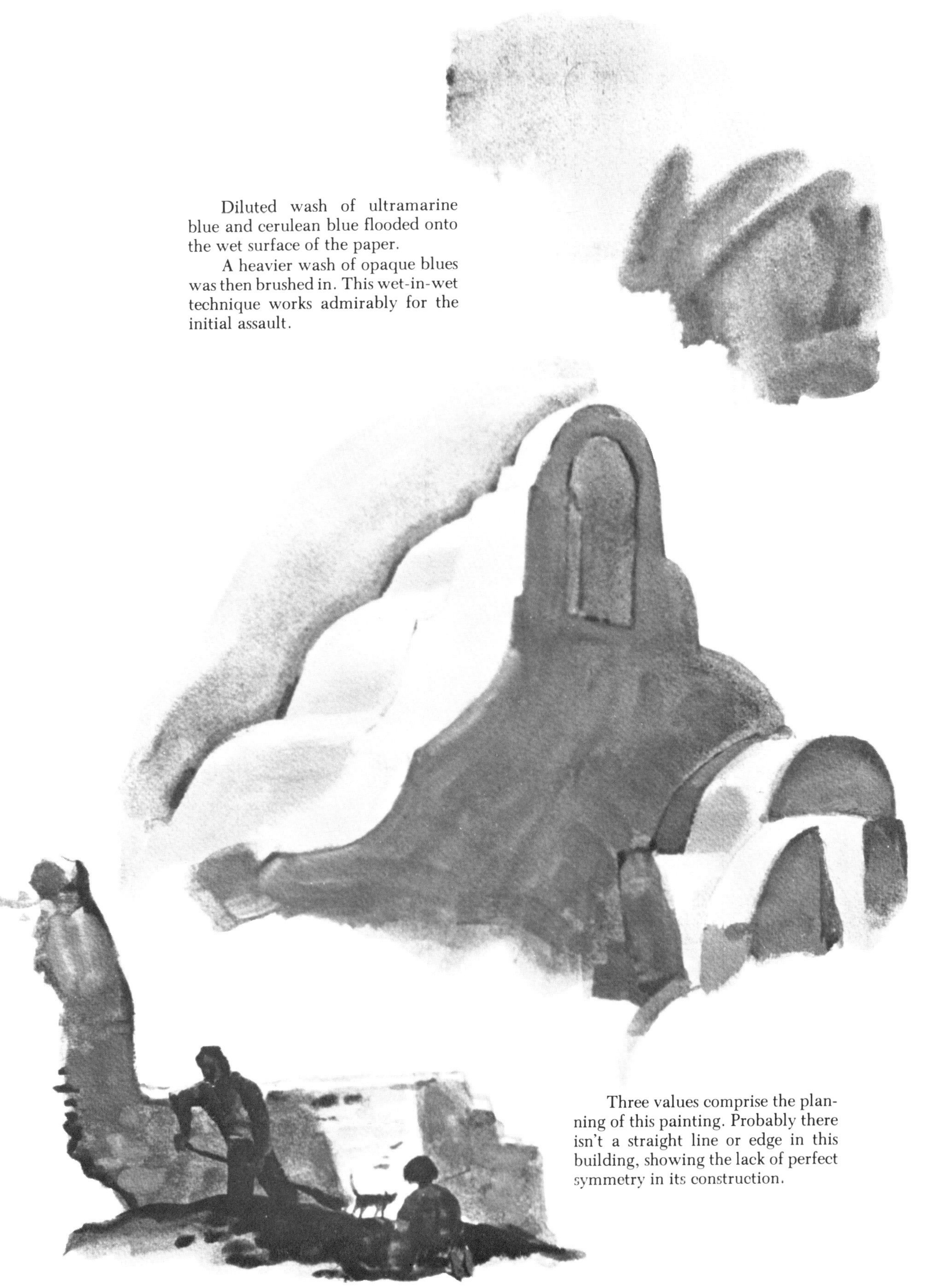

Three values comprise the planning of this painting. Probably there isn't a straight line or edge in this building, showing the lack of perfect symmetry in its construction.

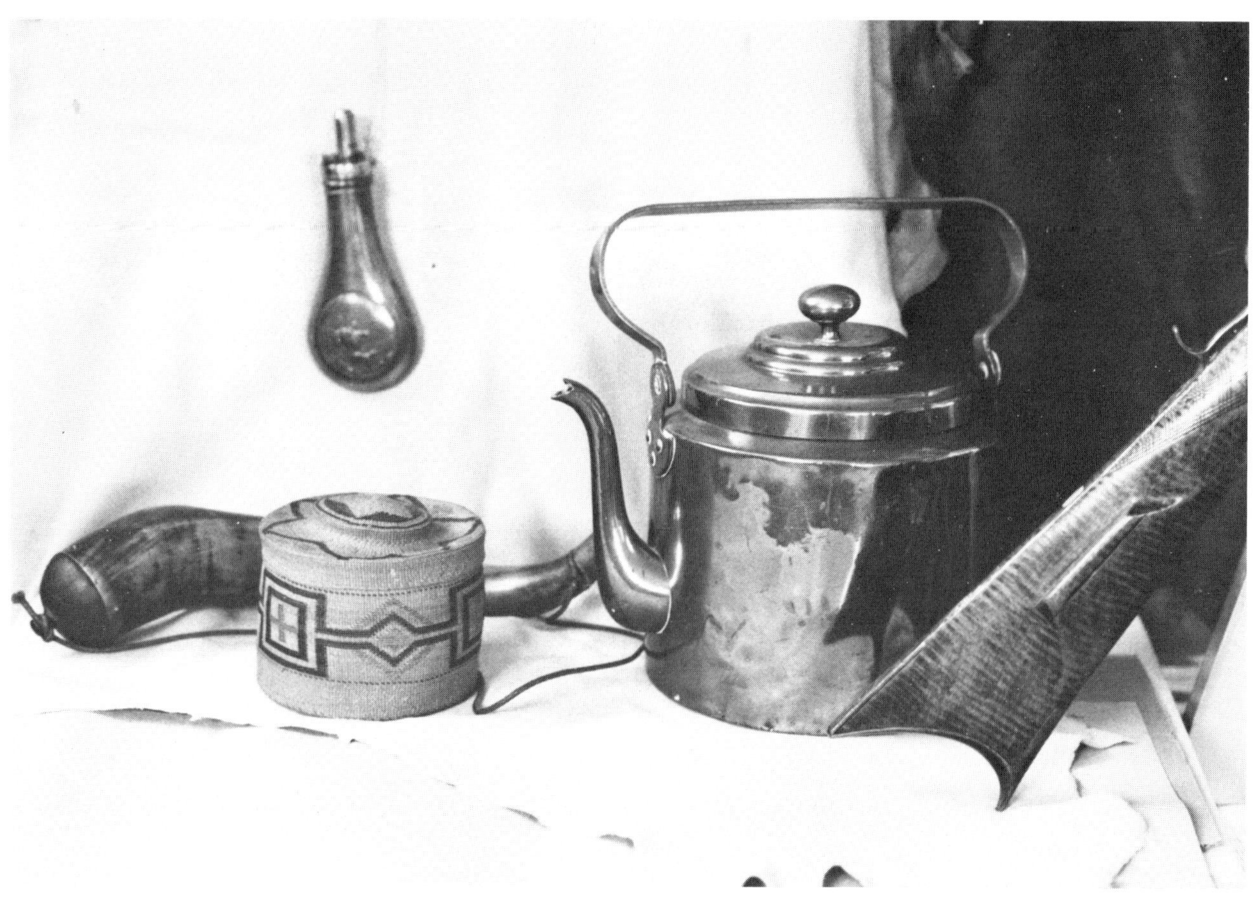

Still Life—Composing and Rendering

The still life painter has several advantages over the portrait or landscape painter: he does not have to contend with changeable or adverse lighting and weather conditions or interrupt the flow of his brush strokes to rid himself of irritating insects. And, he does not have the portrait painter's concern for his subject, the choice of working in complete silence or lessening the strain by providing entertainment. (John Singer Sargent kept his sitters partially hypnotized by playing record after record of screechy music from his new-fangled gramaphone.)

In still life painting, you have the opportunity of selecting and arranging objects that reflect your interests without distractions, thus heightening the enjoyment of painting. Also, because of your total control it is a fine way to study composition.

Shown here is a photograph of an arrangement of objects of some historical interest from my home plus a beautiful old highly polished copper kettle which I borrowed from a friend.

The objects in the composition above were chosen for their repetition and contrast of shape, size, texture, line, and color. In this case the gleaming copper kettle was my focal point.

The finely woven Alaskan basket was selected for its shape, texture, and light color. The powder horn leads the eye into the center of interest, the kettle. A copper powder-flask, beautifully embossed with a Scottish hunting scene, hangs on the contrasting light gray elk hide which forms a more neutral background. The powder-flask, besides filling an otherwise empty space, adds variety of shape and repeats lighter hues of those in the kettle.

To keep the viewer's eye focused on the kettle near the center of the composition, an old backwoods rifle was placed on the right in an upright position. The tiger-maple stock lends pattern, its horizontal lines reflecting in the copper kettle.

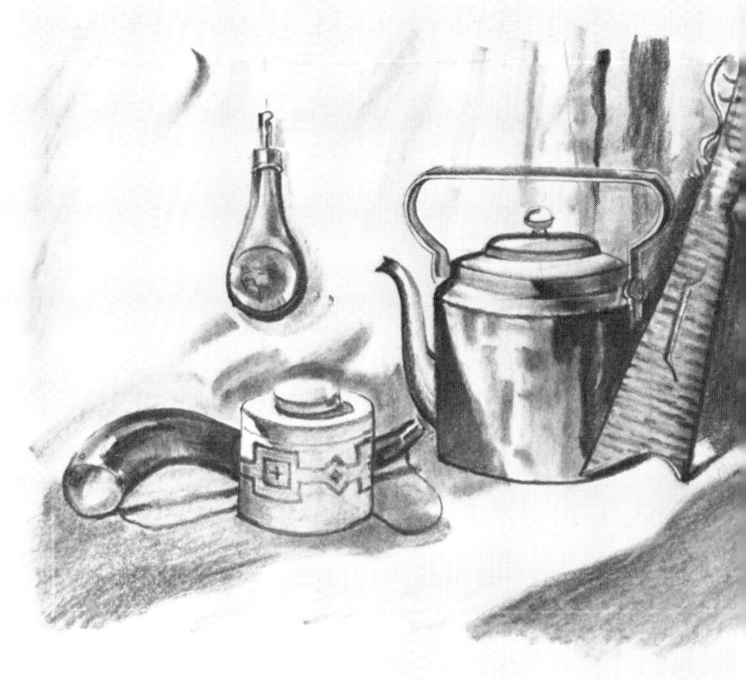

To get acquainted with the subject, I drew a 7 x 9 inch charcoal sketch with a 4B charcoal pencil. A stump (a rolled paper stick) was used to produce smooth tones which are in contrast to the heavy lines and unsmudged areas. The stump smooths the tones, the pencil adds solid tones and accents. A small sketch such as this gives you the opportunity to study the placement of the objects to gain a feeling of the forms and to relate value patterns.

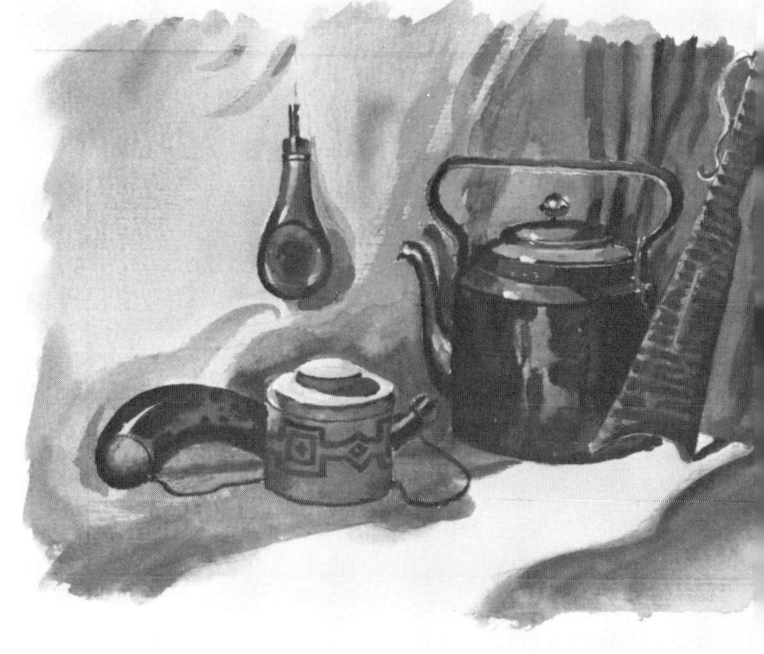

This preliminary color sketch, the same size as the charcoal sketch, serves as a guide or a reference, if needed, for the larger final painting. It also further acquaints you with the composition and color values that will be used later. Needed changes and corrections can be foreseen, enabling the final work to proceed with more confidence, freedom, and speed.

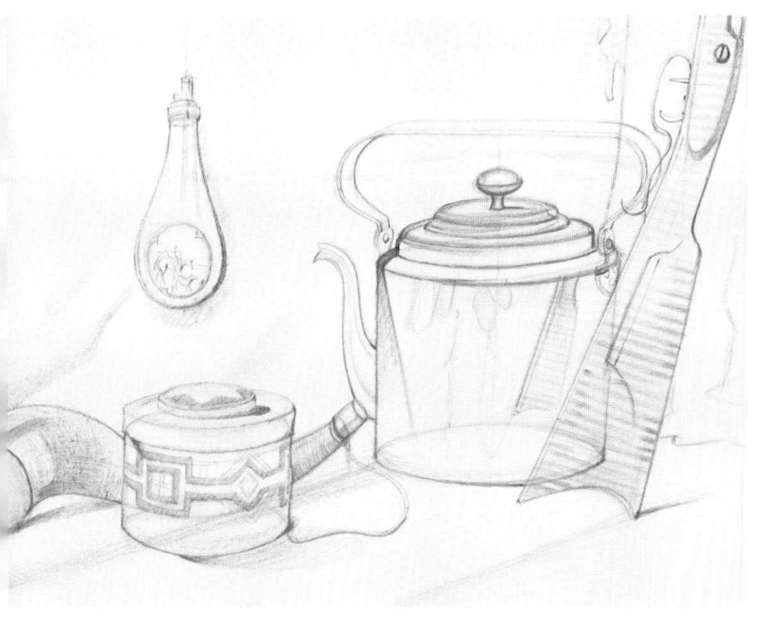

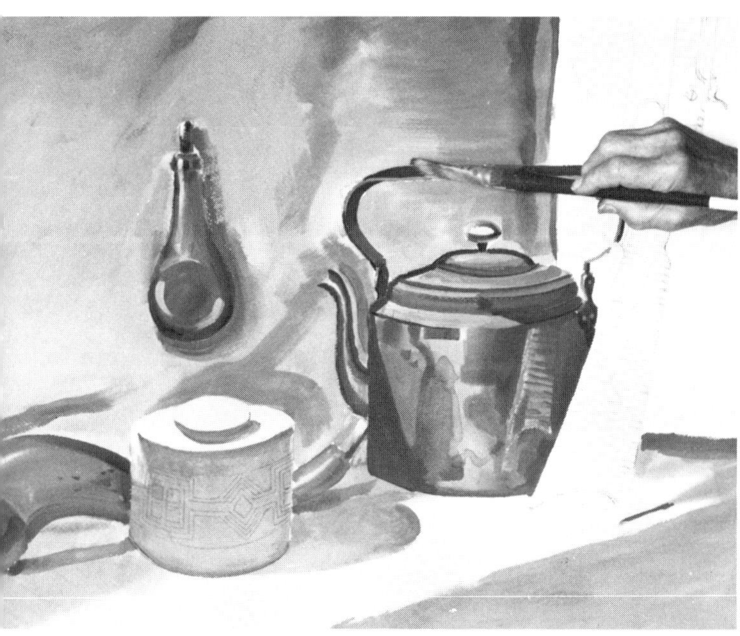

Next, a pencil drawing is made on layout paper. This paper is the same size as the watercolor paper (20 x 30 inches) to be used for the final painting. The drawing will position and establish the sizes and proportions of the objects in their relation to each other, as in the smaller sketch. After studying these relationships with half-closed eyes, the objects were freely and lightly sketched in before beginning any detailed drawing. This drawing was mainly linear.

The kettle, which dominates the composition, was first sketched in; the other objects were then drawn in relationship to the kettle. Even though parts were hidden, each object was drawn through thinking of the solid objects as though they were transparent, being certain that the bulk of one object did not invade the space required by its neighbor.

When the drawing was completed, the back of the tissue was smudged with charcoal dust, thus enabling the drawing to be traced onto the watercolor paper. Any weak lines of the tracing were strengthened with a charcoal pencil.

More experienced painters may wish to eliminate this step of drawing on tissue, preferring to sketch directly on the final paper. But beginners may feel more relaxed correcting their drawing on the tissue, leaving the watercolor paper fresh for their painting.

Before laying out the opaque colors on your palette, again study the relationship of values and hues—their lightness and darkness, warmth and coolness, and their intensity. Although colors look somewhat different on the palette than on the paper, you may find it helpful to place any hues you lightly mix on your palette next to one another as they will appear on your paper. Remember to mix a larger quantity than for the smaller painting. If your palette seems crowded, use two palettes.

The painting procedure for the larger painting, working from the actual still life, was much the same as the small color sketch. A palette knife was used to mix the background tone of ultramarine blue, raw sienna, and cerulean blue. Using a 1½-inch flat brush, the tone was washed over the dampened surface of the paper. The wash was kept on the thin side and applied wet-in-wet.

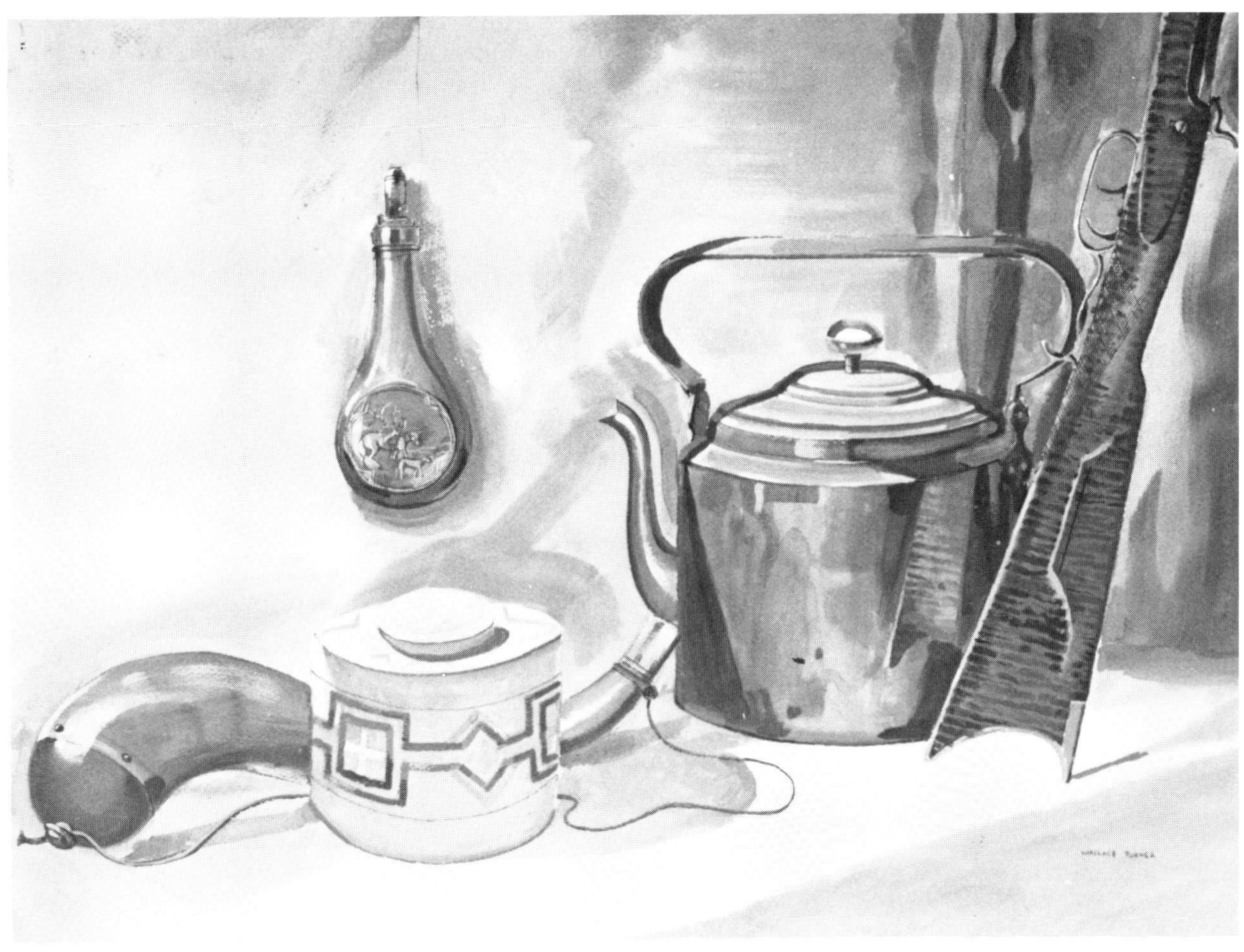

While laying in the background tone, a broad beam of sunlight crept onto the foreground of the setup, giving the entire still life a more brilliant effect; the copper objects glowed even more in the new light. I hoped I could capture this glowing quality in my painting.

You must work rapidly and freely, improvising as you go along. The reflections on the copper surface of the kettle shifted so rapidly that it was frequently necessary to refer to the charcoal sketch for values. The kettle was painted in warm intense tones—flame red, cadmium red light, cadmium orange, and burnt sienna mixed loosely right on the paper. Before these brighter tones completely dried, the dark tones of the reflection (alizarin crimson, burnt sienna, and burnt umber) were flowed into the lighter tones, as soft edges were desired. The reflection of the rifle stock was indicated on the surface of the kettle. Details would be left for later.

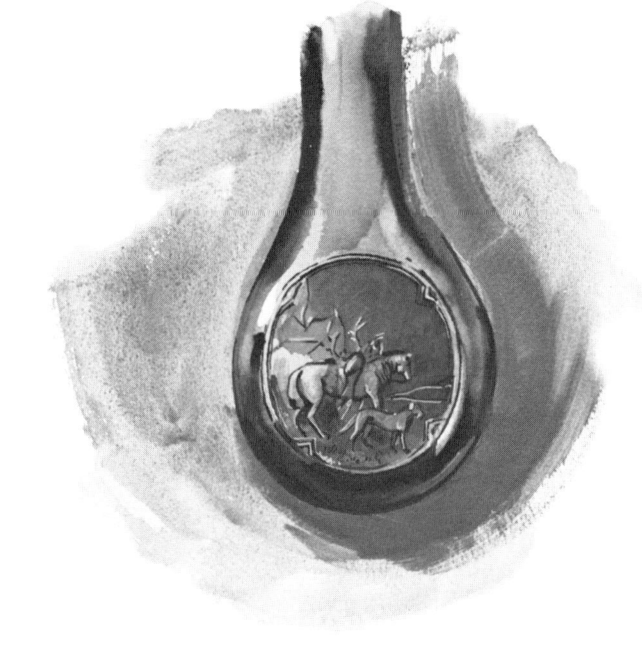

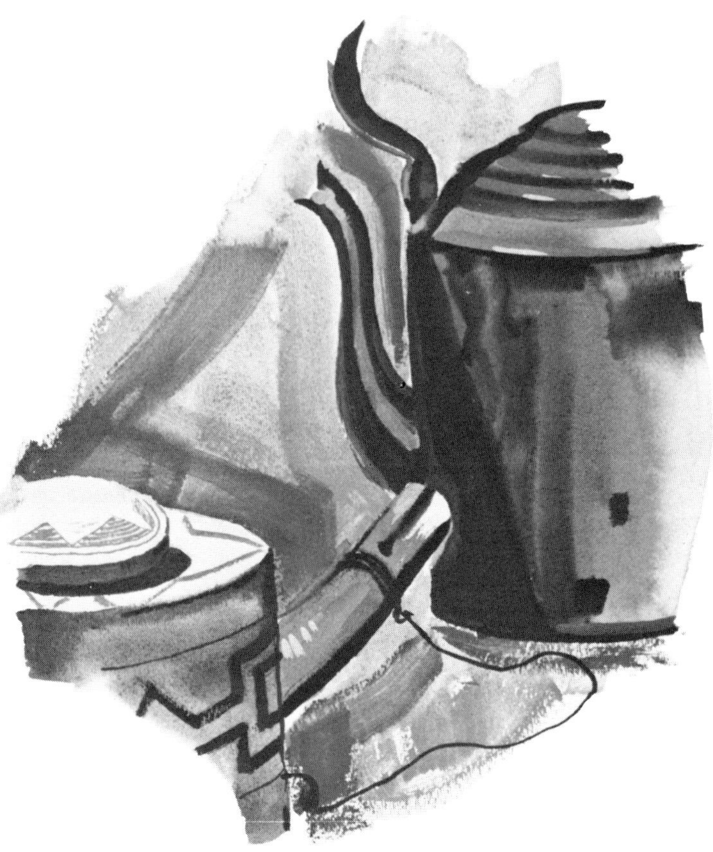

A muted color range for the powder flask was obtained by adding blue or violet to cool the warm tones mixed for the kettle. So as not to compete with the coppery hues of the kettle, a darker version of the background hue was used to form a cast shadow to the right of the powder flask.

Working from back to front, a dark hue of burnt umber with Payne's gray was mixed for the powder horn. The curving shape, accentuated by the brass tip, made an excellent pointer leading the eye to the kettle.

Of all the units shown here, the Indian basket has the greatest value contrast. The lid of the basket was painted with lemon yellow and white, while burnt sienna, raw sienna, and Payne's gray were used for the body of the basket. If the lay-in was painted strongly enough, some areas could be left as finished art which would give a greater feeling of freshness and spontaneity.

Colors for the gun and deerskin behind it were burnt sienna, burnt umber, and Payne's gray. The darker folds of the skin were rendered wet-in-wet, with attention given to the delicate sweeping curves of the brass trigger-guard of the rifle so as to avoid any appearance of clumsiness. Detail and highlights on these metal surfaces were left for the finished painting. With the exception of the highlights which add sparkle to the painting of the metal areas, the flask was left as it was originally rendered. The vignette on the flask was painted (see pull-out) to help explain the embossing of the powder flask. More value contrast is shown here between the tones than in the small sketch, helping to clarify the action of the horse and deerhound. The section showing part of the basket with the powder horn leading to the kettle emphasizes the overlapping of these two objects. Overlapping helps to unify what might otherwise be a scattered composition.

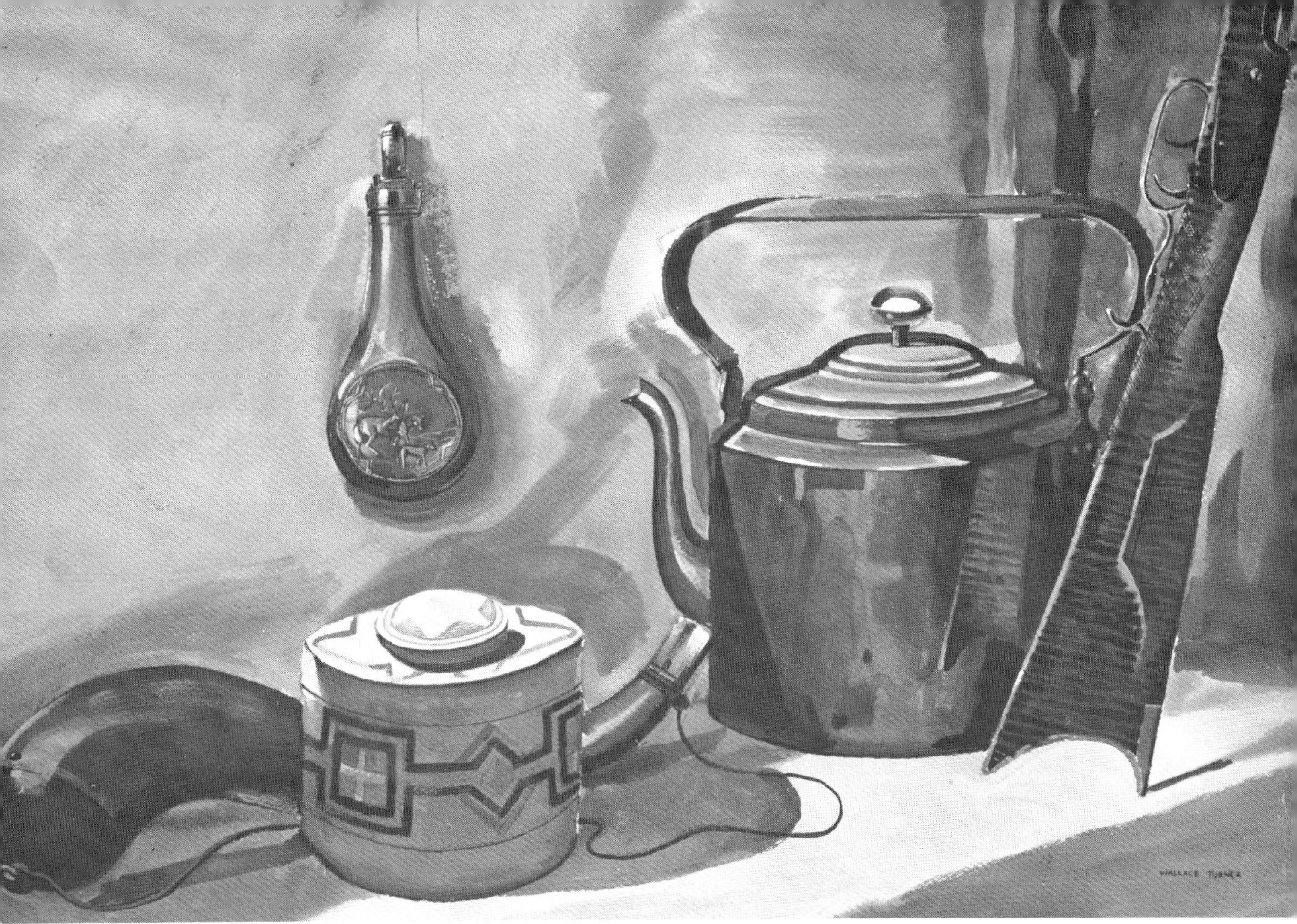

With the lay-in broadly indicated and the shapes advanced to approximately the same degree of workmanship, stop to evaluate before going on, noting any needed correction in drawing, or the changing of a tone for better contrast.

The important details in this last stage are mainly the highlights on the brass and copper metallic surfaces as these add great sparkle and authority to the painting. The curving highlights, a mixture of white and cadmium yellow, accurately follow the ellipses of the kettle and other objects on which they are painted with a lesser degree of intensity. Putting the big flat brush aside, a good pointed sable brush #5 was used to paint in the highlights with heavy pigment.

Here is an example of beginning a still life by using some of the interesting props that are shown in the photograph. After some trial and error, by making innumerable thumbnail sketches, you can arrive at a viable composition.

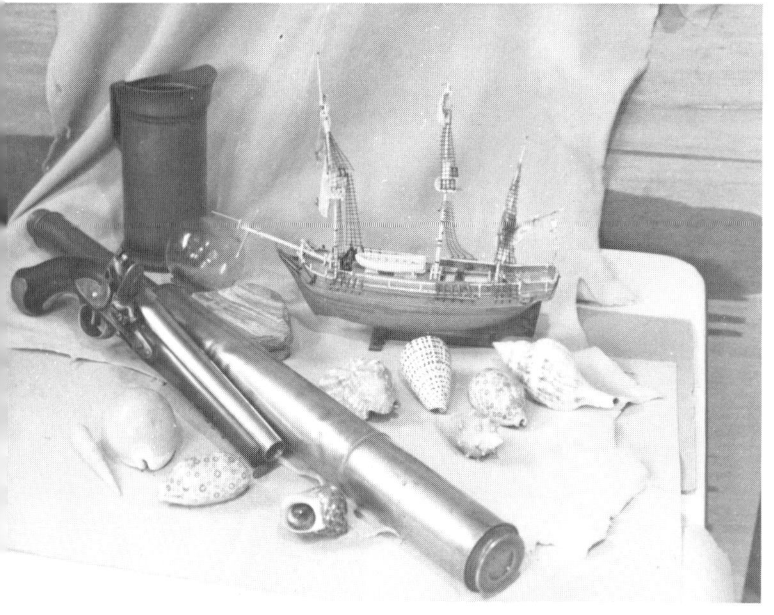

Observe how in the photo of the props something is missing—in this case the something was the need for verticals. So I stood the spyglass on end and hung the dagger point down. Then I elevated the ship, HMS Bounty, to make it more dramatic and to create a middle height. Next, a path of the shells was made to lead the eye into the composition. The pistol points into the picture from the left. The ship does the same thing from the right. By using an old parchment map as a background, I felt I had completed the composition.

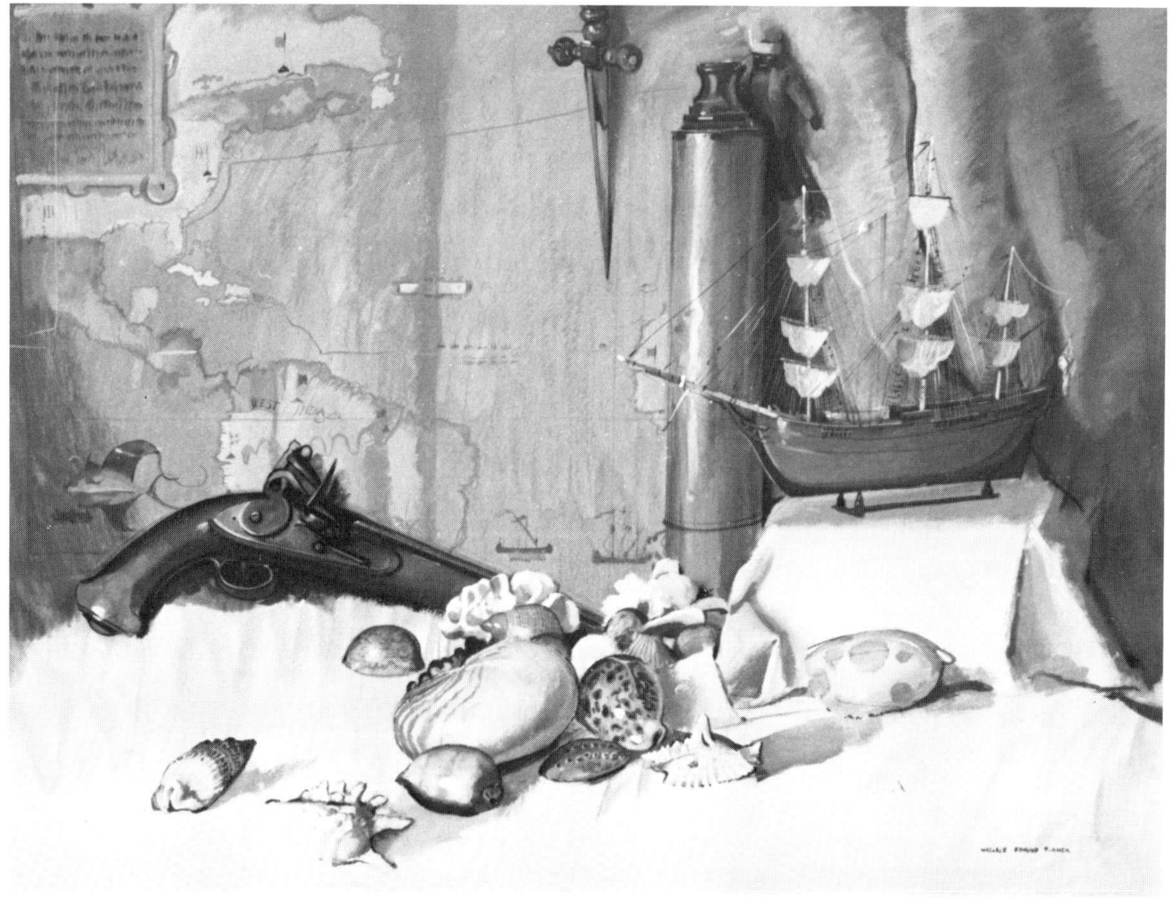

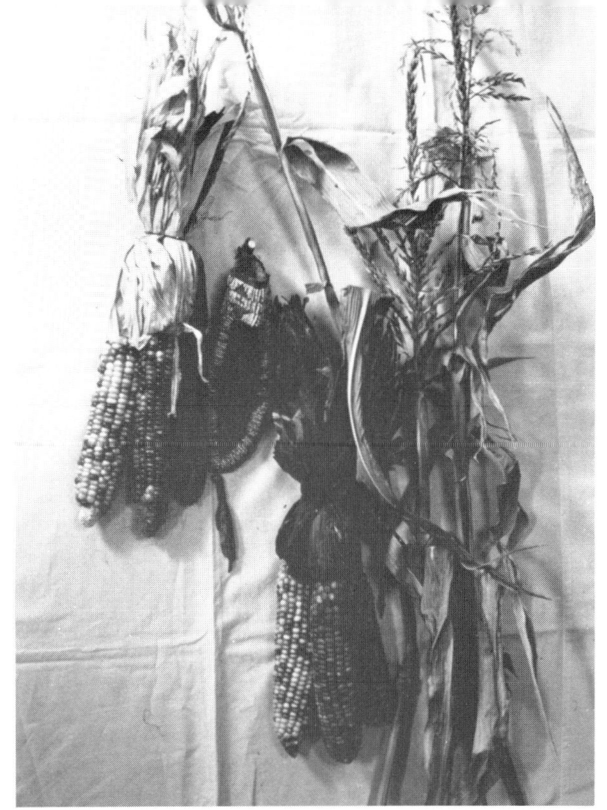

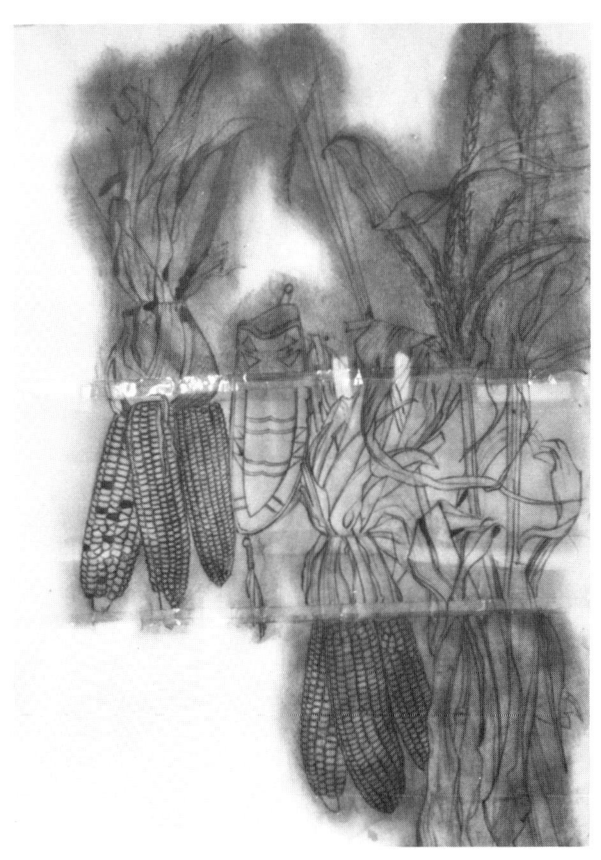

Opaque Watercolor with Pen and Ink

Pen and ink used in conjunction with opaque watercolor is an effective medium with which to accentuate a rendering. It works well in defining and strengthening the drawing, in pointing up what needs to be emphasized and in establishing a textured contrast. If an opaque painting takes on a chalky appearance, a sharp pen line can reinforce the rendering. However, its application should not be a complete pen and ink drawing in itself, but should act as a supporting role. It is best to develop dark masses in pigment rather than in pen and ink.

To illustrate the technique of applying pen and ink to opaque watercolor painting, I decided to bring a bit of Nova Scotia's autumn colors into my studio. I chose the multi-colored ears of corn, referred to in early days as "Indian corn." The set-up for my composition is shown in the photo at the top of page. The Indian corn suggested that an old Plains Indian knife sheath be a part of the composition, placing it so as to give variety to the spacing. A few corn stalks completed the composition.

The preliminary drawing was with a 4B charcoal pencil on tissue as it was to be traced to a sheet of Hi-Art Illustration board, 30 x 21½ inches.

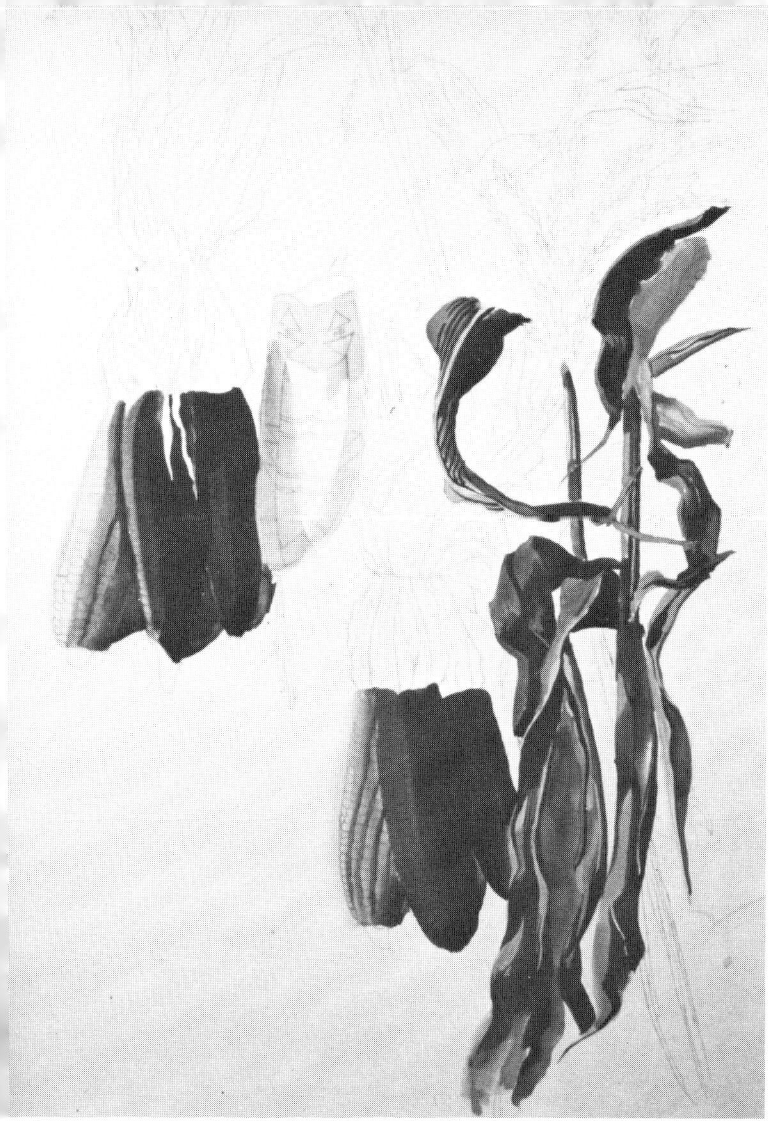

Here all the bright reds are in use—flame red, alizarin crimson, cadmium scarlet, and Parma violet. For the red ears of corn, an undercoating of flame red and alizarin crimson was mixed for the light side and alizarin crimson, burnt sienna, and a touch of Payne's gray for the dark side. These hues served as a background for the hues to follow for the individual kernels. The variations of these colors of the kernels add interest to the painting. Many of the kernels were painted with cadmium red mixed with cadmium orange, while the darker kernels were rendered in alizarin crimson, Parma violet, and a touch of Payne's gray. There did not seem to be an end of color in any one ear of corn. In painting the light side of the kernels in the yellow ears of corn, white with cadmium yellow light was used, while for the shadow side yellow ochre was mixed with burnt umber and Payne's gray.

The group of corn leaves on the left was painted with cadmium yellow and yellow ochre in contrast to the leaves in shadow painted with yellow ochre, burnt sienna, and a touch of ultramarine blue. For the purplish cluster of leaves near the center, alizarin crimson and flame red were used, with ultramarine blue replacing the flame red for the shadow side. A variety of hues—warm yellow greens, cadmium orange, yellow ochre, and raw sienna—gave warmth to the clump of leaves and stalks to the right. Both warm and cool greens were employed in this area; for the darker greens—alizarin crimson and Hooker's green, or ultramarine blue and burnt sienna, both striking combinations.

Cast shadow patterns on the background consist of ultramarine blue with a bit of yellow ochre.

The final touch was to paint highlights, using white, on some of the individual kernels and where the painter wished to draw attention.

The only pure white in this painting is the white of the beadwork on the knife sheath and the highlights on the corn. No black pigment and little Payne's gray is used.

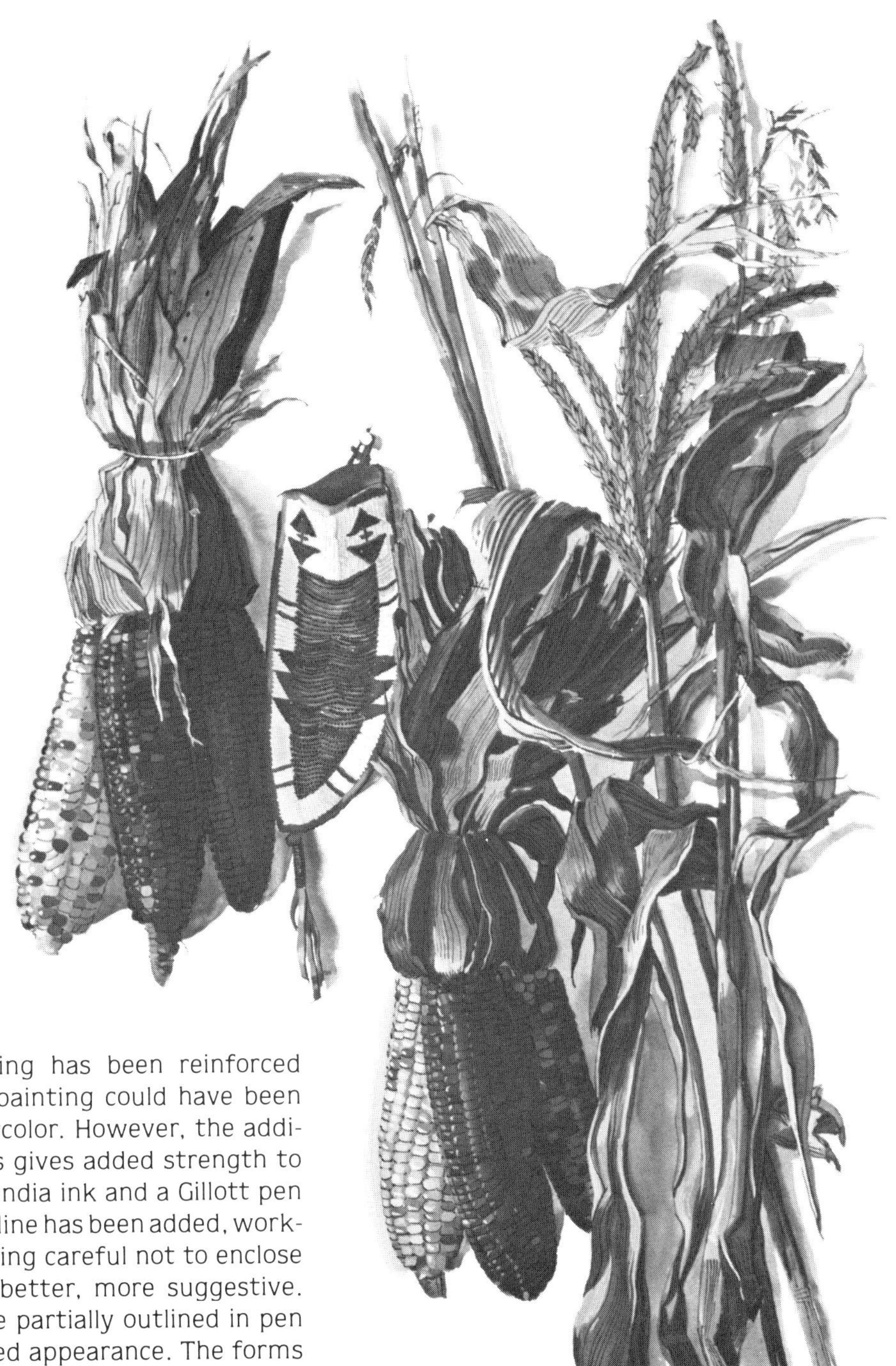

The completed painting has been reinforced with pen and ink. The painting could have been left as an opaque watercolor. However, the addition of pen and ink lines gives added strength to the composition. Using India ink and a Gillott pen point #170, a broken outline has been added, working around the units, being careful not to enclose them; a broken line is better, more suggestive. Just a few kernels were partially outlined in pen and ink to avoid a labored appearance. The forms of the ears of corn with the different colored kernels and twisted leaves demand a thick and thin pen line treatment. Pressure on the pen increases the thickness of the line.

In contrast to the sharp pen and ink line, a blurry effect can be obtained by drawing a loaded pen over a damp surface; this will create a sort of halftone effect. Sometimes pen and ink or brush and ink are used for the basic free drawing over which a tone is washed when the ink is dry or partially dry, also giving a blurry effect. By experimenting along these lines, you may discover a technique that more fully expresses your own aspirations.

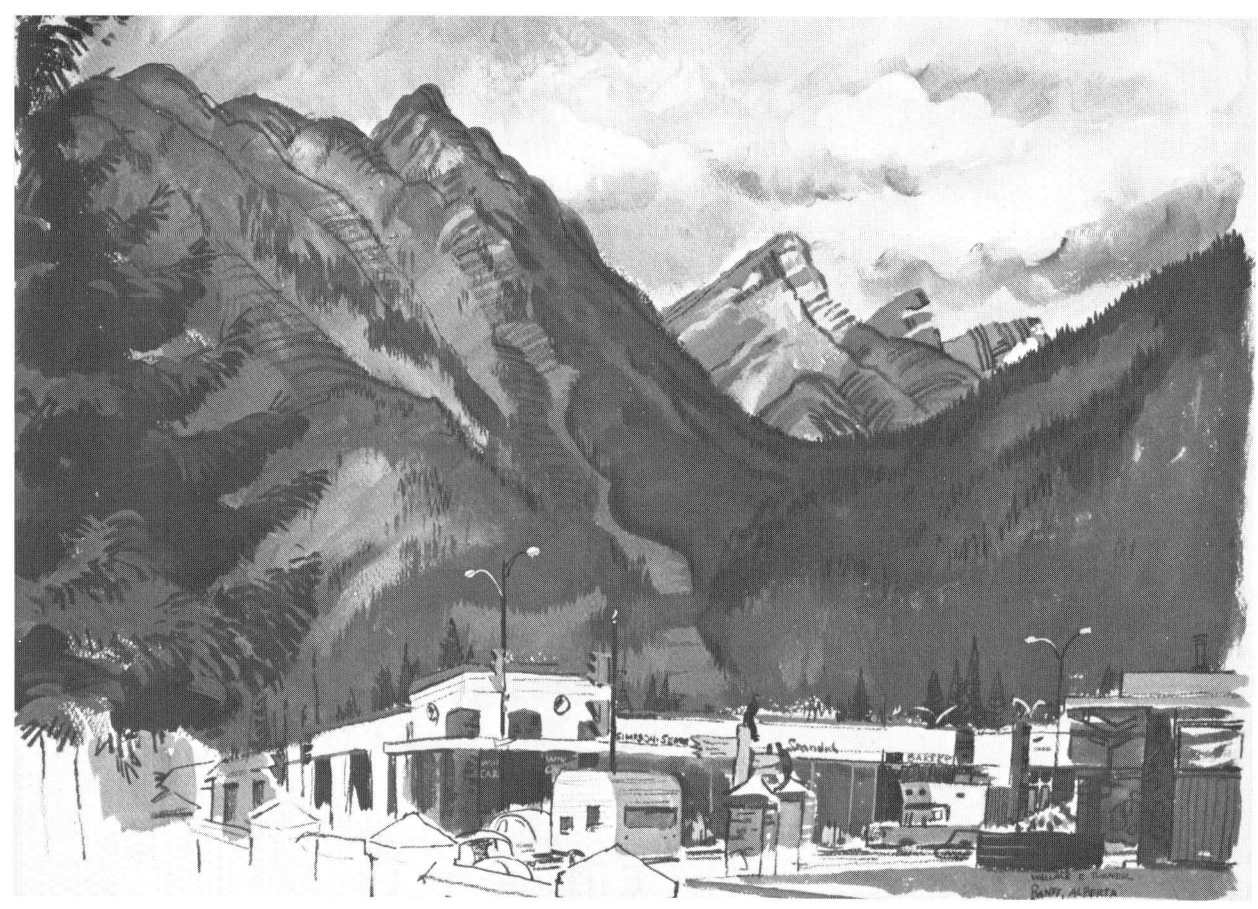

BANFF, ALBERTA
Opaque watercolor with prismacolor pencil

CHAPTER 6

Painting on Location

On-the-spot painting always presents problems. Certainly it is a less predictable procedure than working in your own studio. As you are probably aware by this time, I like to work on location and have done so in many parts of the world. For me each painting is a unique experience, and the problems of doing it enrich the final result.

There are few pictures I have done on-the-spot that do not have a little story or anecdote connected with them. They run the gamut from hostile dogs to unexpected rain squalls. Actually, very few have lasting negative connotations; indeed, a number have been rewarding experiences in their own right, and in some cases more memorable than the resultant painting. If you are not already addicted to painting on location I urge you to give it a try. It takes some initiative, but you'll soon realize your position as an artist gives you special license and a kind of universal respect and tolerance.

In the next several pages I'll offer some step-by-step accounts of a couple of my on-the-spot painting sessions.

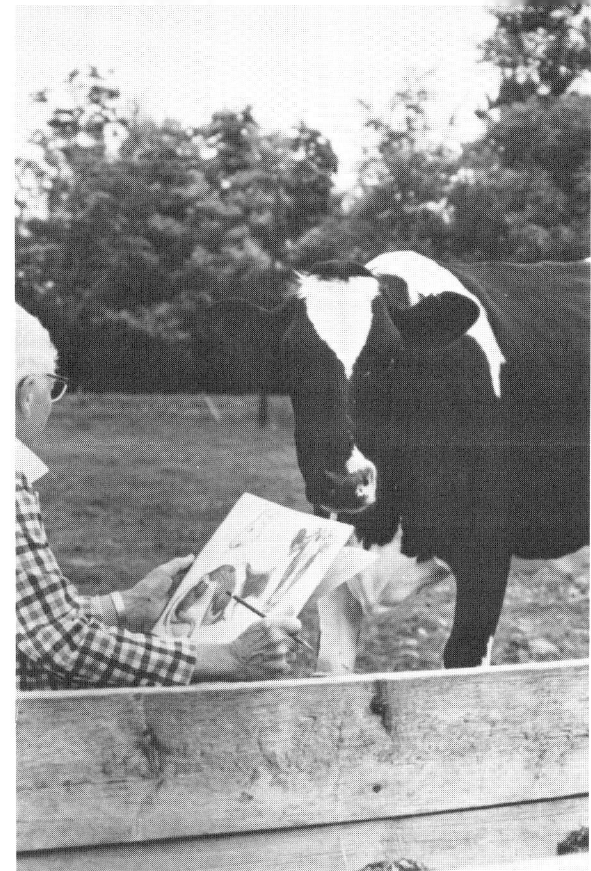

A scene on the Cogswell Farm just a few miles from my home in Wolfville, Nova Scotia, first attracted my attention due to the stark simplicity of the silo with its strong vertical movement upward to the cloud-filled sky. The horizontal movement of the lower buildings, broken by the treetop shapes, unified the scene, adding contrast of movement and tone, variety in shape and spacing. The cows in the foreground added life and interest.

I knew I would include some cows in the picture, so I decided to sketch a few of them before starting to paint. I moved right into the herd. They surely were curious, but in a little while they were accustomed to my presence and came right up to look over my shoulder.

Before deciding on a composition, I walked around the scene, viewing it from different angles and distances. Then I chose two locations from which to make the 8 x 10½ inch sketches.

The view with the Holsteins grazing amid the various greens of the foliage and the sunny grays of the buildings offered possibilities.

For the second small sketch, a large tree with its dark foliage masses and shadow area dominated the foreground. Though the sketch seemed well composed, the silo which had first attracted me was of secondary importance. Its prominence was further diminished by its distance and the branch overlapping the dome. Not satisfied, I resumed my search for a better composition.

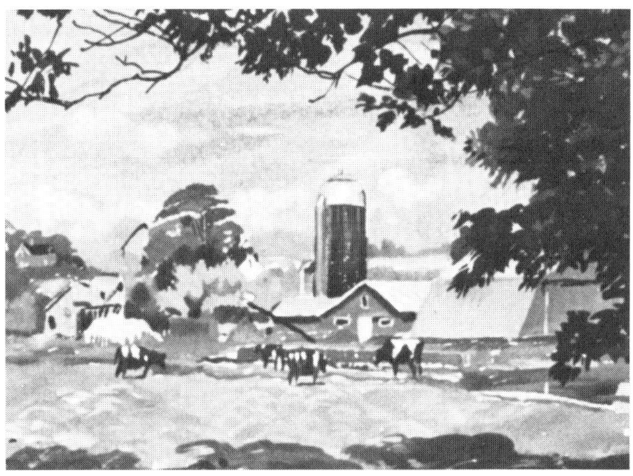

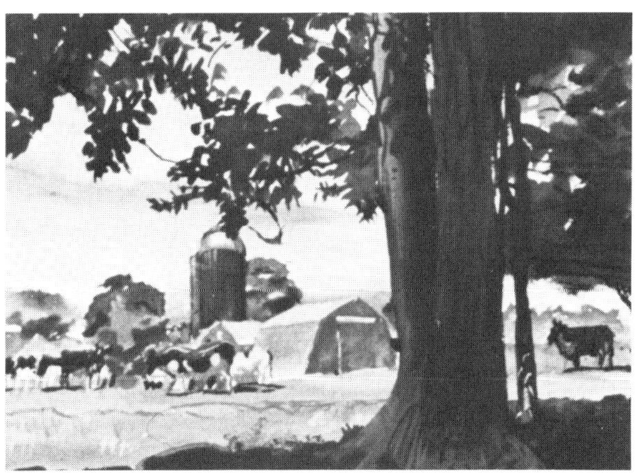

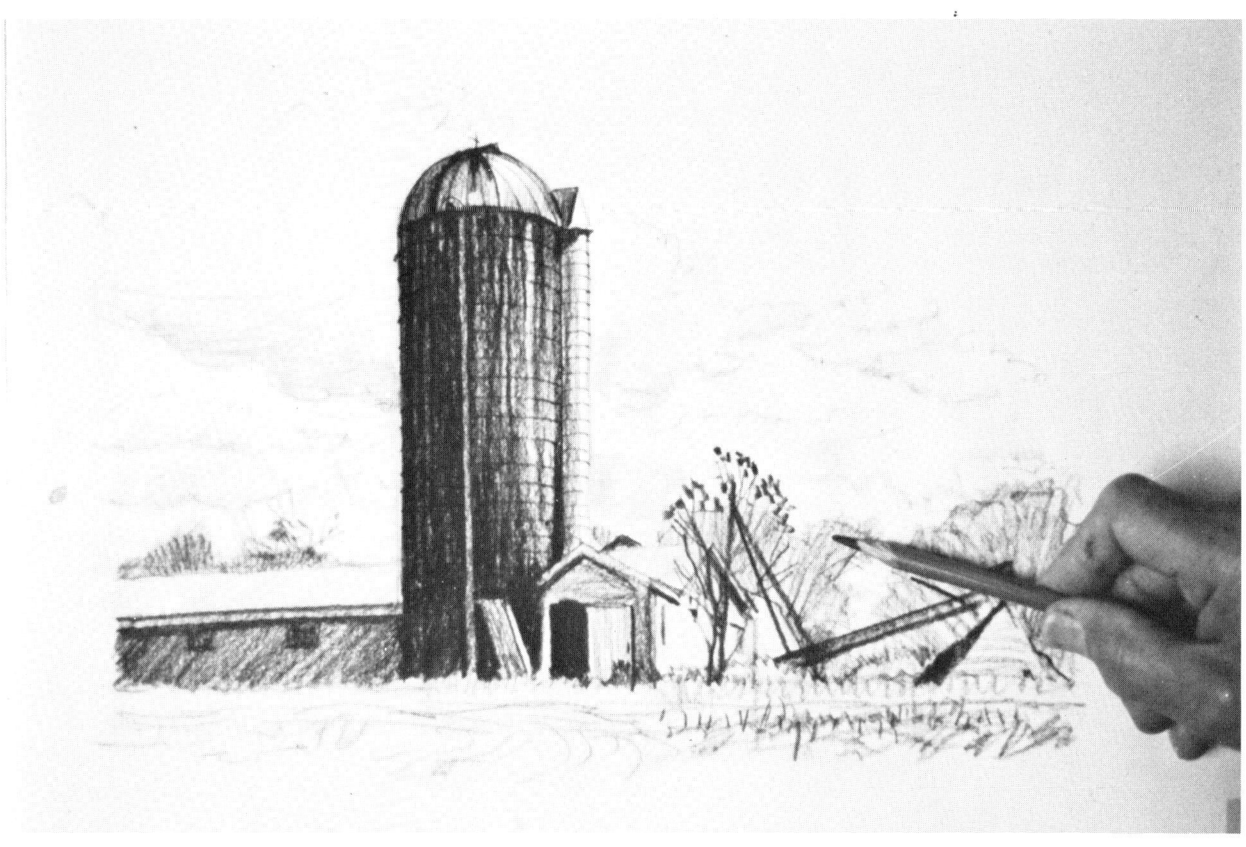

For my third try I selected a position directly in front of the imposing silo. Feeling certain that this way my best vantage point for the composition, I decided this time to first do a 9 x 12 inch charcoal pencil sketch using a 4B charcoal pencil and bond paper.

This charcoal sketch emphasized the simplicity of the vertical and horizontal lines, giving more impact than in the two previous sketches. The dark rectangle formed by the doorway of the building at the base of the silo acted as an invitation to wander into the picture.

The round ribs or ellipses that circle the silo were drawn carefully with dark lines so that washes to be added later would not obliterate these important charcoal lines. The ellipses became flatter as they moved down to the horizon line at the base of the silo and buildings. Note how the lines from the roofs of these buildings slope down to vanishing points that are on the horizon line to the left of the silo. This vanishing point is quite a way out, while the vanishing point to the right is close in.

After completing this small charcoal sketch, I made an 8 x 10½ inch painting in opaque watercolor. Then I started my final composition on a 22 x 30 sheet of Strathmore watercolor paper, again drawing with the 4B charcoal pencil. This drawing was mainly linear in treatment, showing little tone or value as excess charcoal dust has a tendency to muddy the color applied over it. Charcoal pencil is preferred to charcoal stick because it does not break as easily.

You might ask: why not use a drawing pencil as used for sketching in the small compositions? The answer is that charcoal pencil gives a stronger dark which can be easily lifted with a kneaded eraser if desired. Also, charcoal pencil does not resist the application of watercolor as the greasy surface of a soft pencil does. In the smaller sketches less and lighter drawing was required, so

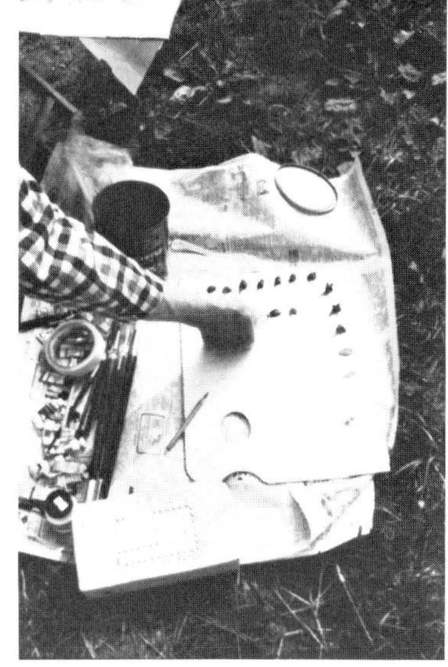

there was no problem of erasing.

Now that the final composition had been sketched in and all other drawing completed, I was ready to lay out my palette. Because both warm and cool colors would be required, a full palette was needed. With the block of disposable palettes on the ground within easy reach beside me, the colors were squeezed from the tubes in the following order: white on the upper right, then through the yellows and reds to the earth colors, on to the greens, the blues, and Payne's gray.

No black was used as richer darks can be obtained from combinations of viridian green and alizarin crimson, or ultramarine blue with burnt sienna. Other combinations also give deep rich darks without relying on black.

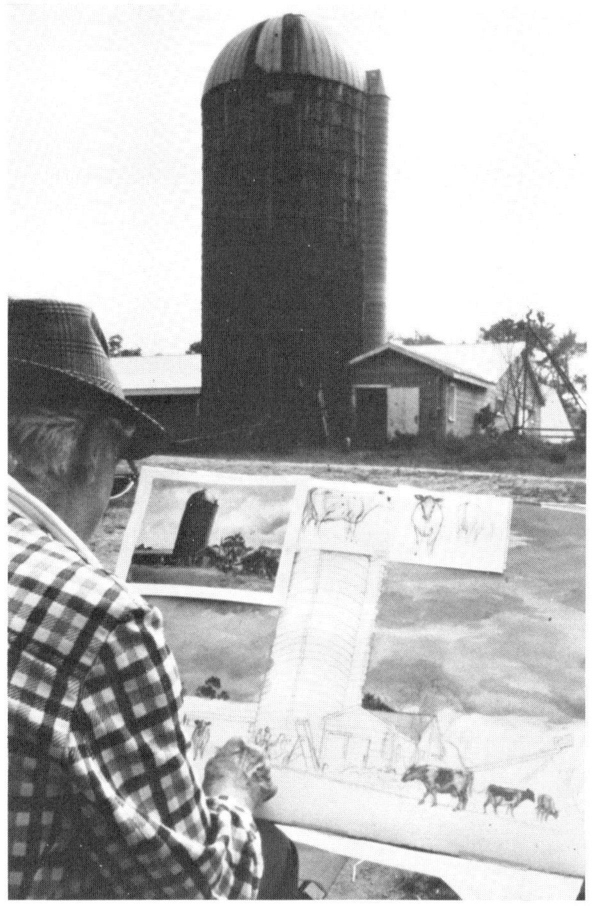

Working rapidly with a 1½-inch brush, I started with the sky, using a mixture of ultramarine blue and cerulean blue. This was washed into the dampened surface of the sky area. The small opaque painting and the charcoal sketch of the cows were taped to the upper left side of the large paper for quick reference if needed. Notice that the photograph here shows the sky cloudless and duller than indicated in the preliminary sketches. Although skies in Nova Scotia are moody and change rapidly, I felt I could not wait. This was when the small painting proved of value for reference, aiding my memory in painting a similar cloud-filled sky rather than the duller cloudless sky before me.

Viridian green with burnt sienna were painted into a wet surface to form the background of trees. A combination of burnt umber, Payne's gray, and yellow ochre was painted wet-in-wet on the silo area and allowed to flow down the paper, giving a streaky appearance. Ultramarine blue and alizarin crimson were added to this dark hue as the tone reached the left hand edge of the silo, reflecting the cool tone from the sky. The dark hue of burnt umber and Payne's gray, running from top to bottom of the silo as the paper was tilted, did not completely cover the dark charcoal elliptical bands which would be painted in later with a fine-pointed brush. The strong streaky texture of the silo was reinforced by a darker value of the same basic hue, partly wet-in-wet, partly dry brush.

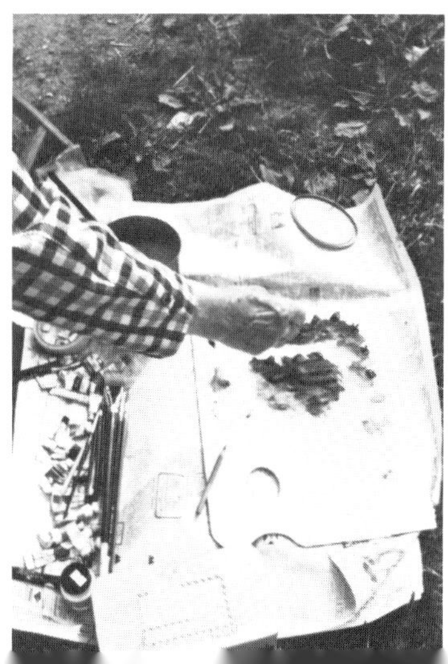

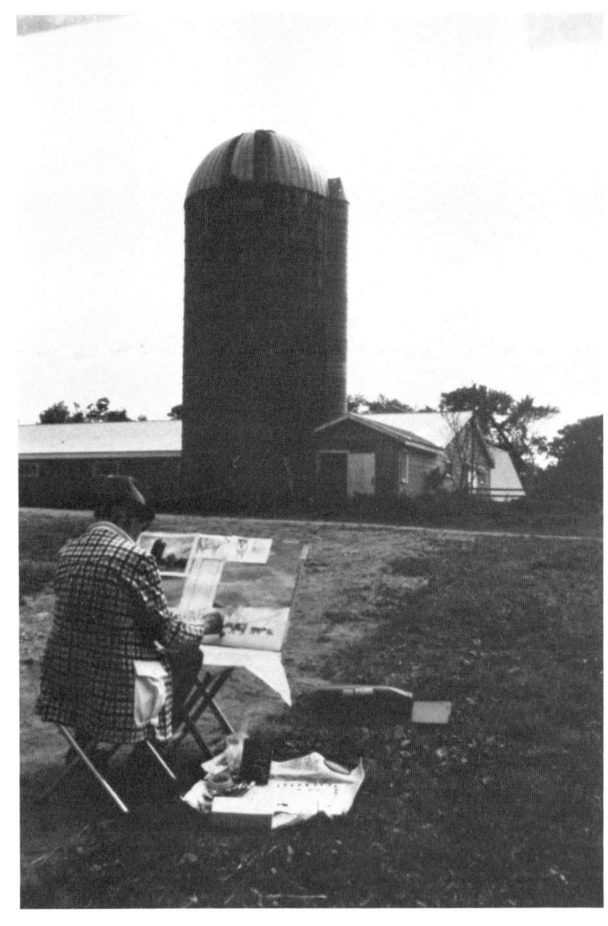

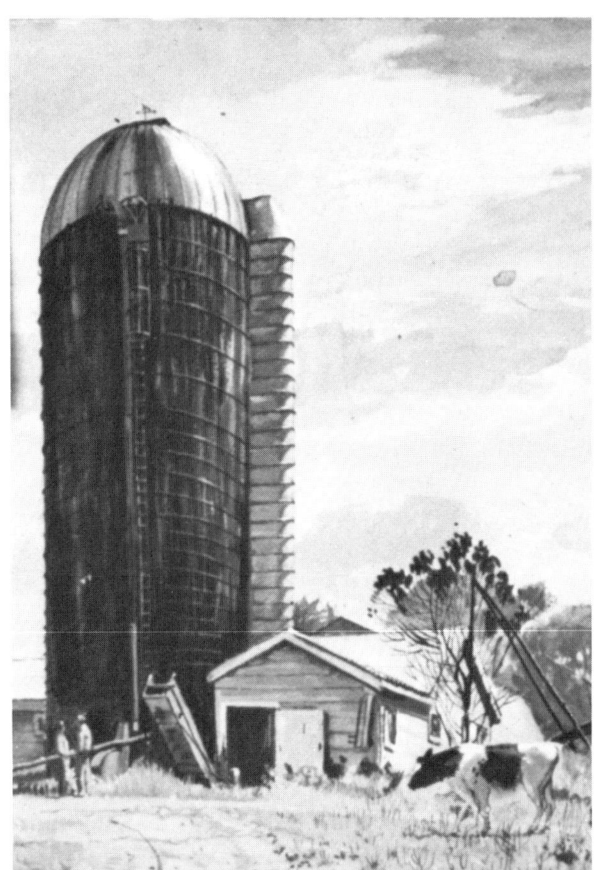

The silo was painted with a 1½-inch flat brush. For the bands, ladder and other details, smaller round brushes, #5 or #6, were used. As said before, the brush must fit the job. To get a free sweep of the arm from top to bottom when rendering the silo, the paper was frequently turned sideways. The wet-in-wet technique was found especially valuable here.

Turning now to the metal dome on the top of the silo, a heavy high-key value of white and yellow ochre was mixed and applied to the dampened highlight area. While still damp, a surrounding darker value of ultramarine blue, Payne's gray, and yellow ochre was painted in. As the edges fused, the highlight on the dome gleamed forth. Later an almost pure white was added as the highest-key light. As the hue of the dome reached the left hand curving edge, a strong dark value was painted into the tone. The ribs defining the rounded form of the dome were then added along with the weathervane on the top.

Speed was essential here. While the tones of the dome were still damp, a large round brush loaded with burnt sienna was swept in to define the deep tones of the reddish-brown rust running down the curved sides of the metal. These rich hues of burnt sienna which I eagerly seized upon and which greatly enlivened the otherwise cool color scheme of the dome were completely lost on the farm's owner to whom the rusted area meant only costly repairs.

Two main values comprised the painting of the adjoining buildings, one for the light side, the other for the dark side. The values were painted with white, yellow ochre, Payne's gray and cerulean blue. The use of flat brushes was found to be best. The strong dark values under the eaves and in the open doorway were painted with a combination of burnt umber and Payne's gray. The openings in the background trees were painted just a tone or so darker than the background sky. Treated in this manner, they did not appear as holes in the trees. The circular bands around the silo were painted carefully with a dark fine line because these ellipses were important in establishing a convincing appearance to the structure.

The ladder and other details are also indicated

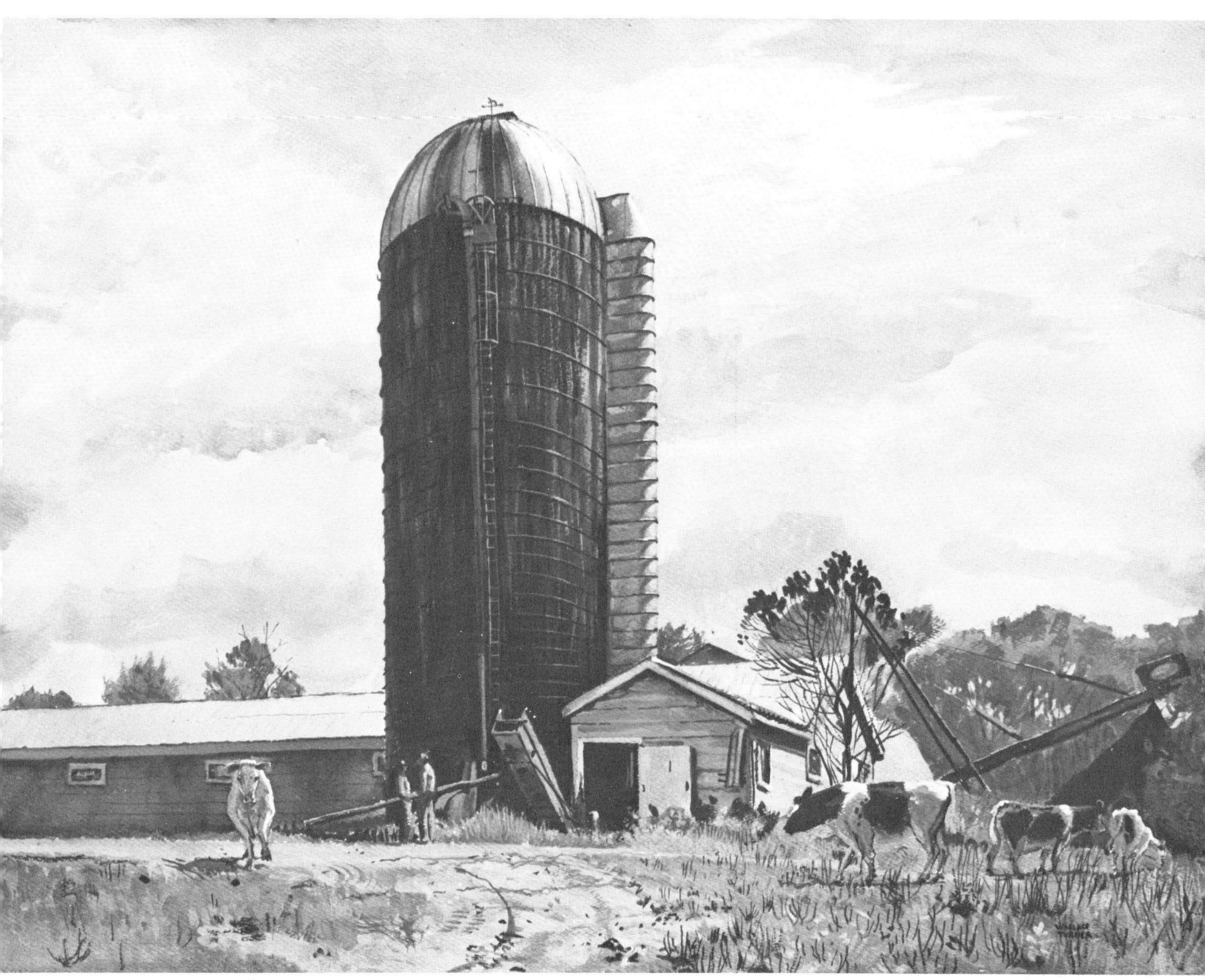

COGSWELL FARM

on the silo. As this is a working farm and contributes its share to the economy of the region, some of the equipment used is shown in the proximity of the silo.

The foreground is now given attention. Note that the curve of the road leads the eye toward the silo and the two young farmers who give scale to the composition. Interest in the foreground area was heightened by adding bright yellow-green grasses and weeds typical of the area. The suggestion of light wagon tracks and the curve of the road carry the interest to the two young farmers and the base of the silo. The rendering of the cows was completed and the dark line of the skeleton of the tree against the shed was added.

I should add that I do not always go through all of these preliminary steps. They have been included here because they may be helpful.

It's a great privilege to paint amidst the ancient ruined temples of Egypt built so many centuries ago, but still casting an aura of wonderment and amazement among all who venture within their confines. An artist, armed with only a few brushes, some battered tubes of watercolors and other painting gear, will face the unflinching gaze of these kings from centuries past.

As a composition, the profile view of the pharaoh had much to offer. The massive parallel rows of sculptured columns on each side framed an oblong of light which made the statue of Ramses II the dramatic center of interest. The light of the sun striking from the left illuminated the crown and side of the face of the pharaoh and also bathed the columns at the right in sunlight. The light of the sun was so intense that reflected light can be seen on the columns to the left and on the right-hand areas of the statue. This color was mainly made by using white and lemon yellow, yellow ochre or cadmium yellow medium. Egypt is, comparatively speaking, a hot country with blazing light and deep blue sky. It seemed to me painting this vivid blue expanse with pure ultramarine blue and white took away the warm quality of the country and presented instead a cool appearance.

A drawing was made on a sheet of Fabriano 15 x 20 inches. The sky was then painted in using ultramarine blue, cerulean blue, and a small amount of viridian green. The sky color was thus relieved of an absolutely "cold" look. Using the largest brush, the columns on the left were painted in combining raw sienna, burnt sienna, blue, and white. This called for fast handling, as there are no hard edges in the columns and the large forms had to be kept fairly smooth and rounded.

The legs of another enormous figure of a pharaoh can be seen next to the columns. Here, to the mixture used to paint the columns was added viridian green and burnt umber with some ivory black. The figure of the pharaoh was laid in with somewhat the same combination only adding more viridian green and Hooker's green deep.

The final touches of light on the crown and head and down the right leg of the figure were painted with heavy white with yellow. As shown in the painting, a variety of greens mixed with yellow ochre and burnt umber comprise the lay-in. Over this were painted the highlights. The strong reflected light bouncing back from the sunlit columns on the right side of the painting was painted with yellow ochre and sap green. To the reflected light on the crown was added burnt sienna.

The painting of the head of the pharaoh is an exercise in hard and soft edges. The transition of light to shadow on the cheek gives a softly modeled edge, while the cast shadow on the same cheek has an extremely hard edge. The same treatment can be seen in the double crown, while hard edges exclusively outline the stone wig on the pharaoh's head. The wearing and cracking of the stone crown offer a texture that holds attention on the head which is the center of interest. The artificial beard on the face of the figure is also comprised of hard edges while the rounded forms of the legs are softly modeled. A great deal of squinting was done during the painting to insure that the greatest contrast and interest was centered on the pharaoh.

The columns were first painted wet-in-wet using warm dark tones—burnt umber, burnt sienna, raw sienna, yellow ochre—and stressing the reflected light areas. Following this lay-in, the hieroglyphics were painted in. This was somewhat a hit-or-miss matter as much of this picture-carving was worn away by the ravages of the centuries. In the warm gloom of the columns it was necessary to strain my eyes and squint at the carved figures trying to decipher them. I had to leave the painting several times, walk up to the huge columns and try to figure out what had been depicted. I'm sure my results on paper would confuse an Egyptologist. As the figures were incised into the stone, it was necessary to give this effect in the painting, contrasting dark and light lines, giving the character of the sculpture.

The enlarged head of the statue is shown with contrasting hard and soft edges—the "lost and found again" aspect of the painting. Just the big shapes and values are shown here, the details seemed unnecessary at this point. The head was painted mainly wet-in-wet transparent technique and the heavy white highlights were added in a "touch and drag" fashion.

The sketch on the right shows the development of one of the avenues between the columns of this enormous ancient temple. It also shows the extent of the reflected light on the objects at the left in the painting. It's a good idea to watch for and to be aware of reflected light. It is not confined only to hot countries, but can also be seen in much colder climates in banks of ice and snow.

I imagine that the great Ramses will sit for his portrait through the next three thousand years or so, and many other hopefuls will approach this great work of art with hope of recording it in paint. May you be one of them.

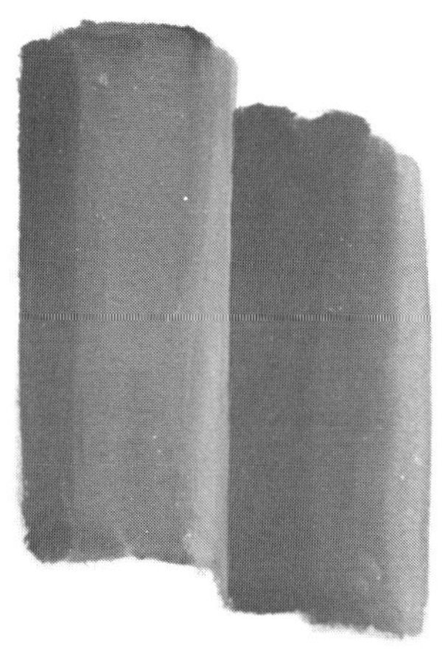

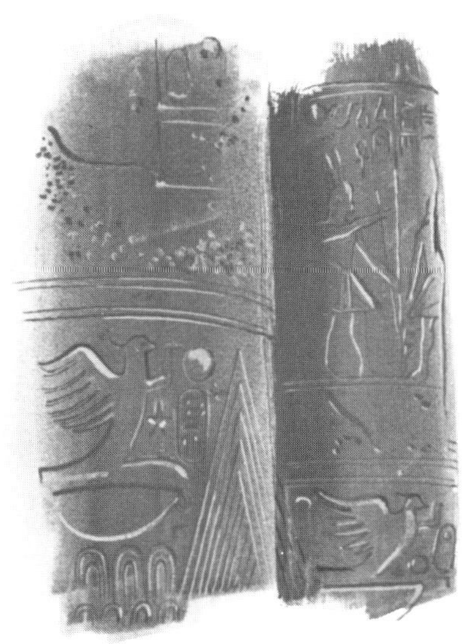

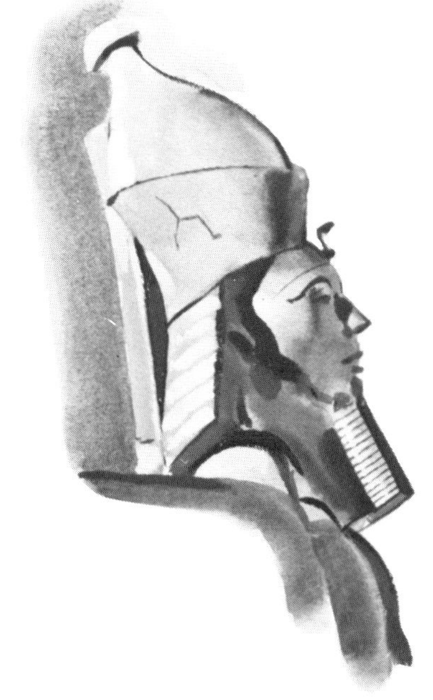

PHARAOH, LUXOR, EGYPT

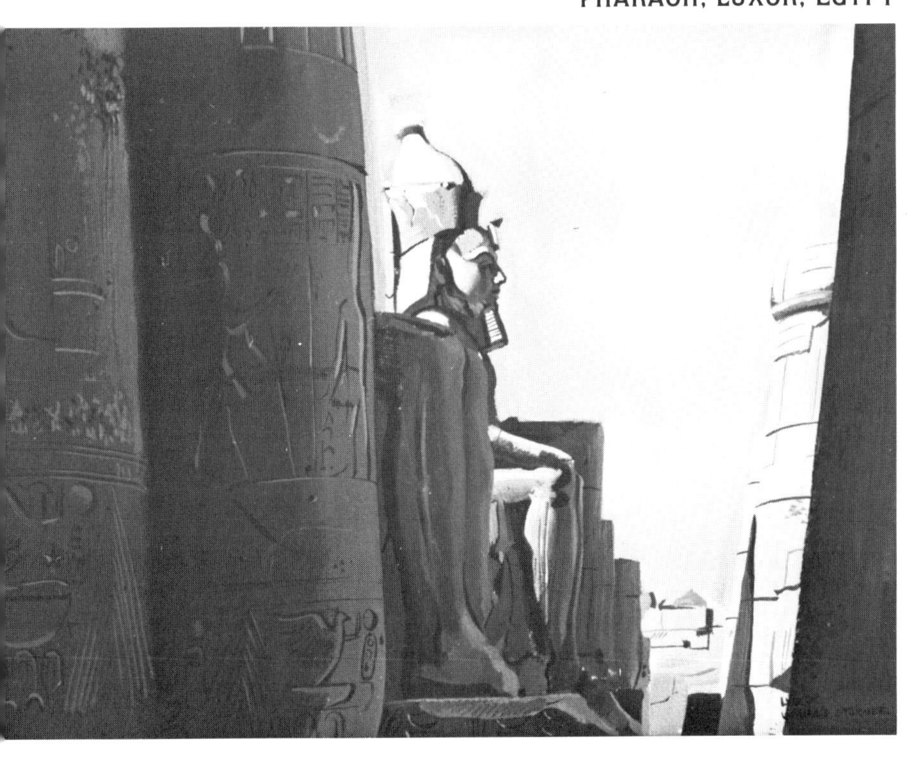

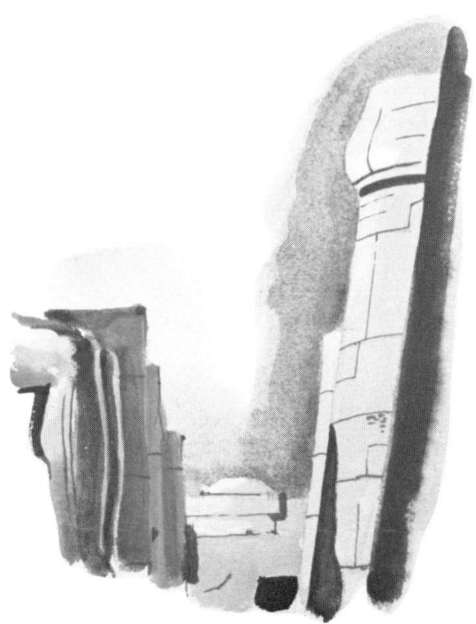

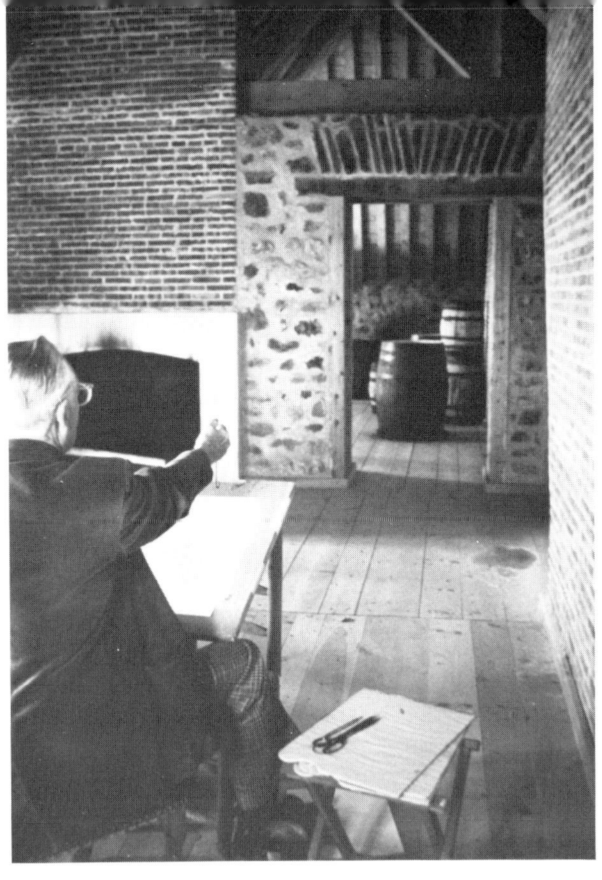

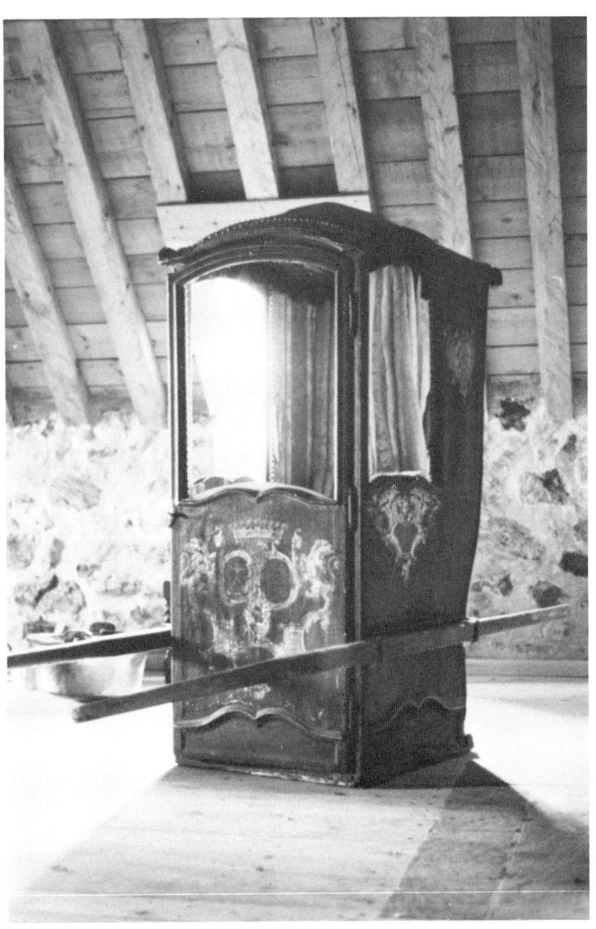

FORTRESS LOUISBOURG

One glance around this attic storeroom above the Governor General's Quarters in the newly reconstructed eighteenth century French military base at Fortress Louisbourg told me this was the interior I would paint. The slanting lines of the great 15 x 15 inch timbers vault upwards in parallel rows, carrying the eye irresistibly to great heights. The blackened opening of the fireplace draws the eye down, only to be taken upward again by the perpendicular lines of the narrow brick chimney. The horizontal line of the beams of the room-divider, surrounded by a textured wall of stone set in concrete, leads the eye into the adjoining room to wine barrels of assorted sizes and colors.

The first photograph shows part of this setting I proposed to paint. The next photograph shows the dark green hues of the original eighteenth century sedan chair to the left of the fireplace. Light from a narrow window silhouettes it against the warm tones of the stone wall and of the low slanting wall. This sedan chair, which has its original paint, shaves (carrying poles) and harness, is of the French Regency period.

I decided I should first make a 10 x 14 inch drawing, using a 4B charcoal pencil on charcoal paper.

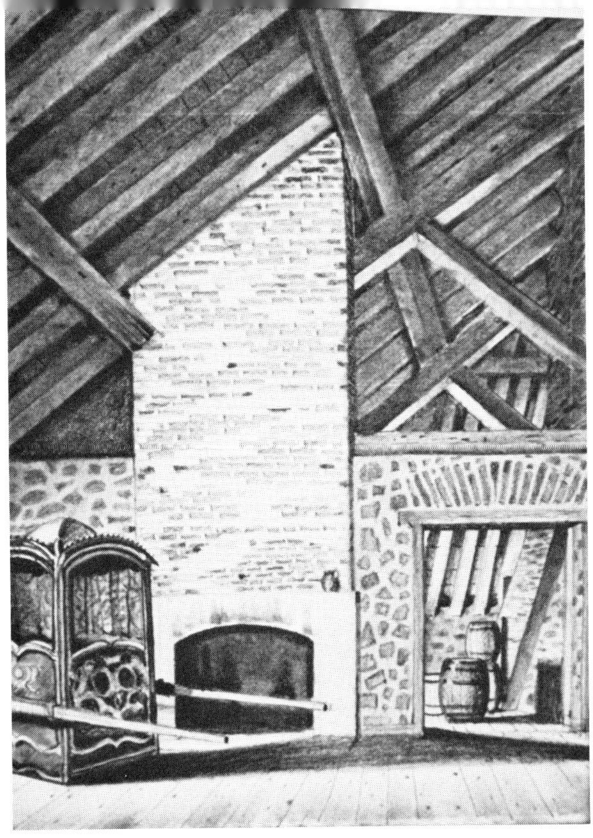

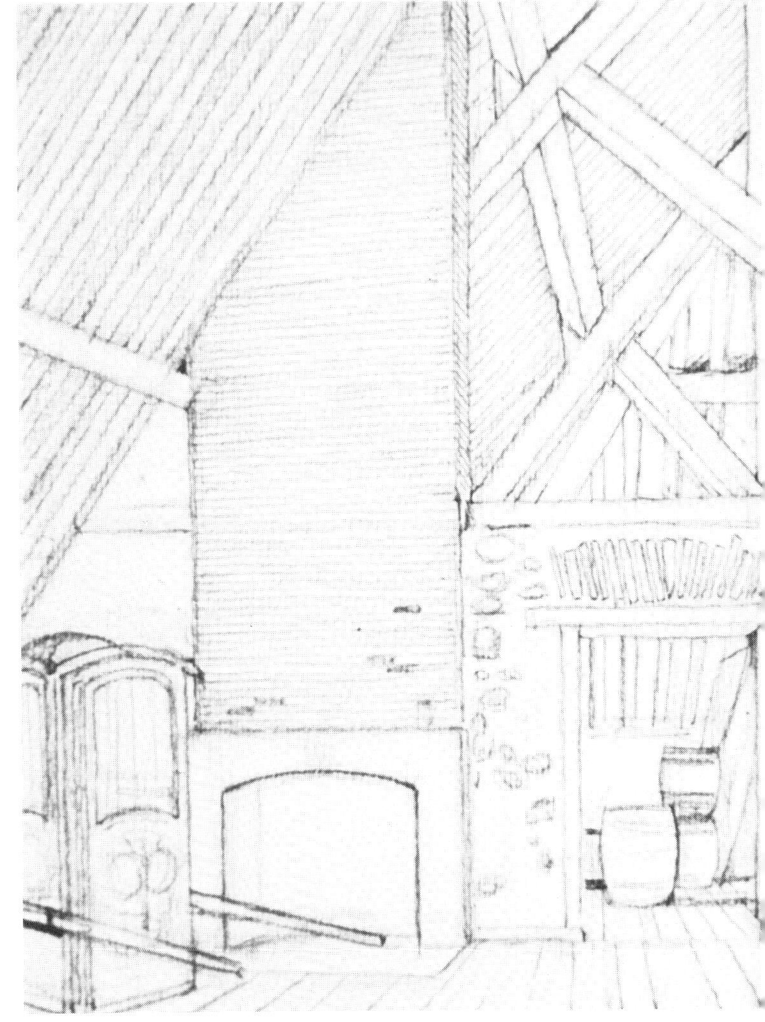

This would acquaint me with the shapes, directions and angles of the pitch of the overhead timbers—all held together by trunnels (treenails)—and at the same time allow me to study the values involved. Starting from the chimney, light perspective lines were drawn. I trusted my eye for their accuracy. Charcoal tones on the timbers were smudged with the stump, showing the contrast between the smooth timbers and the rough stone and brickwork. The varicolored bricks of the fireplace were treated in a suggestive manner. Just a few were rendered to suggest the solid brick construction. A chisel edge on the charcoal pencil helped to quickly indicate brick. An old pitcher found lying on the floor was placed on the fireplace mantel as a point of interest. The coat of arms on the sedan chair was roughly indicated. Daylight was failing through the narrow fortress windows, so at this stage it was important to sketch in everything as rapidly as possible.

Having concentrated on the lines and values, I decided to do a small 10 x 12 inch painting. The preliminary drawing was done quickly with the same 4B charcoal pencil, very lightly suggesting outlines. These charcoal outlines would not be erased as they would be easily covered by the opaque watercolor without smudging the color.

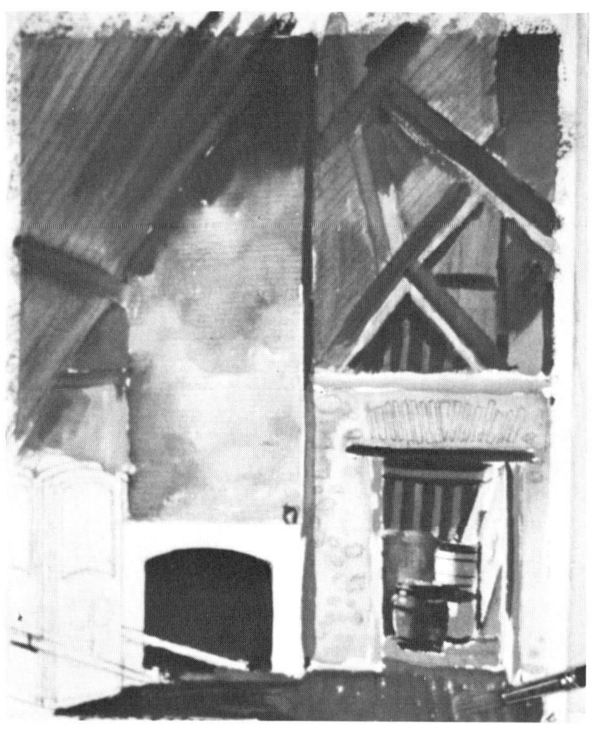

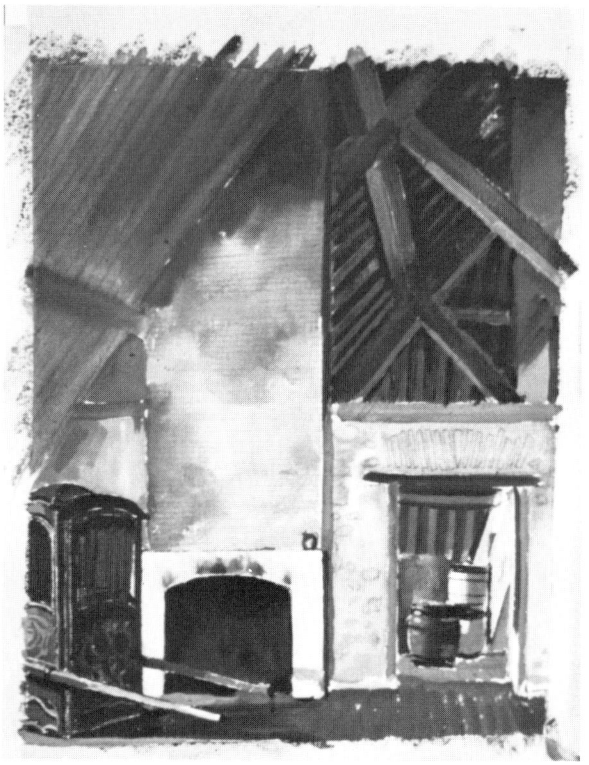

Now the lay-in of the painting was begun, the first step being a thin wash of white, Payne's gray, and yellow ochre was painted over the fireplace chimney. While this first wash was still wet, burnt umber and Payne's gray were added. The overhead rafter area was painted with the same wash. This muted tone would later be treated with darker tones of the same mixture to bring out the square shapes of the timbers.

The barrels seen through the open doorway were painted in high-key pigments, bright contrasting hues, to attract the eye. The highlights on the barrels were painted with white opaque. It was felt that the warm hues of the wall, the rafters and beams behind the barrels, made warm by the light from the window, would also attract the eye to the distant area, giving depth to the composition.

In the next step of the small painting, the basic hues of the sedan chair have been painted, using viridian green, Payne's gray, and burnt umber for the light side. The golden coat of arms was painted with raw sienna and a touch of burnt umber. Wherever more brightness was needed, cadmium yellow was mixed with the basic raw sienna. By squinting the eyes, the correct value of the coat of arms was checked.

Wet-in-wet technique was used in painting the fireplace. Smoke stains of Payne's gray were streaked onto the wet surface and not touched again. The dark lines separating the wide floor boards are important as they lead the eye into the picture.

Keep in mind when painting in opaque, to shift within a general color range from one hue to another and from one tone to another, as when painting the floor boards. Otherwise a painting in opaque can appear flat, drab and chalky; this is especially true if a great deal of white has been added to the mixture.

In the completed small painting the bricks of the fireplace chimney, and the underside of the beams and rafters have been painted. To render these, the paper was turned on the side, applying the pigment from top to bottom in one continuous stroke. When painting the bricks, a variety of reds and earth colors were used, darkening the hues as they approached the rafters. The bricks were spotted in random fashion.

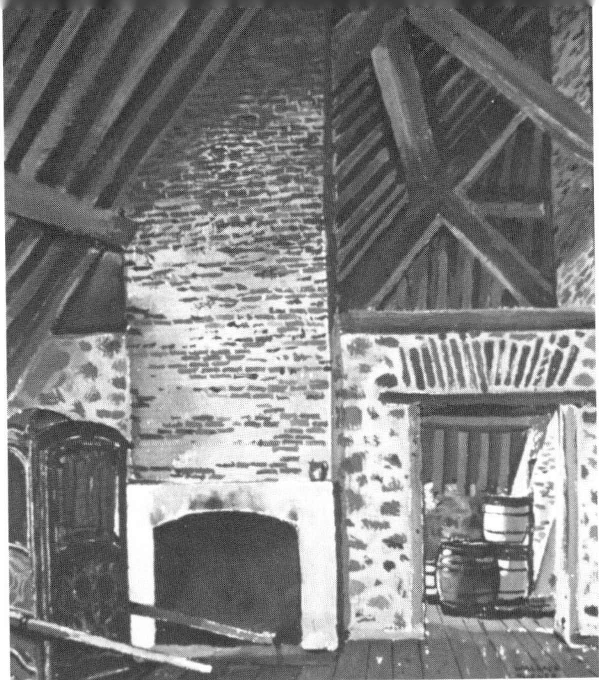

A charcoal pencil drawing for the large painting was begun on Strathmore watercolor paper, 28½ x 17 inches. This time heavy lines were made for the preliminary drawing for the daylight was fading. Here the drawing is shown in progress with the sedan chair, the fireplace, and the barrels drawn in with the 4B charcoal pencil. This drawing is entirely linear; no smudges are used. It was important to draw the timbers carefully, making certain that the angles were correct and that they were going in the same parallel direction.

In the completed charcoal pencil drawing the drapery inside the sedan chair and the general shape of the coat of arms have been added. The perspective lines for the chimney bricks have been drawn and, in some areas, the charcoal lines have been strengthened to insure that they will not be lost under the washes of opaque.

Opaque washes have been flowed into a clear water wash on the chimney and the walls on each side of it. This wash establishes the background values for the brickwork and the stone walls. It consists mainly of thin white, yellow ochre, and Payne's gray. To avoid a monotony of grays, some blotchy areas of raw sienna were introduced on the chimney. The warm hues of the timbers seen through the open doorway were painted in cadmium orange, burnt sienna, and a small amount of white. These rich hues represent one of the warmest color areas in the composition and should help to lead the viewer through the doorway.

On the next page is the progress in painting the barrels. The smaller barrel was painted with a heavy mixture of white and cadmium yellow for the light side, while the dark side was painted

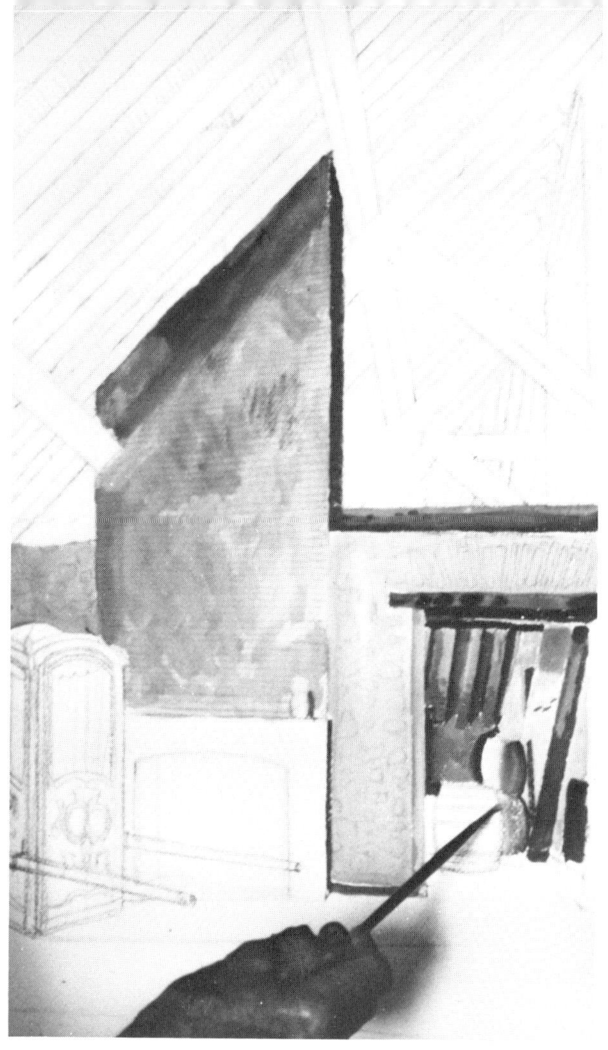

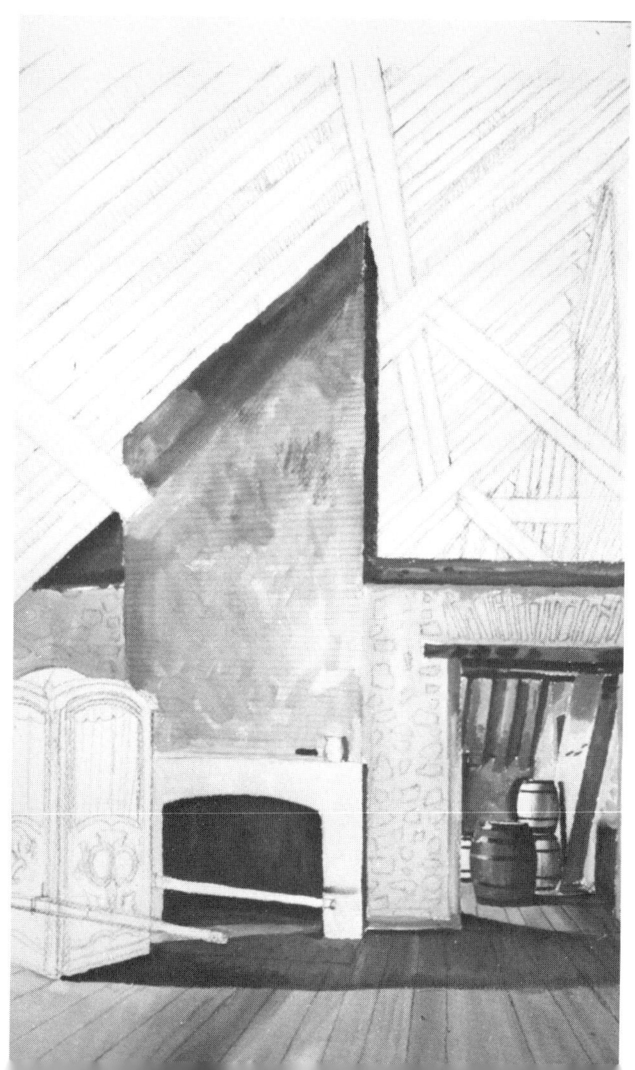

with burnt sienna, Payne's gray, and a touch of viridian green. The barrel hoops will be painted later. The wall colors have been painted, and also the shadows on the wall behind the barrels.

The large barrel has been rendered with Payne's gray, raw sienna, and ivory black, with white highlights used for the iron hoops. The floor boards have been painted with the old standbys for this painting, namely yellow ochre, Payne's gray, and burnt umber, but here the values are more important. The brush strokes for the floor boards follow the direction in which the boards run. At the left, where the values and hues were lightened by light from the window, more yellow ochre and white were added. A good device—and one that was planned—shows the shaves of the sedan chair leading the eye into the painting from the left. To darken the shadows on the floor, darker tones of the basic hues were added.

The interior damask folds of the sedan chair have been painted in alternating vertical bands of blue, white, viridian green, and cadmium yellow. In itself this silk damask drapery is a museum piece. In the painting the folds at the back of the chair have been darkened with Payne's gray and raw sienna.

Now the charcoal drawing of the timbers demands attention. Using the largest flat brush and taking long sweeping strokes, a muted hue of burnt sienna and yellow ochre has been applied. Where the light struck most strongly, cadmium yellow and cadmium orange were added. Because of the complexity of these rafters, it was useful to have the charcoal lines show through. Before painting the darker shadow side of the rafters, each was smudged with charcoal to distinguish it from its neighbor. Each shadow side was rendered in a slightly different tone, using a heavier pigment.

The small painting proved its worth, helping me to anticipate what colors were needed for the next step.

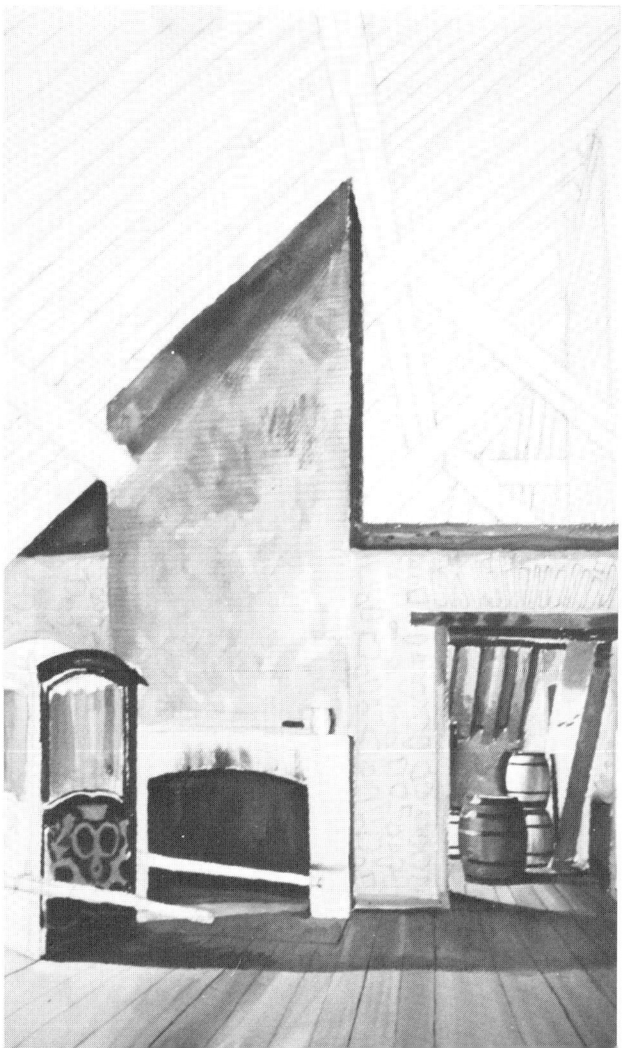

The grayish stones in the walls were then painted with a coarse-haired brush, mixing heavy pigment on the paper and relying on its rough surface to give the edges of the stones a jagged appearance. The hues used for the stones were in the greenish gray range, viridian green mixed with white. Yellow ochre, Payne's gray, or burnt sienna were added in places to represent the different hues and values of the stones.

The bricks of the chimney were painted next. As in the small painting, the varied reds of the bricks were kept in the same family range and in the same proportion. It was necessary to keep in mind the perspective lines that lead to the vanishing point far out to the left.

Only the painting of the coat of arms remained. I wondered what problems the fine craftsmen of 250 years or so ago encountered while working on this fine sedan chair. Their work still looks fresh and bright. They must have used gold dust; I used a combination of yellow ochre and raw sienna enriched with cadmium yellow.

Time ran out faster than expected because adverse weather conditions weakened the light, forcing me to complete the coat of arms at home, using the small painting, my memory, and David's photograph of the sedan chair for references.

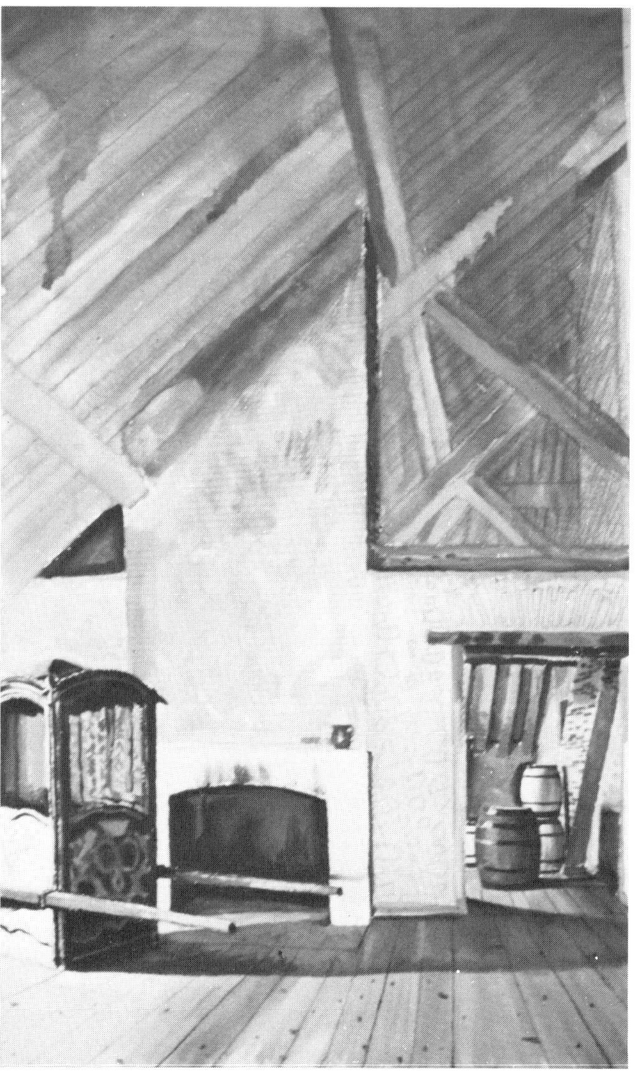

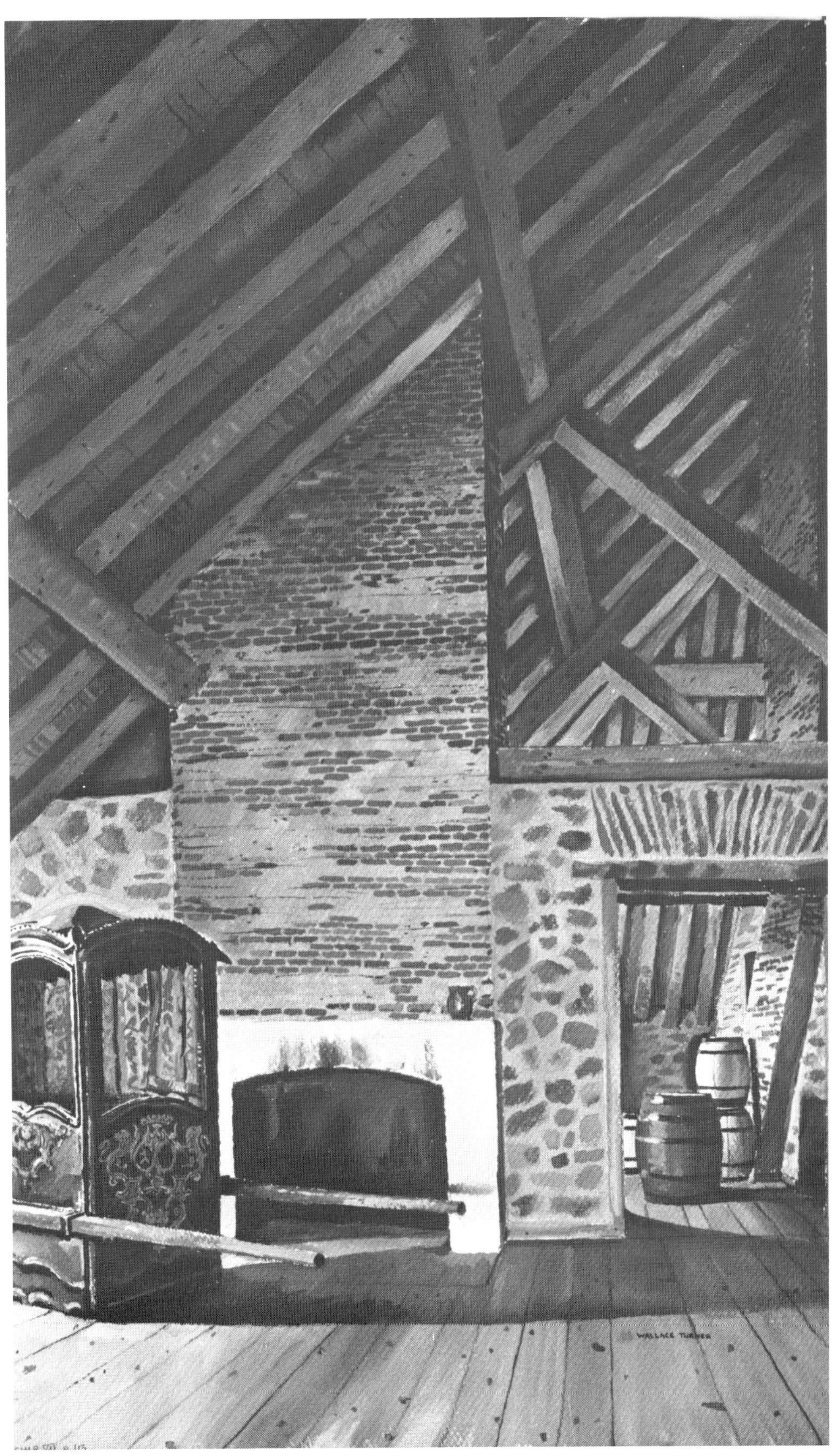

FORTRESS LOUISBURG
Cape Breton, Nova Scotia.

Frank Conrad's Barn

Here is another sequence of pictures showing a painting session done on location. This time I was in the comfort of Frank Conrad's barn. My patient subject was one of Frank's fine Holstein cows. The sketching and painting procedure was much the same as I have already described. I am sure you can follow the steps without further elaboration.

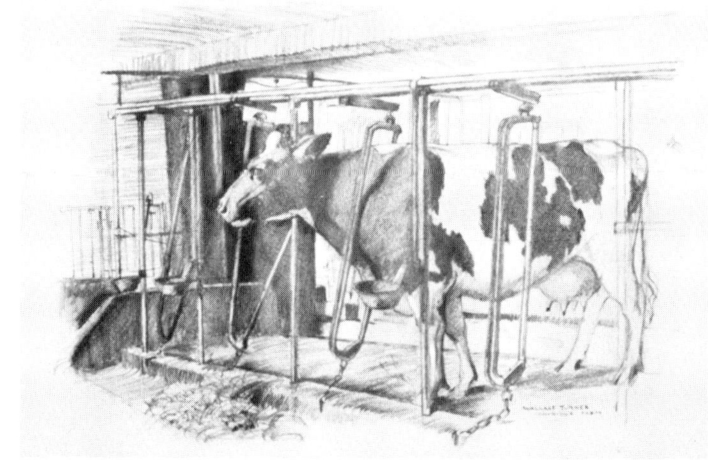

Charcoal sketch

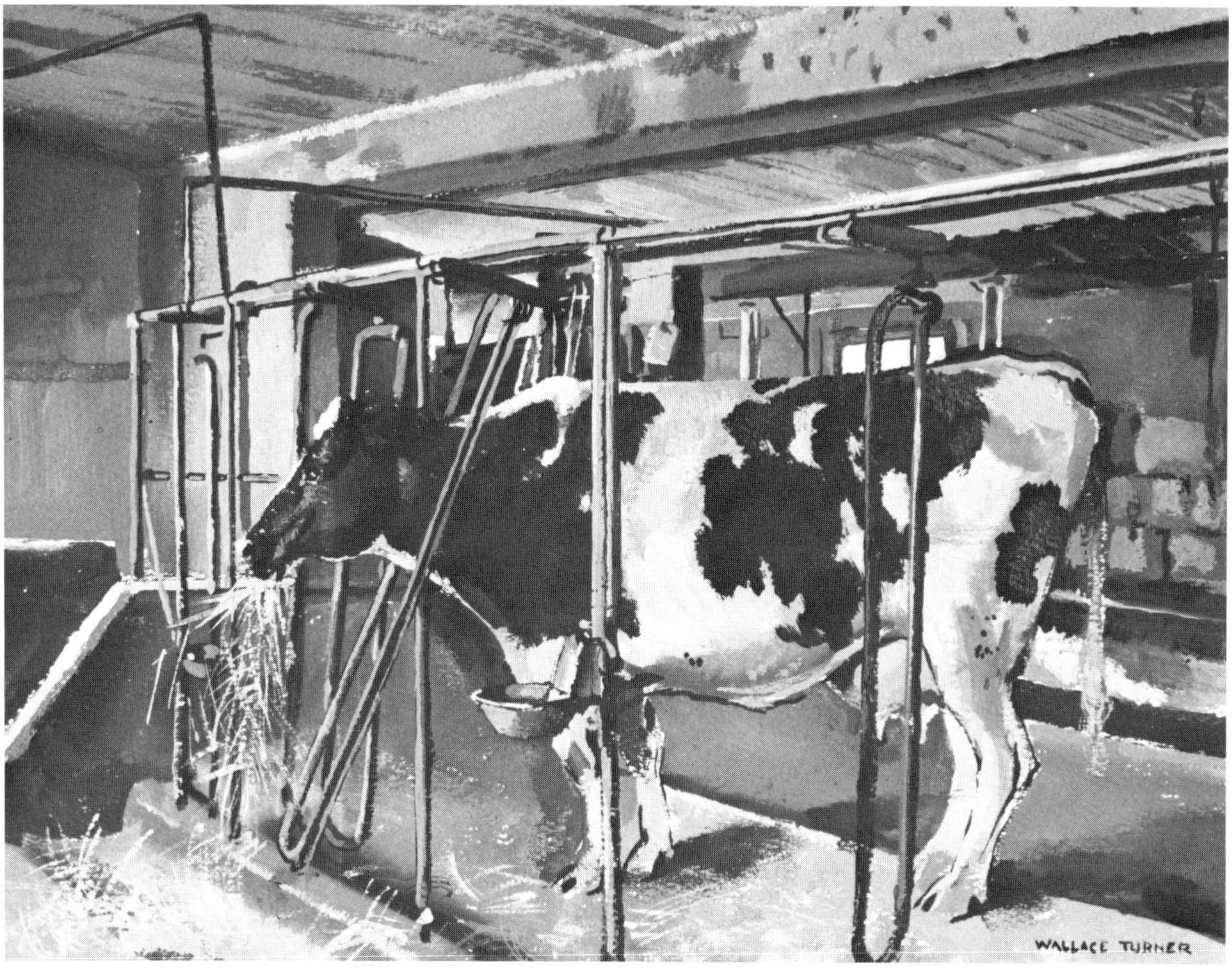

WALLACE TURNER

Small color sketch

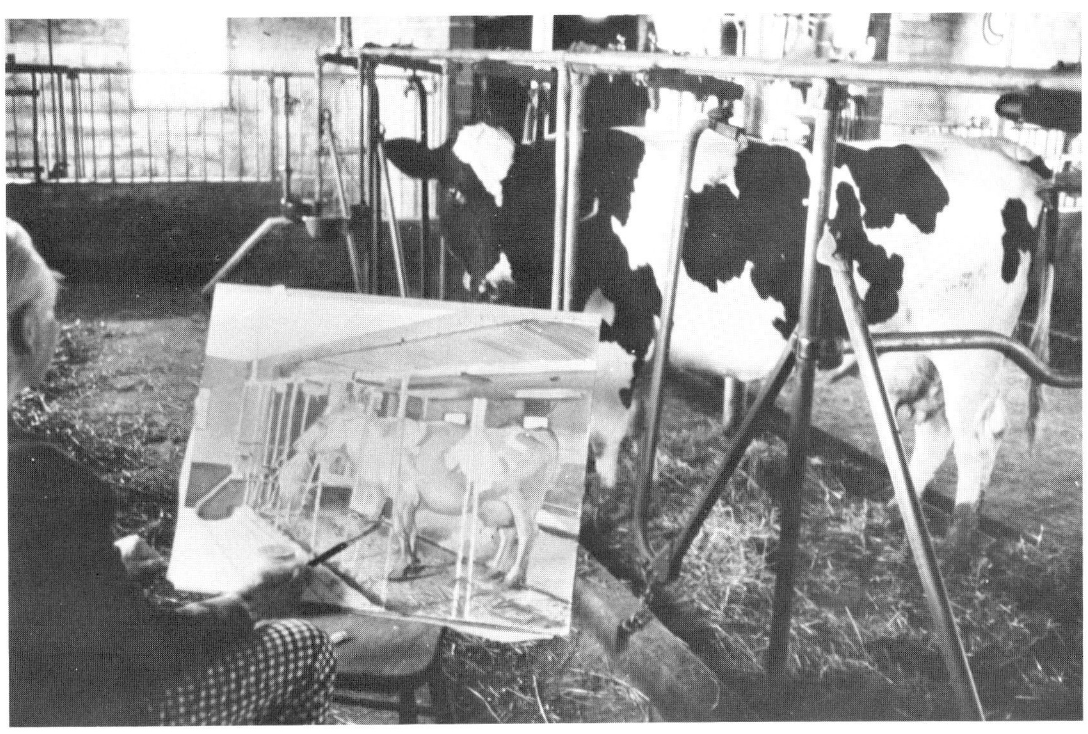

Working on final painting

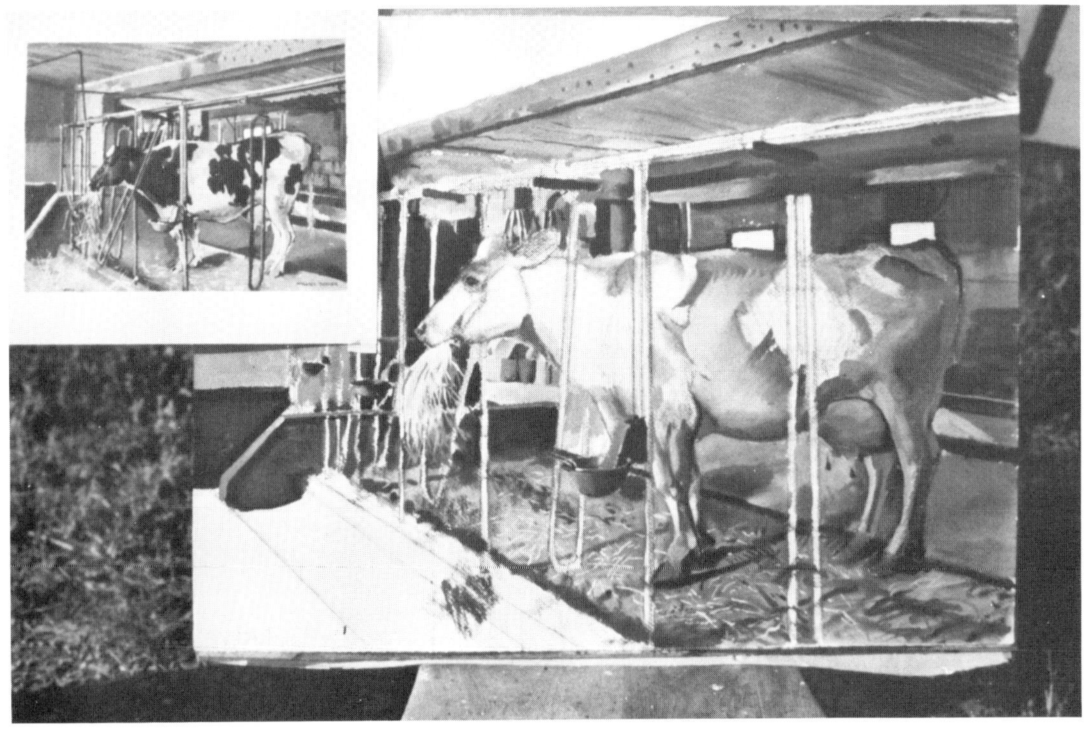

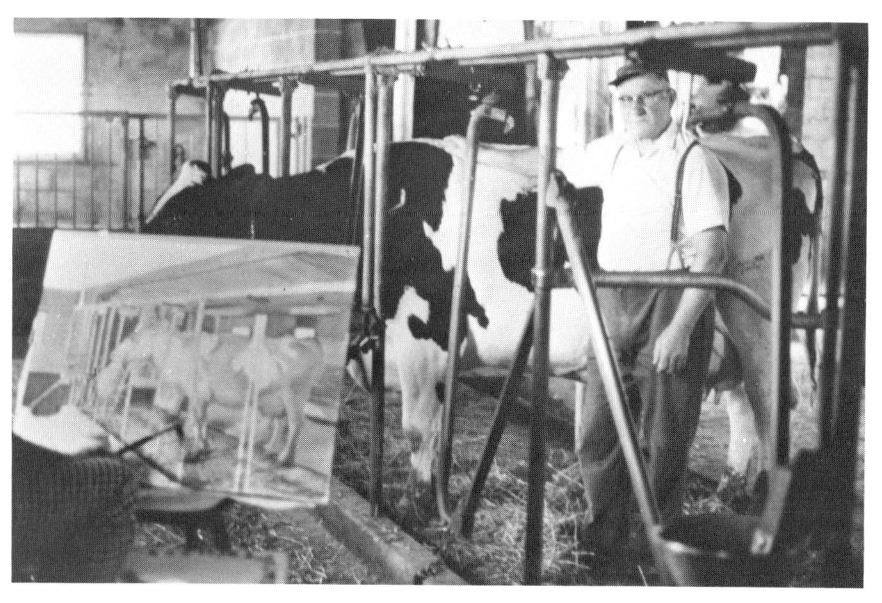

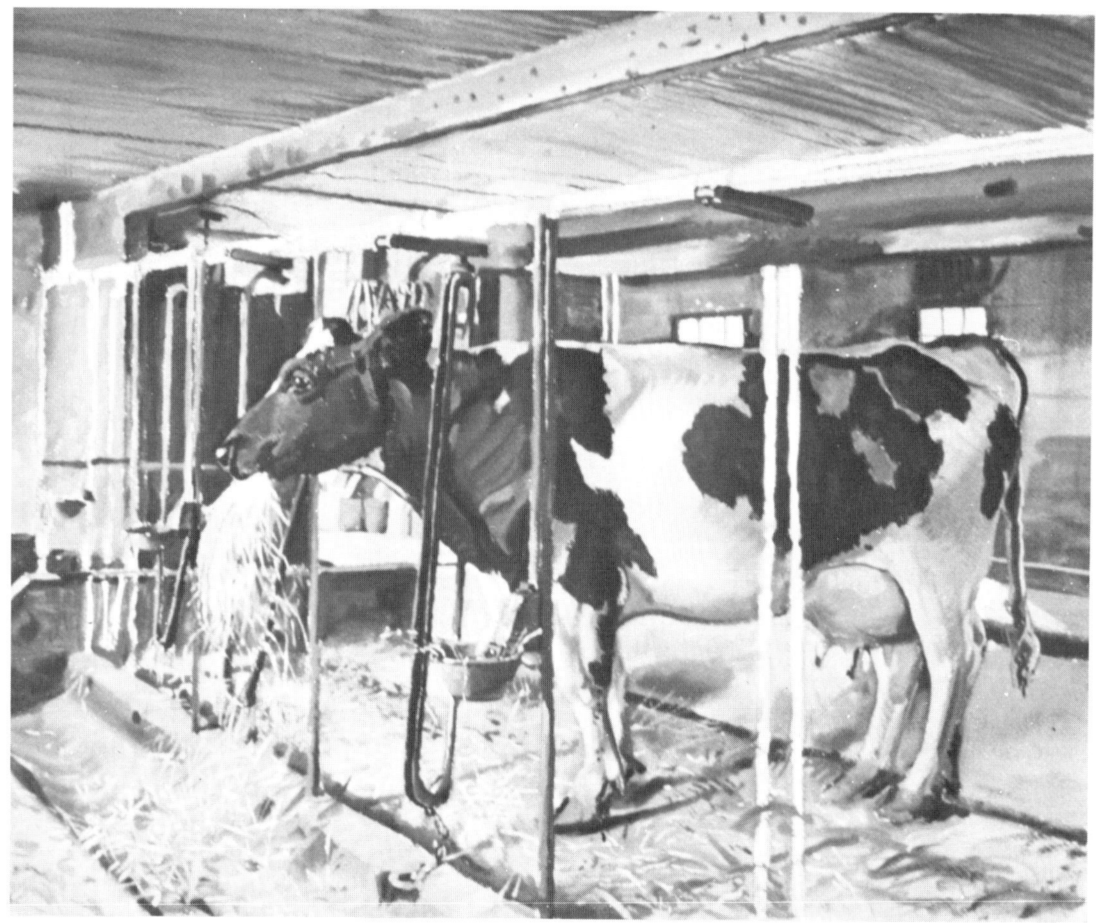

FRANK CONRAD'S BARN

CHAPTER 7
Portraits

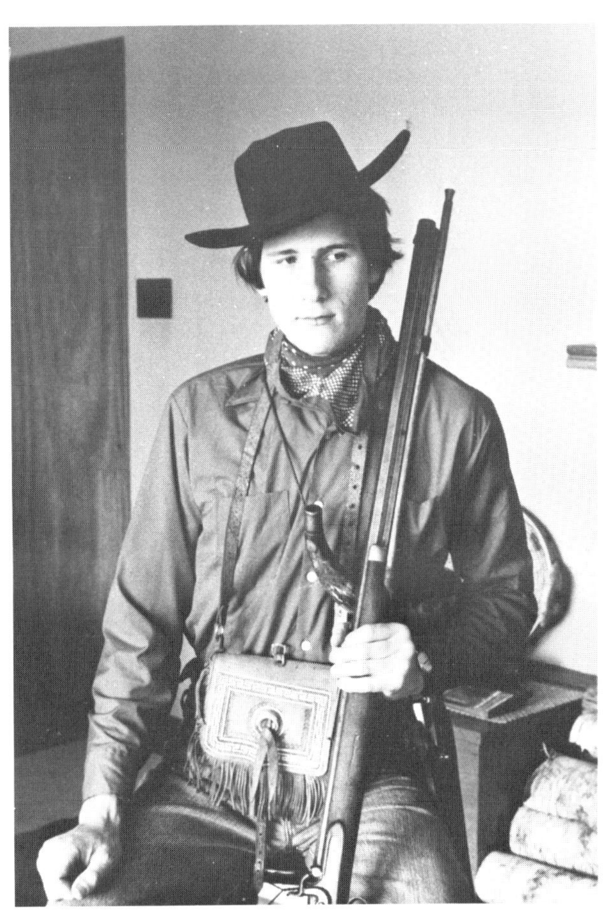

Portrait of Ian James

Because of Ian's strong features and his love of the out-of-doors, I decided to paint him as a buffalo hunter of the old west. Ian is photographed here in his "store-bought" western clothes. Over his bright red shirt, which I wished had faded somewhat, hangs a fringed Mexican pouch. The large bore of the old muzzle-loader indicates that it is probably a buffalo rifle. The side-arm was also used in the buffalo running days. These big pistols can be seen in the hands of hunters on horseback in paintings by George Catlin.

As the model must be comfortable, the butt of the heavy rifle rests on a box, eliminating the strain of holding it. The powder horn hanging around Ian's neck is an essential part of the western gear. The shoulder seams of the shirts of the 1860-1885 western period were about three inches lower than those of today; this change was handled in the painting.

As the painting was to be in the setting of the old west, it would have been more fitting to paint the portrait out-of-doors under the open sky with the cool light on the hat and shoulders, cooling the hot red of the shirt, but weather changes made it necessary to paint indoors. I decided to place my western buffalo hunter on horseback. Needing a background for the western setting, I referred to some colored sketches I had done of the San Jacinto range near Palm Springs, California a couple of years ago. Sketches like these can often be of use in composing a painting at a later date.

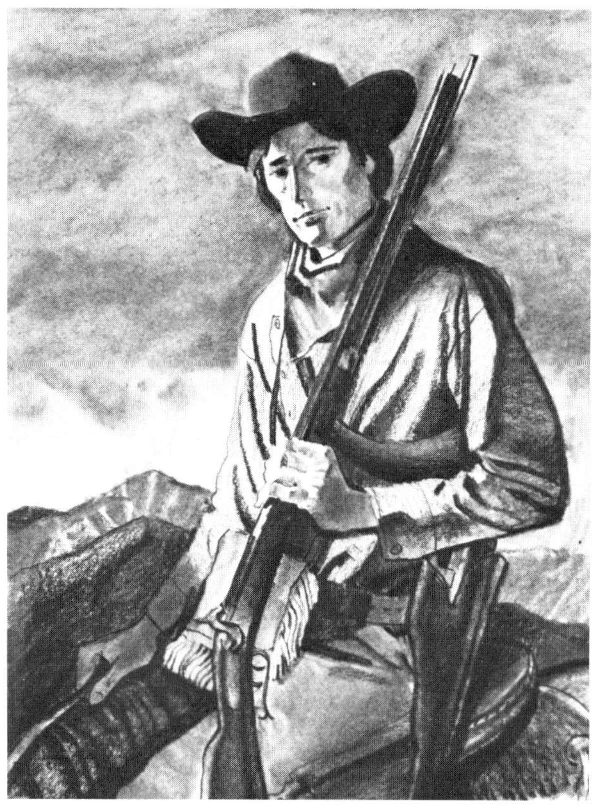

This preliminary sketch is done in opaque watercolor on Strathmore taken from an 8 x 10¾ inch block. The drawing and painting procedures are much the same as those to be used in the larger painting, using in general the same palette with some modifications.

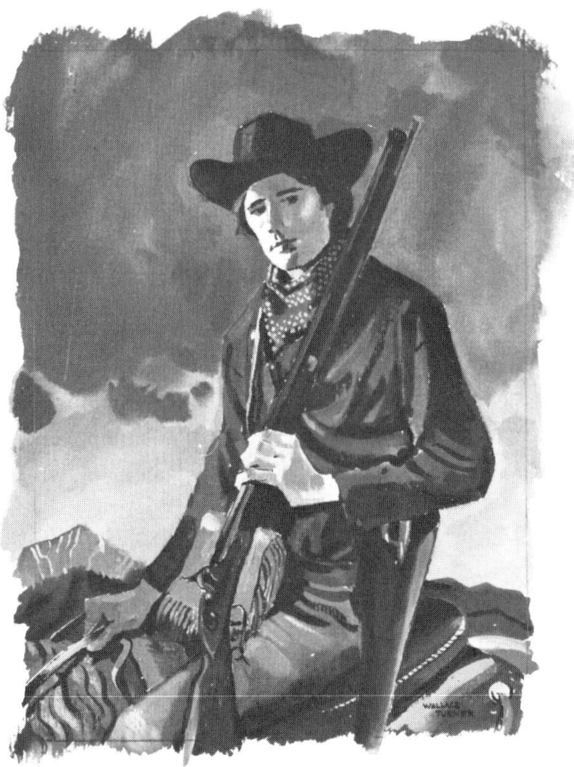

Often portraits are painted directly without any preliminary sketches, relying entirely on the spontaneity and power of hand and eye to capture the character of the sitter. However, I have found that a preliminary sketch is not wasted. Here its main purpose is to help define the features of the sitter and to map out the hues and value patterns, helping to simplify the procedures that will be followed in the large portrait study. It also enables you to experiment with the background, discovering what hues and values will harmonize with the dominant red shirt while concentrating the attention on the head.

Painting a portrait is always a challenge for the experienced artist as well as the beginner. Keen observation and great discipline are required in studying the features, relating them to each other and maintaining the head as a unit. The portrait painter has the choice of painting just the head on which he can concentrate, or the model can be placed in an environment that reflects his interests. Animals, a favorite dog or horse being the most common, are often included in a portrait study. A fine painter, like Augustus John, can reveal the "inner person" of a sitter in a rapidly painted sketch of just the head with no distractions. For the beginner, it is a good idea to paint just the head until experience and more confidence are acquired.

Before starting the small sketch, I decided Ian should be on horseback, showing only the saddle area. In the past, it was the custom of kings and emperors who were having a martial-type portrait painted to sit for the portrait astride a wooden barrel-like conception of the mid-section of a horse, equipped with polished saddle and other royal "tack" or "horse furniture."

In this painting, Ian is placed on a high stool that does not quite approximate the height of a horse's back from the ground.

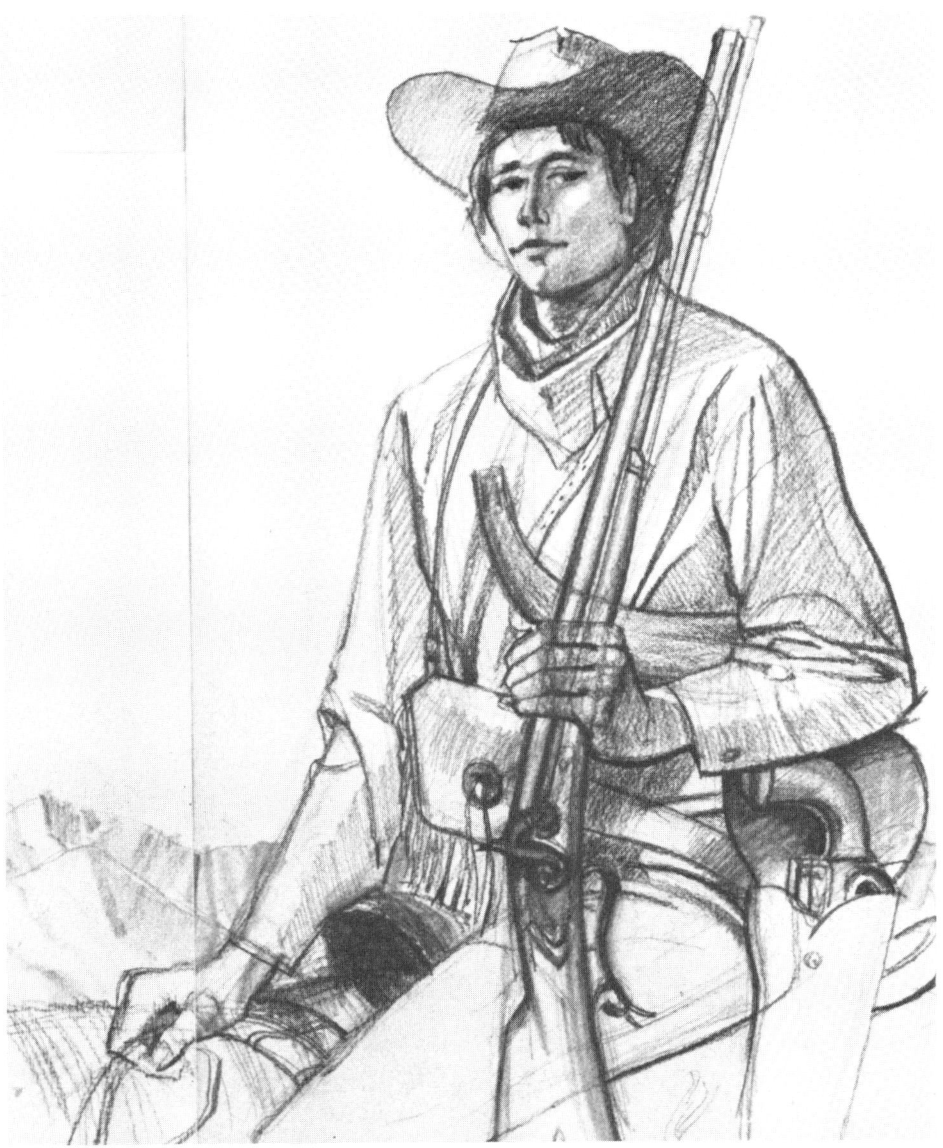

Before starting on a final painting, it is helpful to first make a sketch on tissue or layout paper the same size as the paper for the final painting. When completed this sketch can be traced directly onto your final painting surface. A 6B charcoal pencil along with charcoal sticks for heavier lines should be used.

Here the charcoal sketch is transferred to a sheet of Strathmore watercolor paper rough, 22 x 30 inches, which has been fastened to a sheet of plywood with strips of 2-inch wide carpet tape with an adhesive on both sides to hold the paper firmly to the plywood. No soaking or wetting is necessary. I prefer this method as sometimes soaking the paper flattens the texture of the surface.

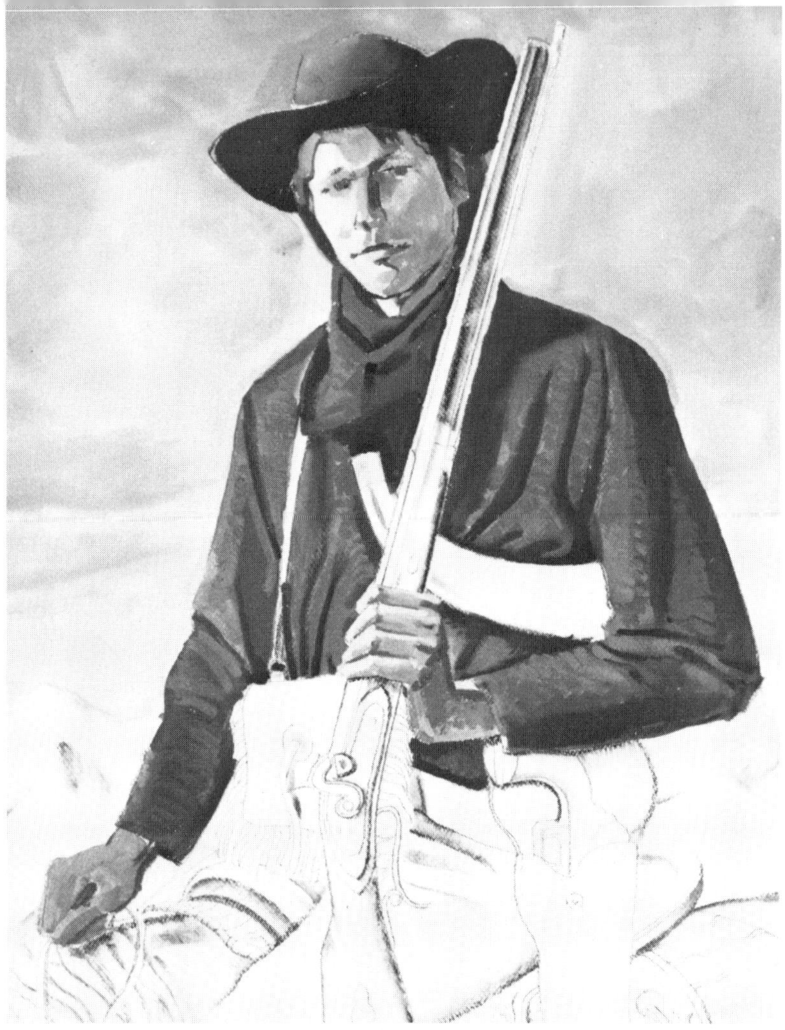

The palette is now laid out with hues similar to those used in the small sketch, only in larger quantities. For me, this requires two paper palettes, one for the warm hues, one for the cool.

The hues, as seen on the model, are mixed side by side on the palette, giving an opportunity of checking their color and value relationship before applying them to the paper, although they will appear slightly different on the paper.

The mounted paper is given a wash of clear water, using a wide flat brush. The paint is then applied somewhat the same as on the small sketch. The light falling on Ian's face at the left is cool, so two mounds of color are mixed, one mound for the cool or left side of the face, the other for the right warm shadow side. No artificial light is used, relying on the daylight that comes in from the window at the left and light that comes from another window over my shoulder.

The color mixed for the warm right shadow side of the face, which is painted first, is yellow ochre, alizarin crimson, and some white. The eye socket in the light left side of the face is included in this part of the lay-in as it is the same value as the shadow side.

For the cool light left side of the face, white, yellow ochre, and a touch of cerulean blue with a bit of alizarin crimson are used. To help the pigment spread quickly, clear water is applied over the facial area. While the surface is still damp, the warm color mixture is brushed into the shadow side of the face. To define the planes of the face, a slightly darker hue is also introduced into the shadow area. Working rapidly, both values—the dark and the light—are painted almost simultaneously so as to fuse the edges of the planes while still damp.

The hair is now painted with ultramarine blue, burnt sienna, and Payne's gray while the pigment for the face is still damp, producing a soft or "lost edge" between the hair and the flesh tones. For the hat, Payne's gray, the dominating value, is mixed with burnt umber with a highlight of ultramarine blue and a little white.

The most vivid reds were used for the bright red shirt: cadmium red light, vermilion with alizarin crimson for the highlights and folds, while the

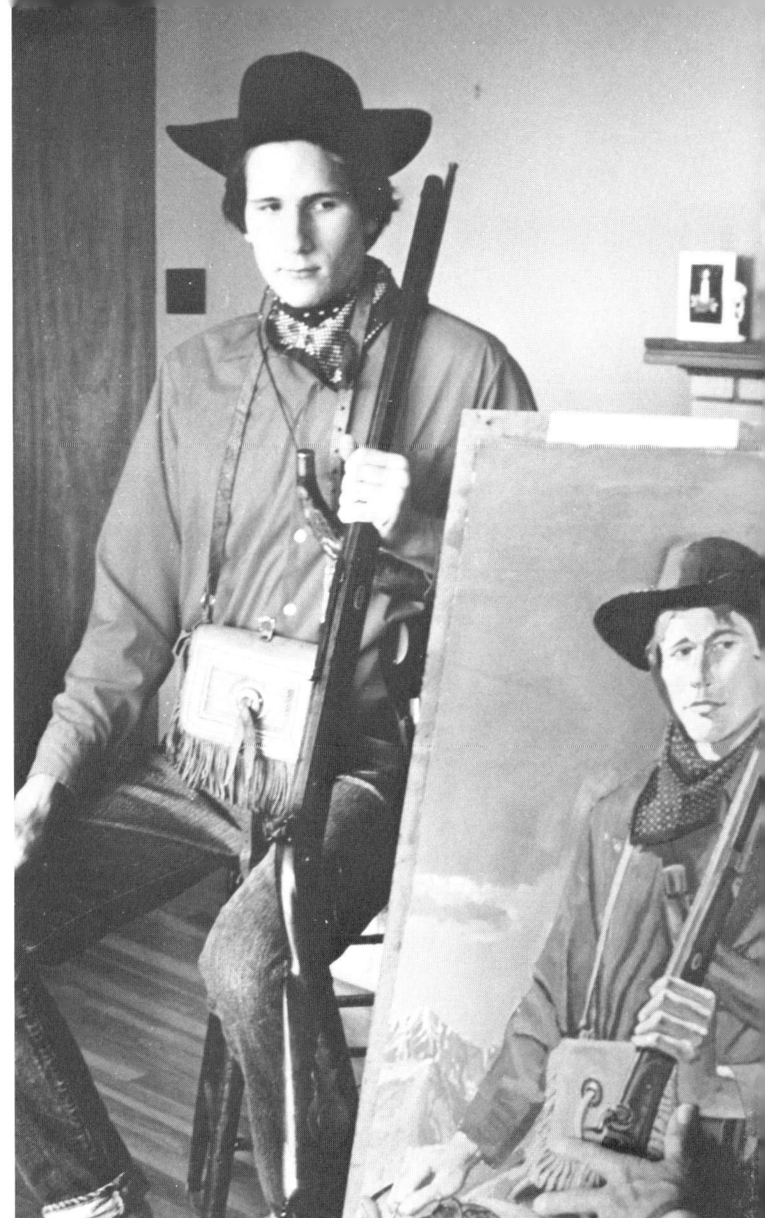

shadows and darks of the shirt were painted with alizarin crimson and burnt umber. Using a 1½-inch flat brush, both of these values were brushed quickly into a damp surface as soft edges were desired in the rendering of the shirt. Into the damp area of the bright reds are painted the darker folds, using the same or similar hues as for the sketch. It was hoped that if this stage of the lay-in was convincing enough, it could be carried along, with a few minor changes or additions, as the finished work.

As the facial tones are already mixed, these same hues, with some additions, are used in painting the hands. So as not to take the eye to the corner of the composition, the value of the hand holding the reins is toned down by adding burnt sienna and a little Payne's gray to the facial mixture.

Two helpful suggestions: (1) If in combining two colors you allow one color to dominate the other, a muddy tone will be avoided. (2) While painting, squint your eyes to eliminate distracting details, and don't worry if your pigment goes over your outlines as this will give your work a look of freshness. However, if this happens to excess, it can be corrected. This is one of the many advantages of working in opaques.

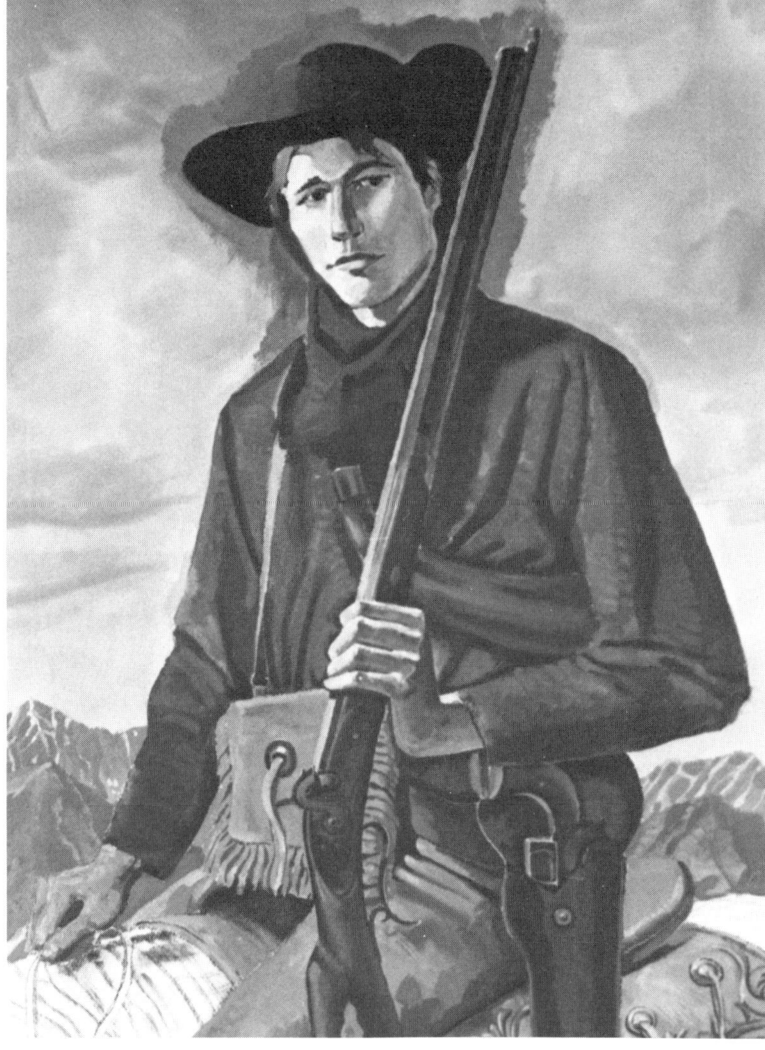

In this step of the lay-in, attention is given to painting the accessories, keeping in mind they are of secondary importance, and the tones must be kept subdued so as not to detract from the face.

Colors used for the accessories are as follows:

The Walker Colt and holster
Payne's gray, burnt umber; the brass trigger guard of the pistol mostly raw sienna with a touch of Payne's gray; highlights on the brass part —cadmium yellow and white.

Powder horn
Muted earth tones onto damp surface.

Pouch
Cadmium orange, cadmium yellow, yellow ochre, touch of white.

Saddle
Burnt umber, yellow ochre, ultramarine blue, touch of white.

Buffalo rifle (wooden stock)
Burnt umber, Payne's gray,
(metal parts) Payne's gray, ultramarine blue, white for highlights.

Blue jeans (although I doubt they were available in the old buffalo days) ultramarine blue, cadmium red light, touch of white.

Neckerchief
Ultramarine blue, Payne's gray, alizarin crimson; white spots were toned down considerably so they would not detract from the head; spots were of different sizes and followed a definite pattern which I did not adhere to.

The lay-in of the sky at the beginning was a thin wash with no further development until now. In this step it was decided to paint the sky as a dark cloud effect on the upper part of the painting so as to emphasize the face, to draw attention to the facial features. For the cool neutral tones of the sky, cerulean blue, Payne's gray, and Hooker's green were mixed. To obtain soft edges for the low clouds, two tones were painted into a damp surface. Lost and found edges add interest and do not detract from the head.

The painting of the San Jacinto mountain range is now completed, indicating more clearly their form and the crevices which hold the winter's snow, for this was late February. Ultramarine blue, alizarin crimson, a touch of burnt sienna and white comprise the hues for the mountains range.

For the saddle blanket, a muted red tartan design repeats the red of the shirt.

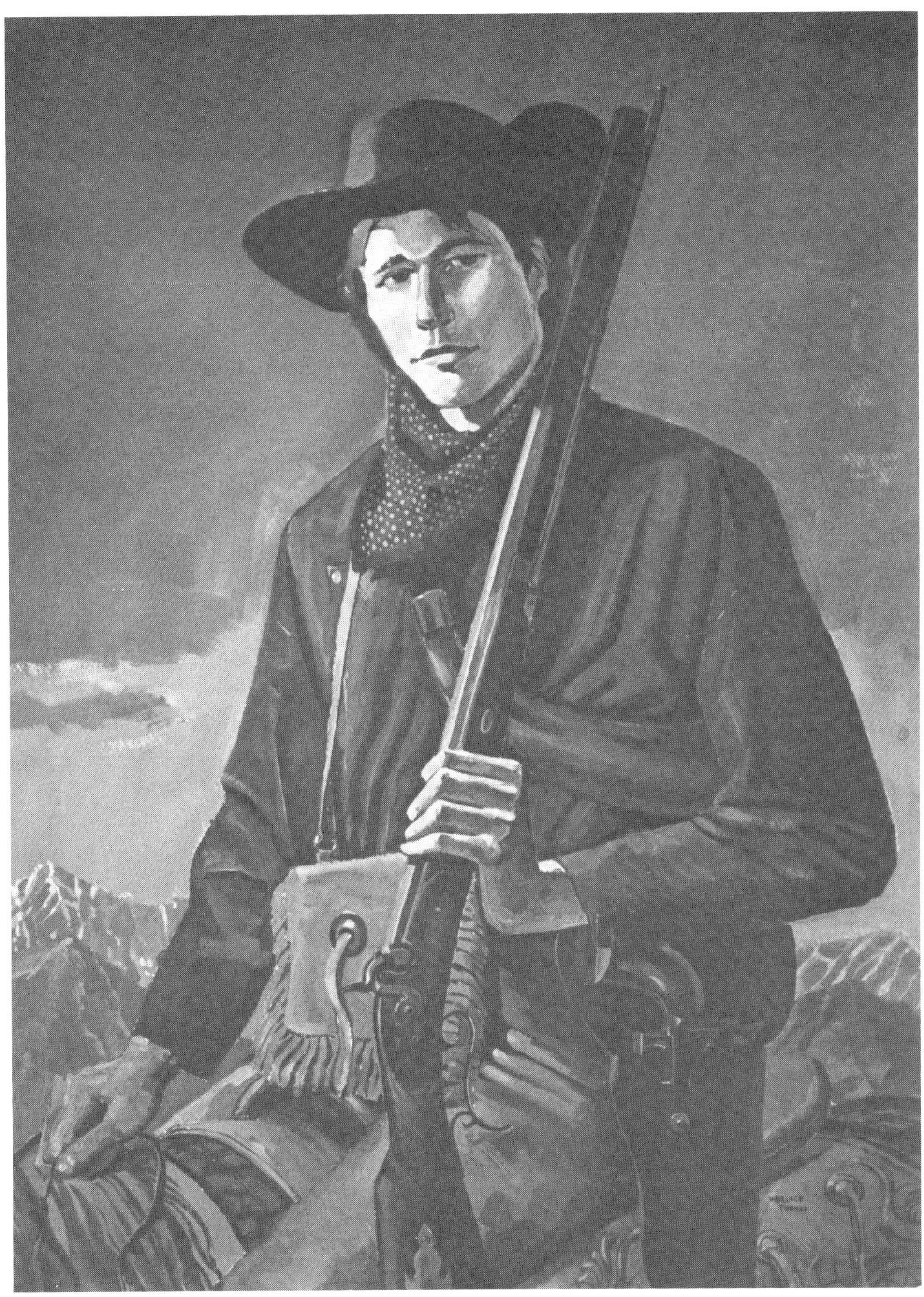

PORTRAIT OF IAN JAMES

Last touches are given to the hands and features. All areas are painted by now and a last check is made for needed corrections or additions while the model is still present.

In the process of painting a portrait, poses will invariably change. Seldom do you end with the first pose. A composition such as this may be thought of as an illustration rather than a pure portrait; as something more than the features are shown. The setting tells the viewer more about the subject portrayed.

In the smaller sketch, the face is that of an older man, but both paintings reflect the height and broad shoulders of our model.

SAMOAN WOMAN

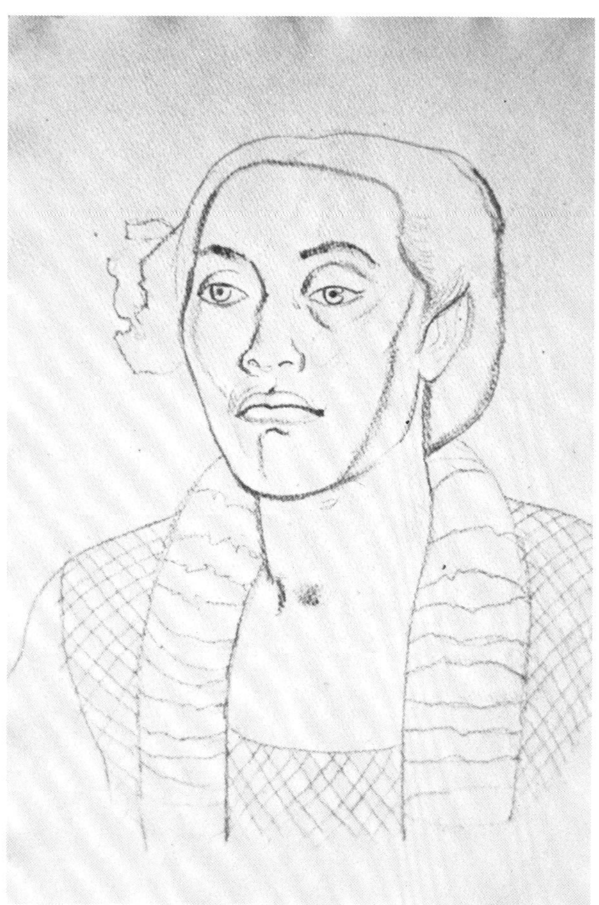

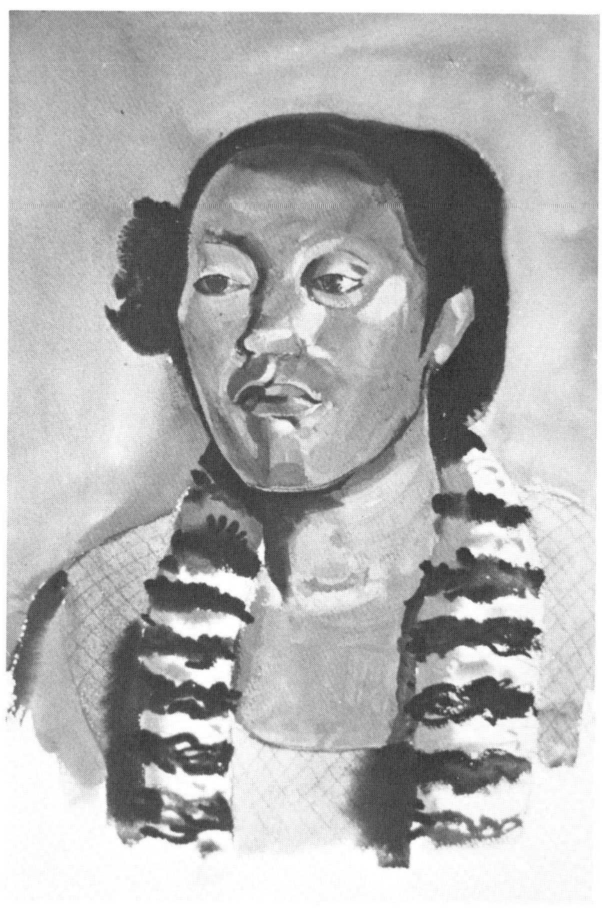

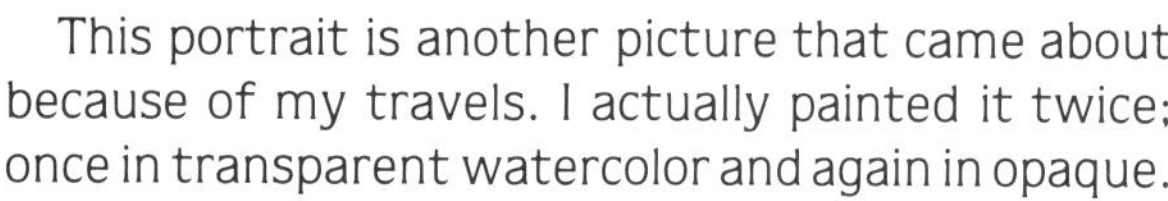

This portrait is another picture that came about because of my travels. I actually painted it twice; once in transparent watercolor and again in opaque.

As you can see, the initial sketch simply stated the pose and established the proportions and features.

The basic color and values were quickly laid in. My main concern was to hold the form and the strong structure of the head. I worked with wide flat brushes to keep from becoming involved with details too soon.

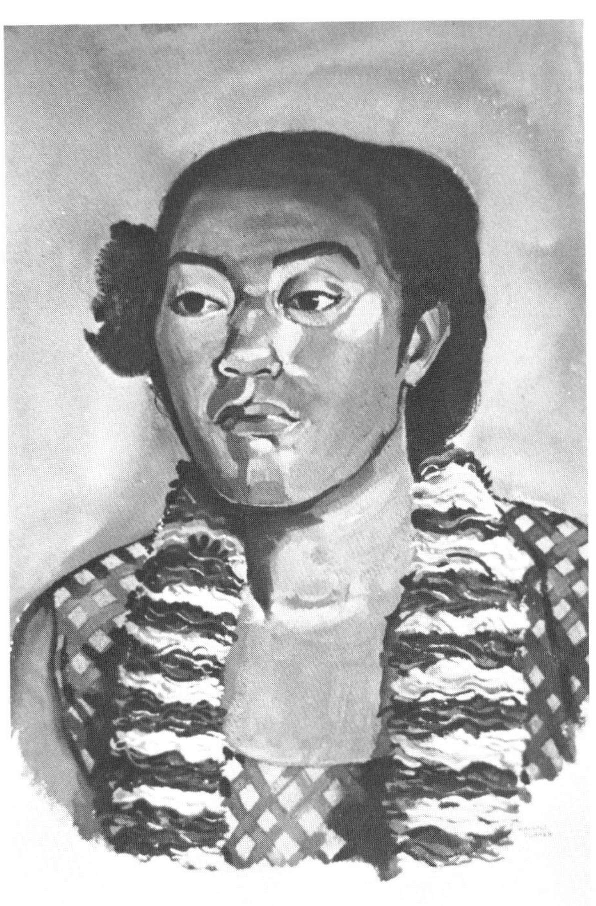

It did not take a great deal of additional work to bring the picture to this degree of finish. If the basic structure is sound the detail will come easily.

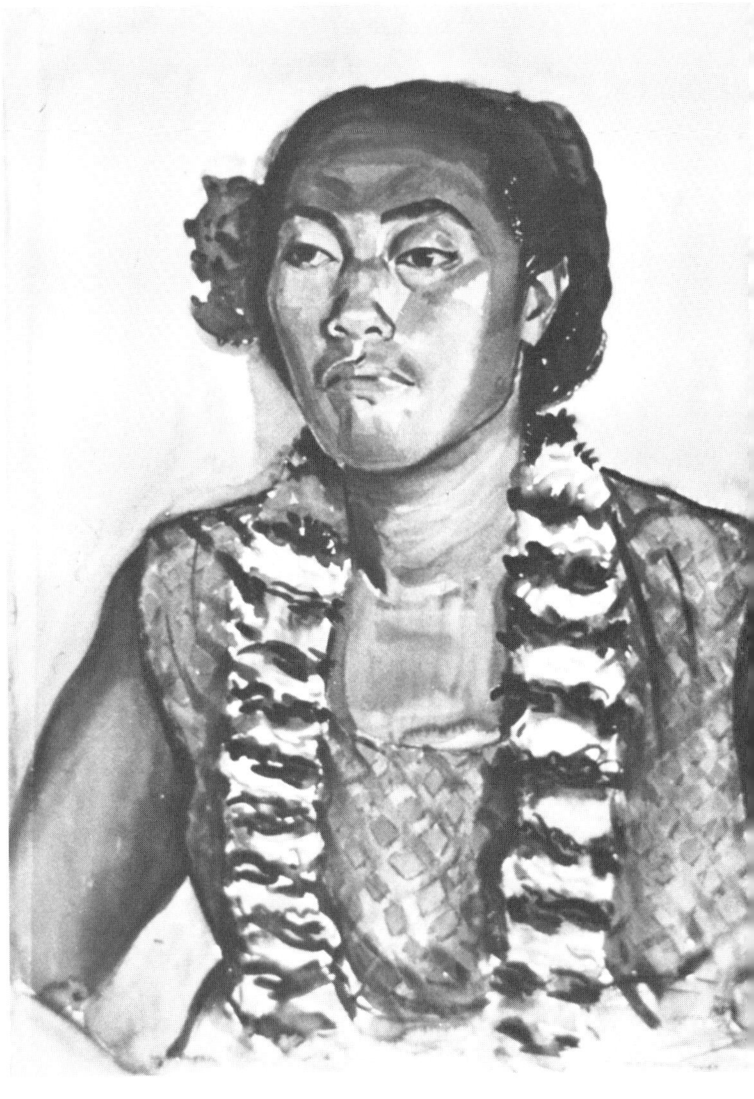

Here is the same portrait done completely in transparent watercolor.

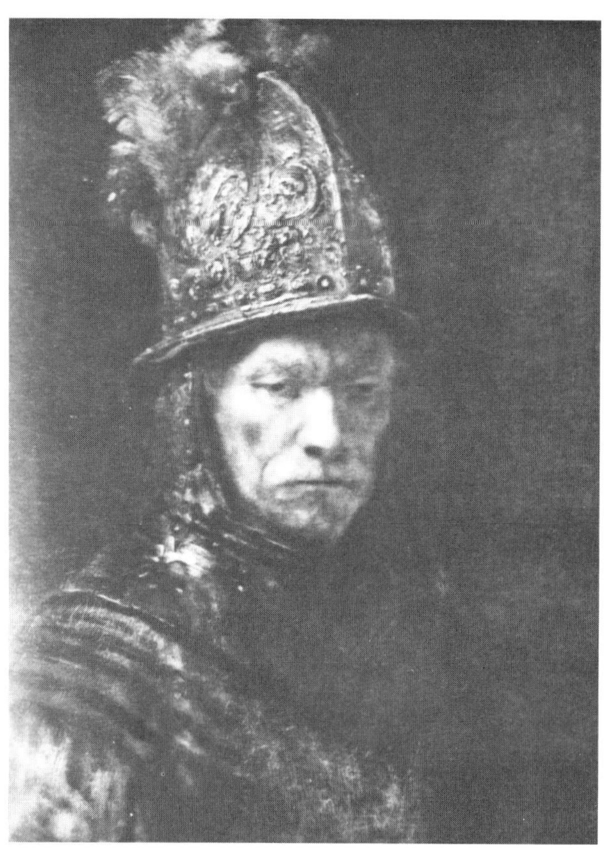

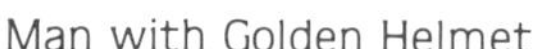
Man with Golden Helmet 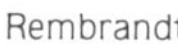 Rembrandt

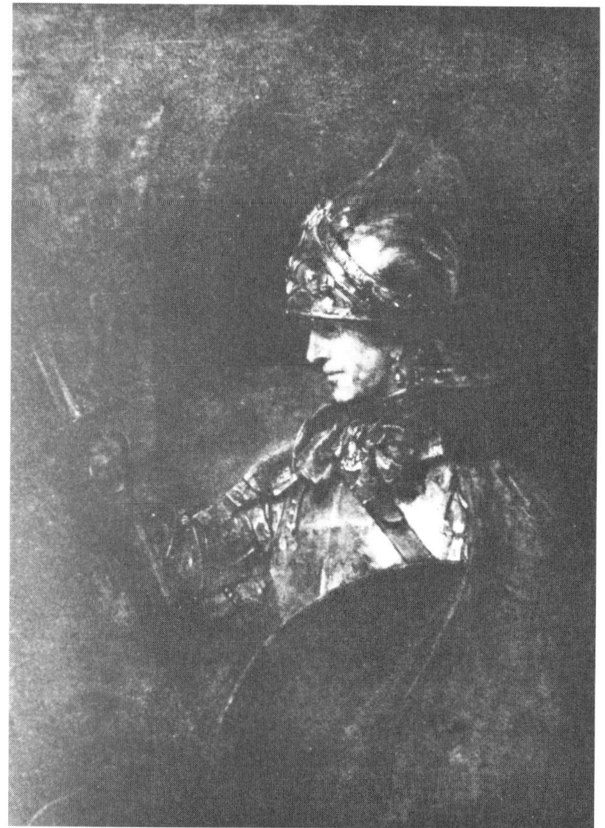

Alexander Rembrandt

CHAPTER 8
Rendering Details

Opaque is a wonderful medium with which to render fine details. In my opinion no other medium will allow you the same kind of control. To make the point, here is a step-by-step demonstration of a rendering of a Renaissance helmet. My inspiration came from Rembrandt's wonderful paintings of men wearing helmets.

As metal, from cars to jewelry, plays a large part in our lives, experience gained from rendering a metal work of art is not wasted. Having available a reproduction of a sixteenth century helmet, I thought it would be rewarding and challenging to paint this armorer's work of art.

Rendering a Renaissance Helmet

With the helmet before me, I began a series of steps in the development of a painting to be rendered in black and white opaque watercolor. Though this helmet is a reproduction, it shows how light coming from one source is distributed over an uneven surface; the edge of a raised area closest to the light being the first surface to catch the light. The same holds true for embroidered cloth or folds of drapery. In a simpler form, the rendering of this artifact reveals how the heights, or ridges, catch the light while the valleys remain in shadow.

As this is a parade or showpiece helmet fashioned for the nobility, the embossed design of the surface includes mythological figures, foliage and various beasts.

In the first step of the drawing, 2B and 4B charcoal pencils are used on Strathmore Kid Finish 14½ x 15 inches. The height of the helmet in the drawing measures about 12 inches, just under life size, while the actual helmet is about an inch longer from the top of the comb to the bottom of the neckpiece.

The raised figures, as in Rembrandt's helmets, catch the light, further heightening the relief effect. Rembrandt painted the helmets in thick oil pigments and the rest of the portrait with thin pigments.

While working on the drawing of the helmet, a visitor asked what a painter would use for a subject if he were not fortunate enough to have a Renaissance helmet. My answer is—try painting any metal object—a tea kettle, a brass watering can, a copper pan, pewter mug, tin cans of various metals, a coal scuttle or milk can—the older and rustier the more fascinating to paint.

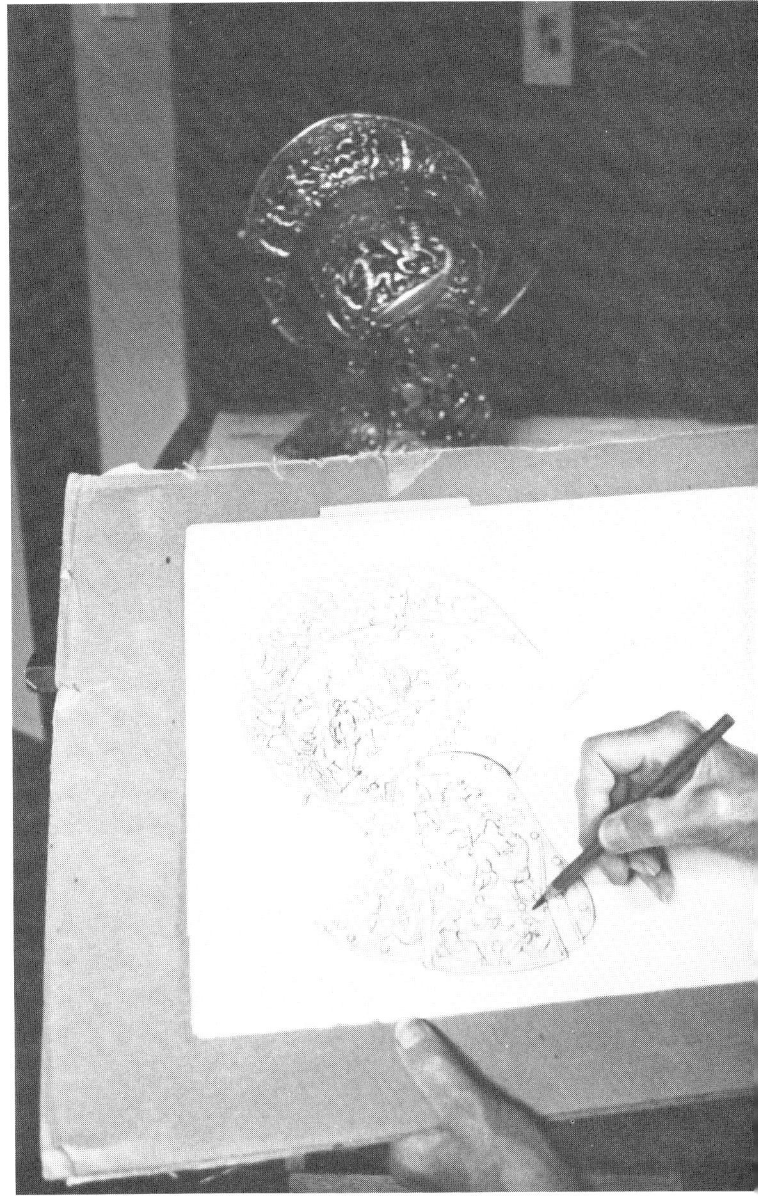

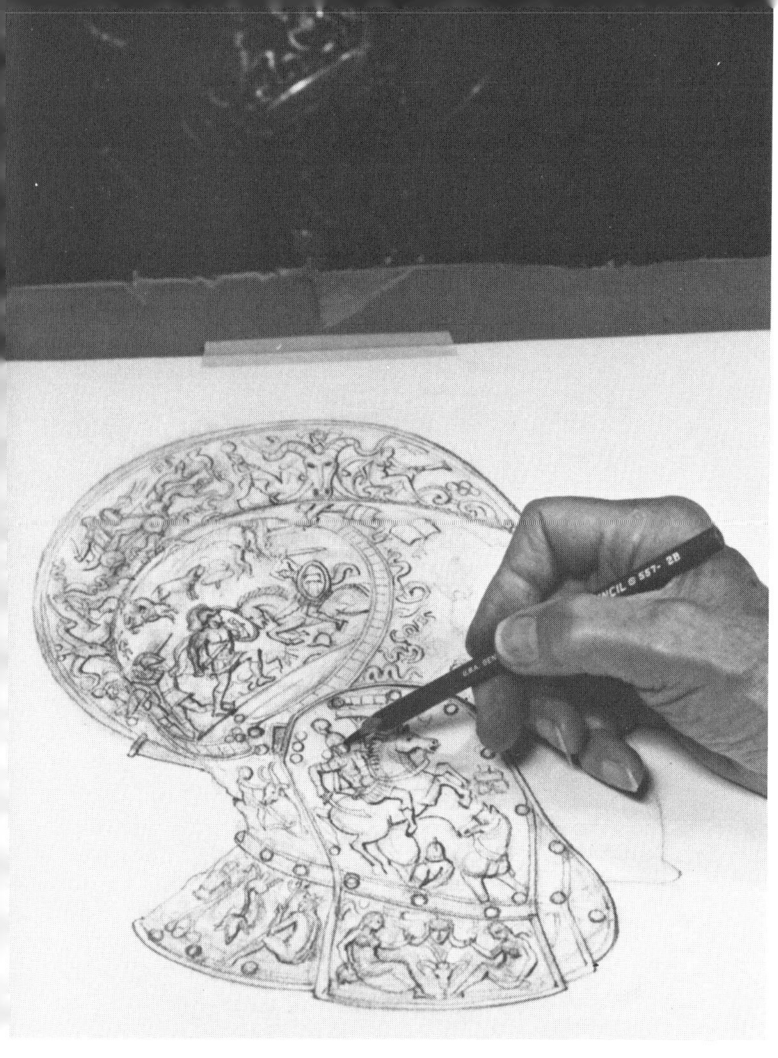

When sketching in the main shape of the helmet, the helmet was thought of in parts—the comb, crown, visor, and cheek pieces—and their relation to one another in size and shape. Each part was carefully drawn to form the general shape of the headpiece. To increase the effect of the figures in relief, a thick and thin line was used for the shadow side of the reliefs.

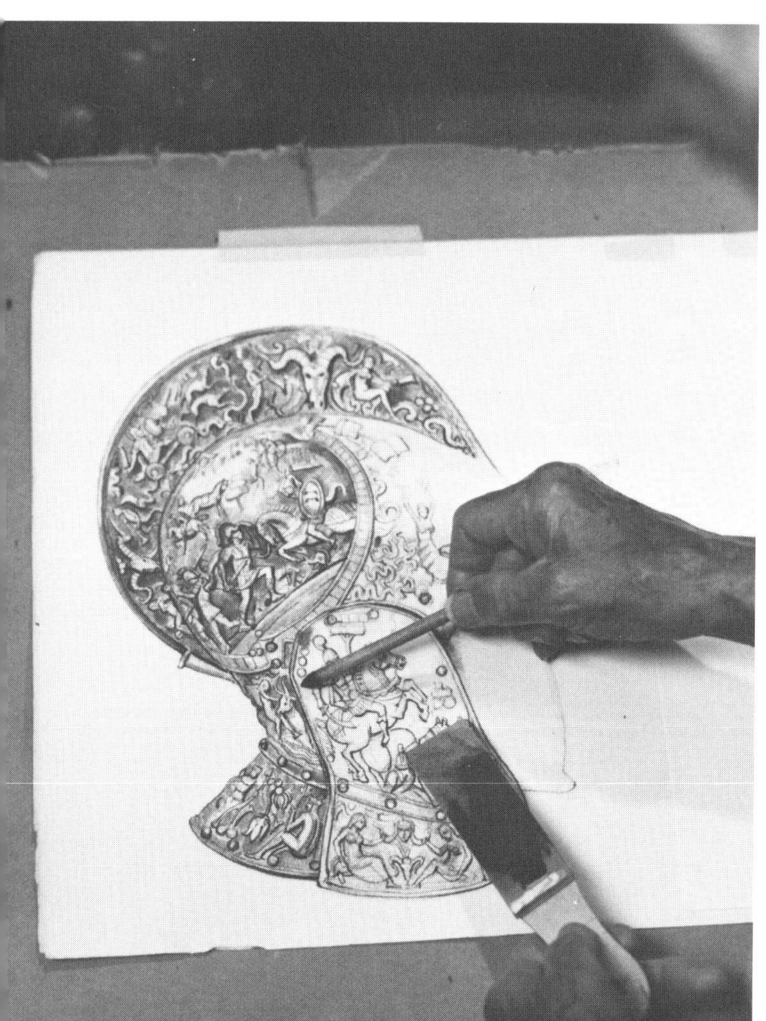

Following the basic outline drawing, tones were established by using a stump. Dust from the sandpaper pad was picked up on the stump to spread onto the drawing. This "smudging" technique created the values on the helmet surface. The lighting was kept consistent. The white of the paper was left as the highest light on the surface, and the values around this highlight darkened as the charcoal dust was rubbed onto the surface, refining and modeling the raised figures. The charcoal dust was applied generously to the sunken areas between the raised figures as well as the shadow side of the figures. Keen observation was necessary here.

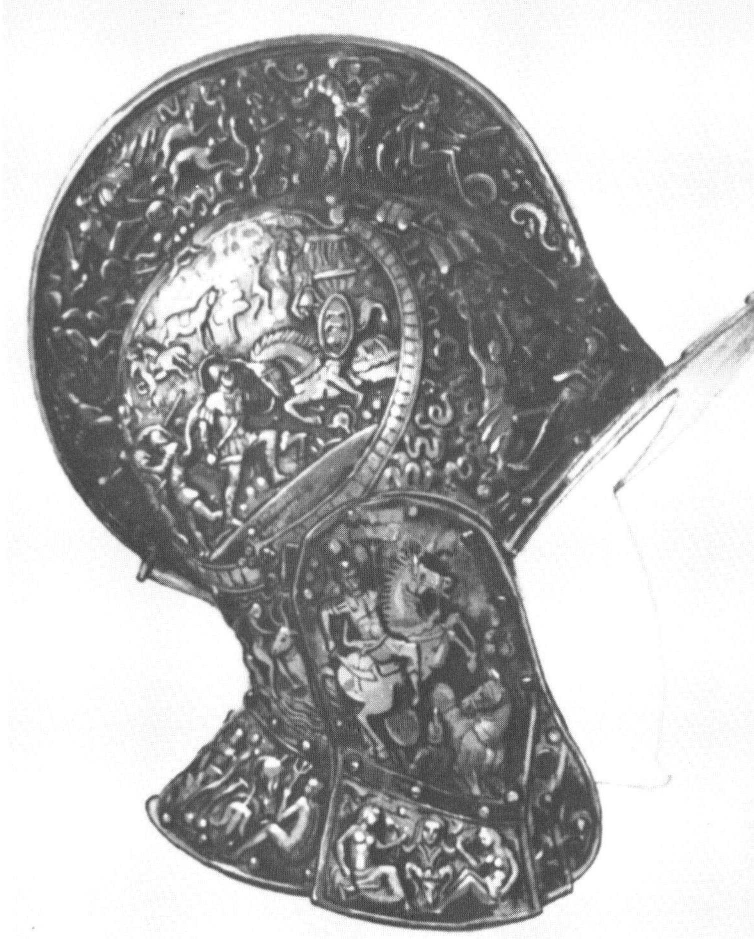

Having applied the basic values with charcoal and stump, a wash of clear water was then rapidly applied with a large brush. A water wash will not disturb the charcoal drawing to any great extent but will tend instead to pull the charcoal tones together. Following this, a thin wash with a touch of ivory black was rapidly washed over the drawing with the exception of the highest light which was left the white of the paper. Remember that this wash was kept thin so as not to conceal the charcoal drawing underneath. The helmet now appeared as a solid and heavy piece of metal.

The light wash of ivory black gave a background for the painting of the embossed figures with white and gray opaque. The figures, treated with these grays, began to stand out from the background. In rendering the raised figures, I thought of them as separate units to be painted, yet kept them within the general tonal scheme. I wasn't concerned when some of the tones of the pigment went over the drawing lines of the figures. Some raised sections were flattened by 450 years of existence, and many of the figures had been blurred by time.

In painting the highest light, heavy white opaque was used and even built up to catch the light. A thinner white with touches of ivory black was mixed to paint the figures furthest from the highest light. As the helmet took on a more solid appearance, it looked heavier. I thought about the weight of metal that was worn by the nobility of this period. This heavy helmet was just one part of an entire suit of steel. Even suits worn just for processions and parades must have been heavy to carry.

The final touch was to use a 1¼-inch wide flat brush in wetting a band of the paper next to the upper and lower sides of the helmet, charging this area with a wide single sweep of the brush loaded heavily with ivory black. This brush stroke was applied swiftly, with the idea of creating a soft edge away from the helmet. Ivory black was used throughout this rendering. Ivory is a warm black.

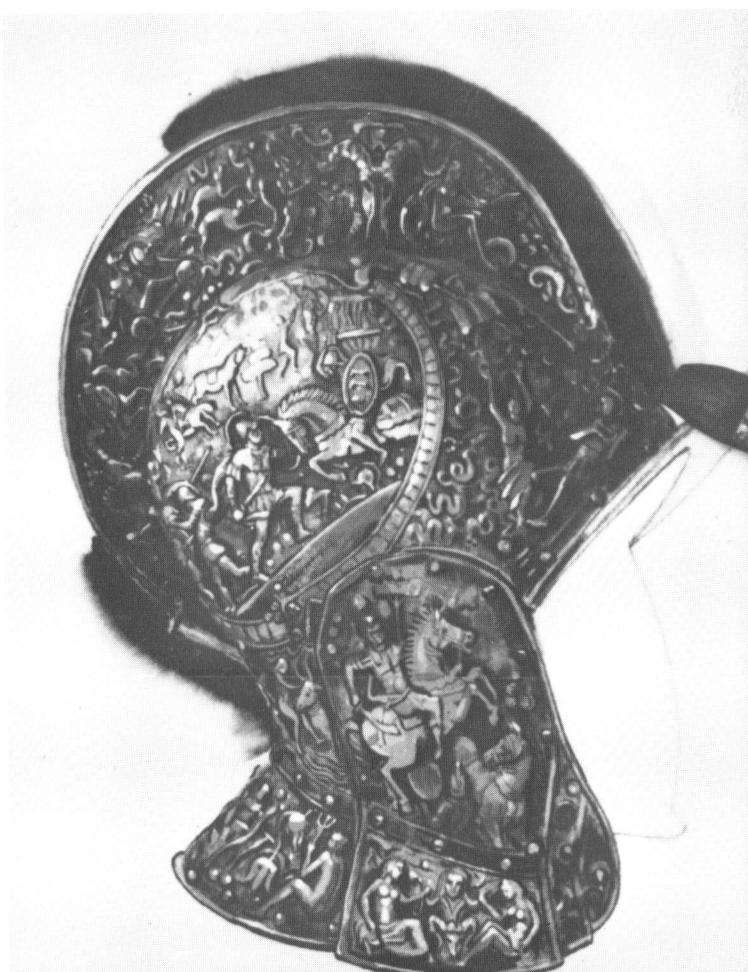

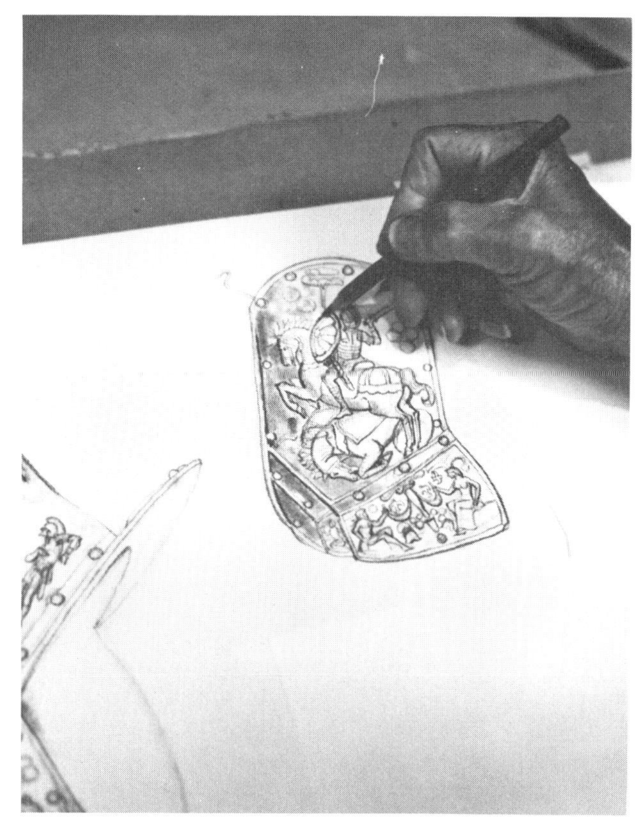

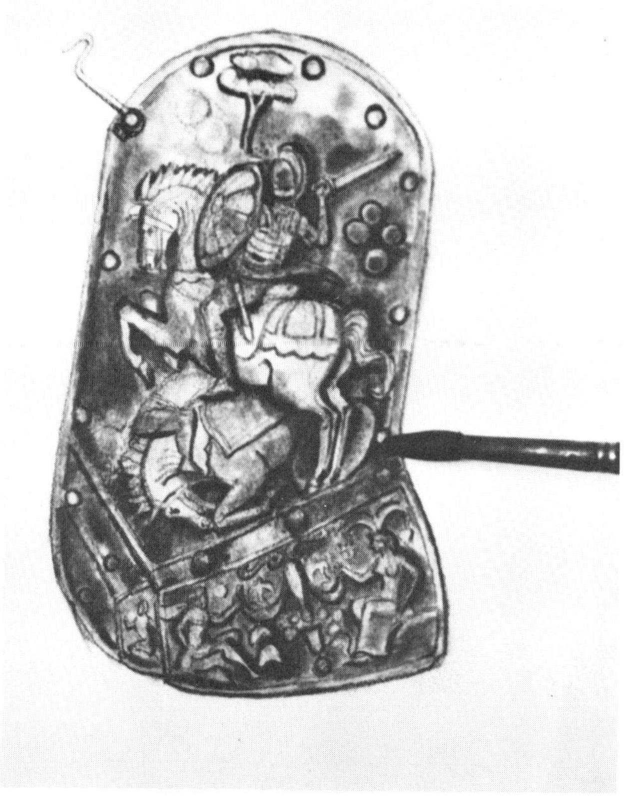

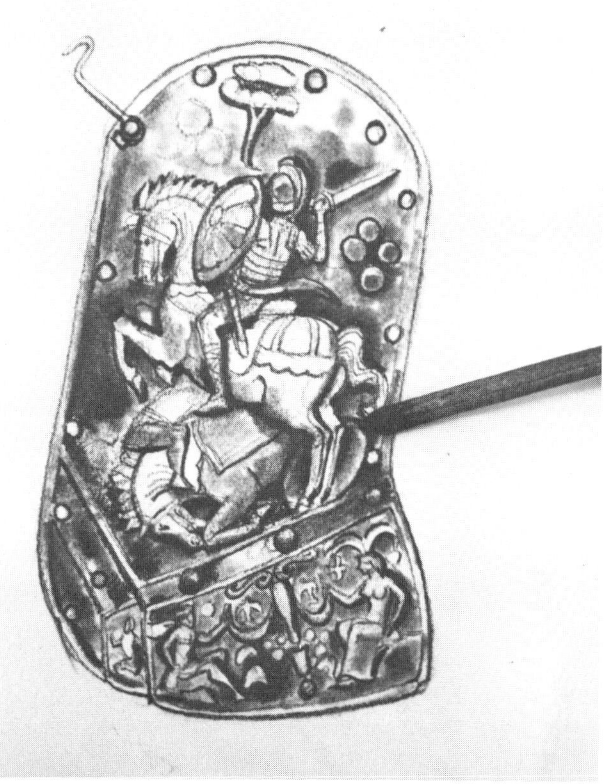

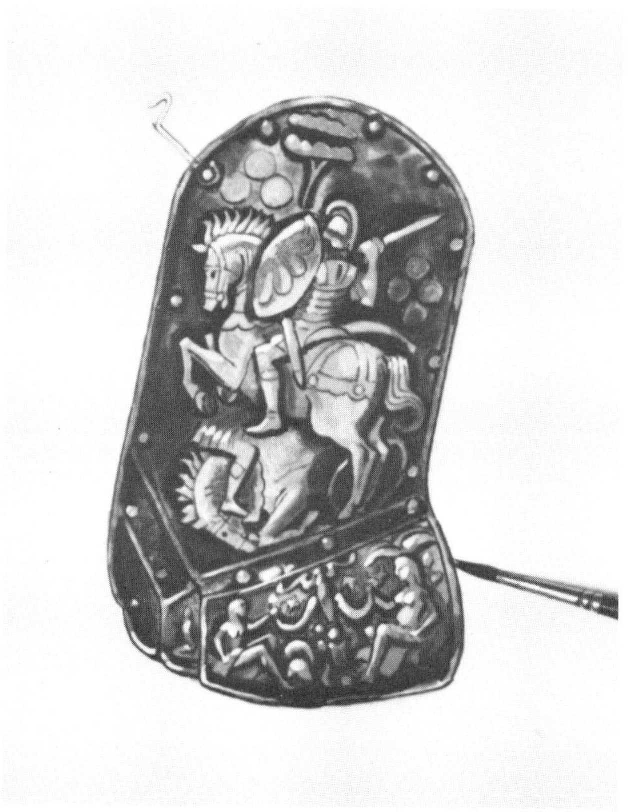

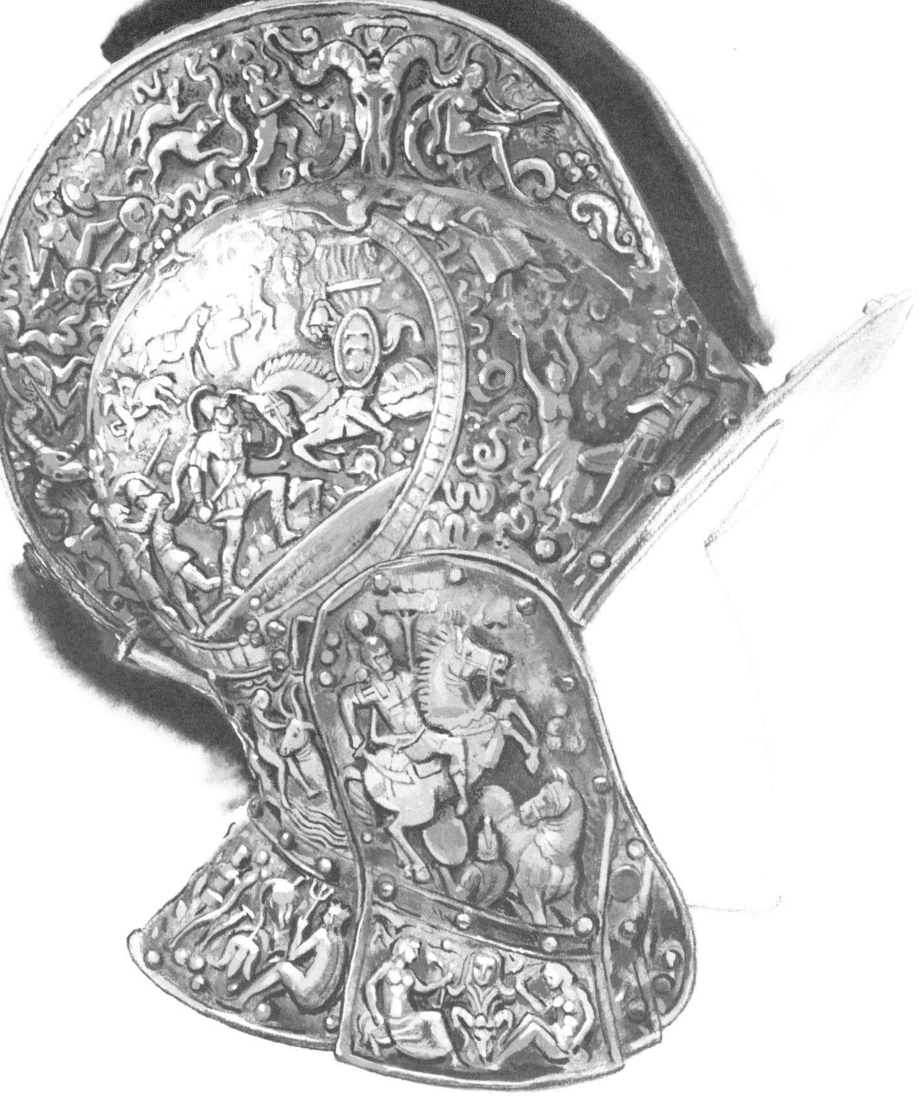

Following the same procedures already described, I added the detail of the ear covering on the opposite side of the helmet.

When I finished the last wash, I looked back over the steps from the beginning flat charcoal pencil drawing through the gradual step by step development as the work took on the appearance of a rounded heavy metal form. It is sometimes amazing the deception that can be accomplished with brush and paint guided by a steady hand and mind. Was it Rembrandt who said there should be no break between the mind and the hand?

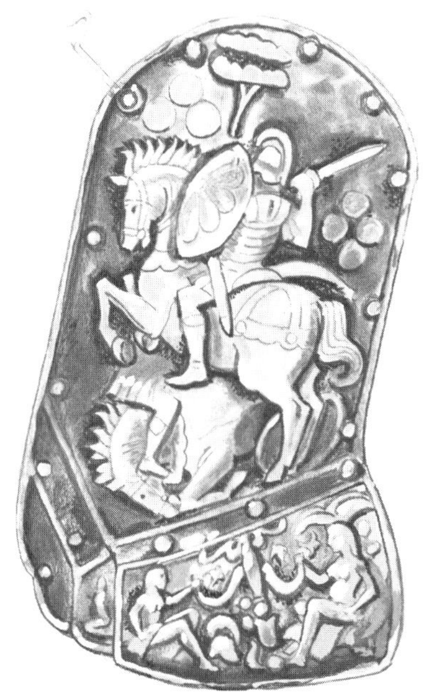

The challenge here was to capture the quality of the old metal of the can. The other elements served as foils in texture, color, and shape.

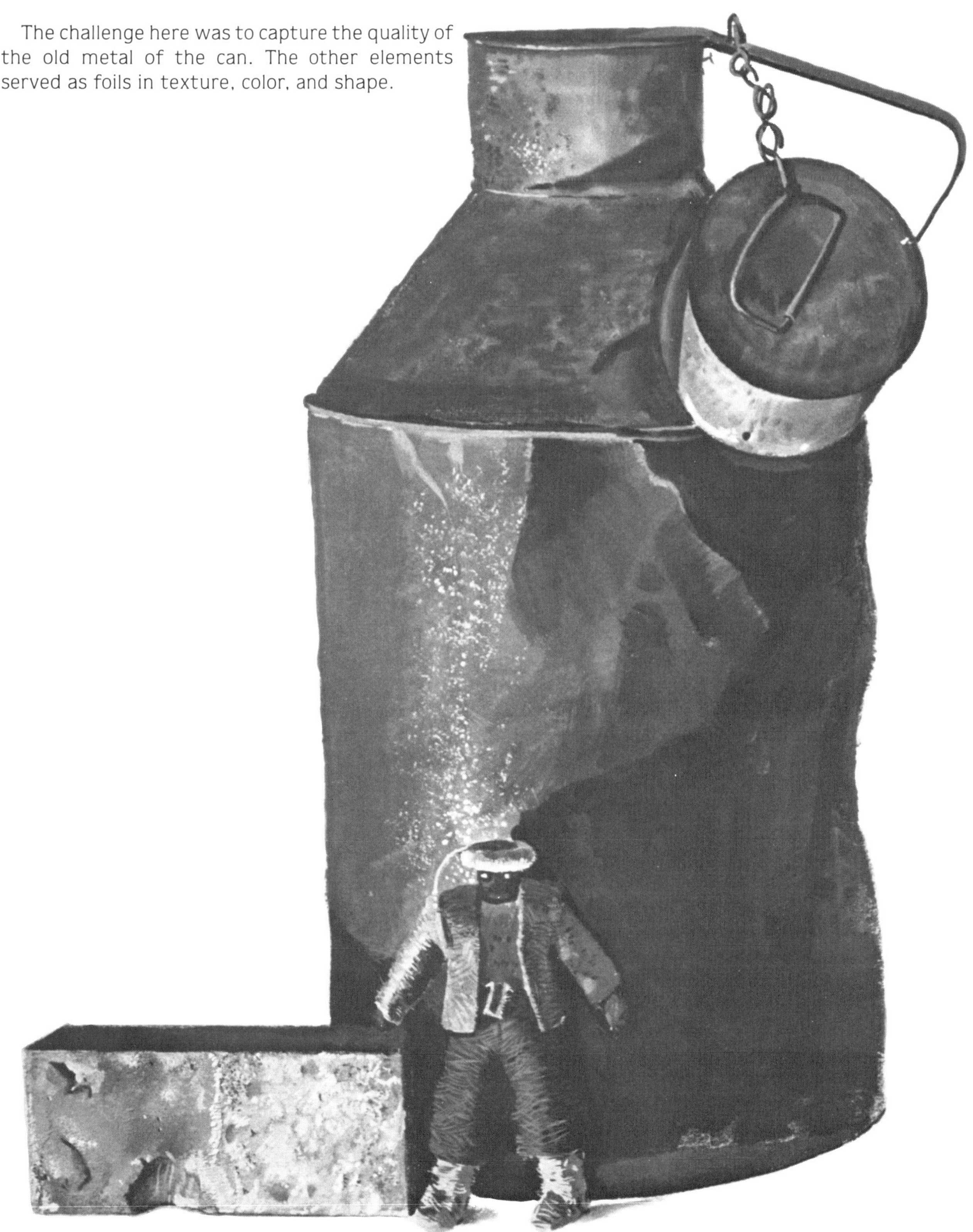

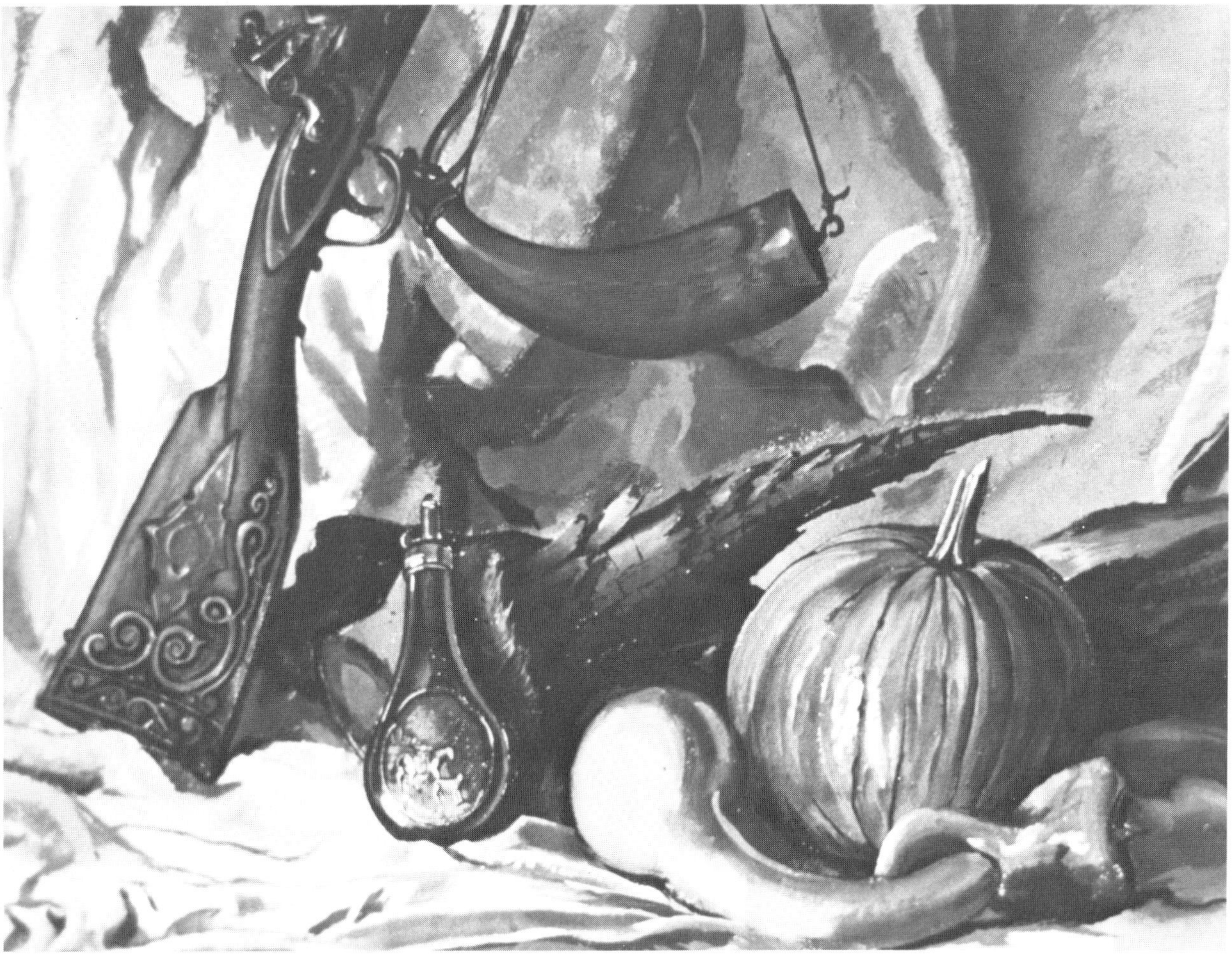

This still life is full of intricate detail, but here they are held subordinate to the picture as a whole. What I was striving for was a well-composed picture with an interesting variety of shapes, color and textures.

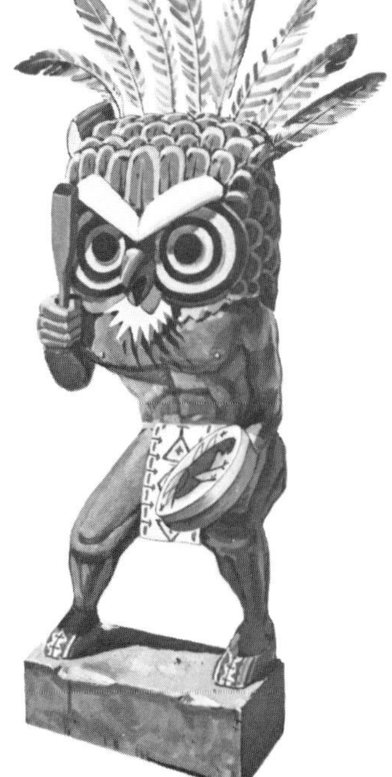

The Indian Owl figure is an example of hard edge painting with many details. The overall texture had to appear constant to maintain the feeling of a carved artifact.

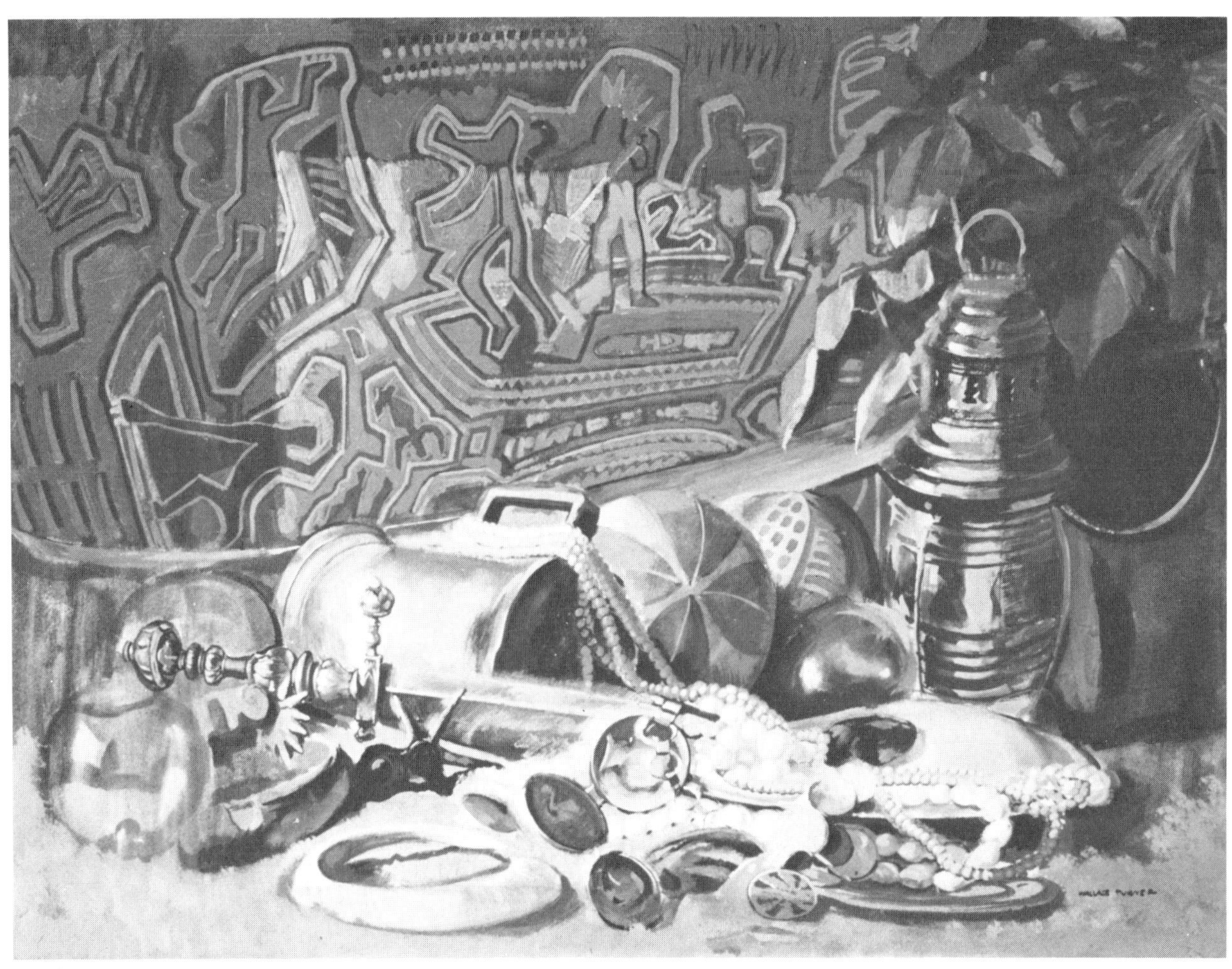

LOOT OF THE CORSAIRS

The multitude of objects, their texture, color and detail carry the main thrust of this picture. Without the detailed rendering much of the interest of the picture would be lost.

CHAPTER 9

Gallery

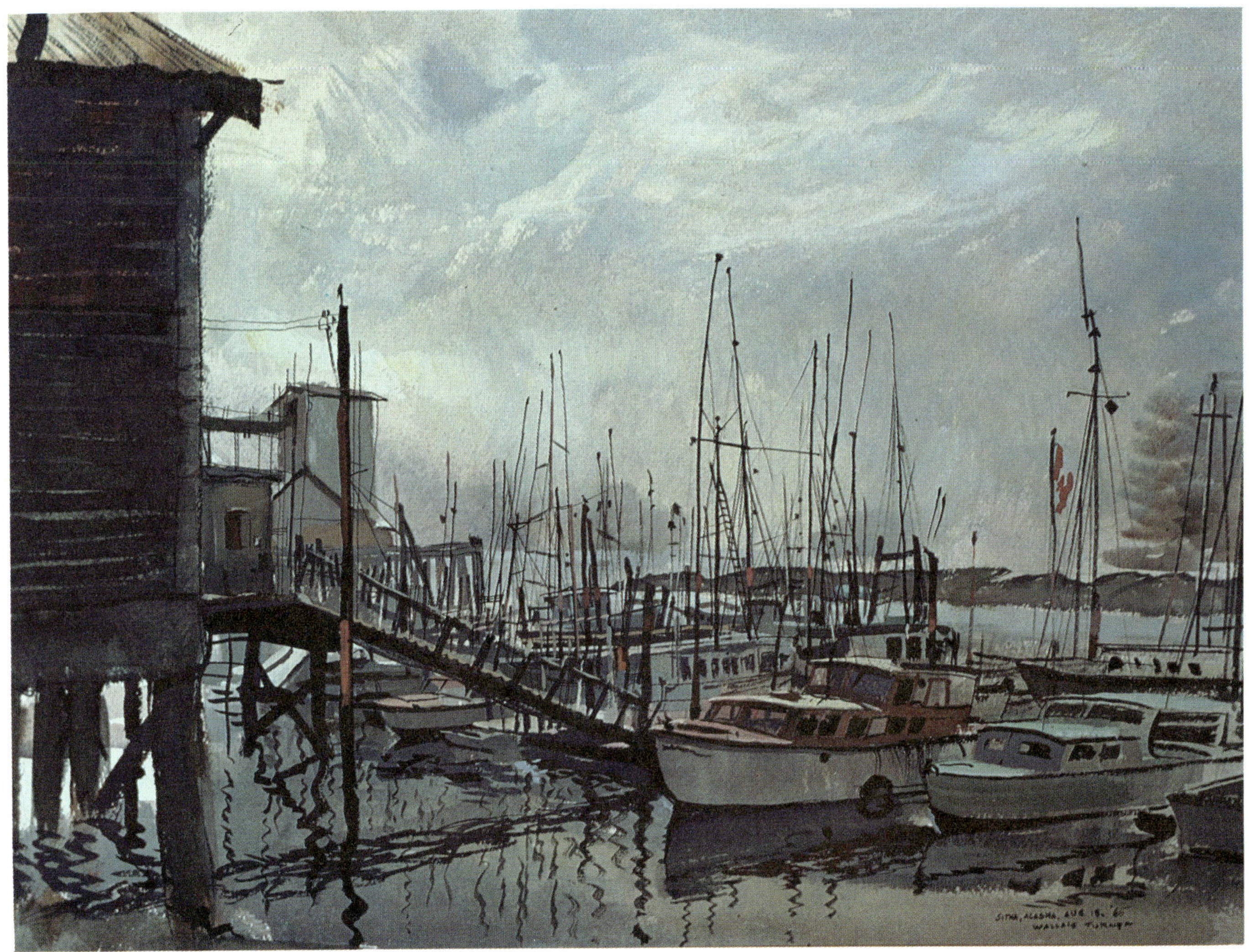

SITKA HARBOR, SITKA, ALASKA

This old Russian capital of America presents a strong pictorial setting. The dark building on the left with downward sloping ramp leads the eye down to the boats, the center of interest. The boats are drawn carefully, making certain that they are immersed in the water, not just sitting on the surface. Although there is a great deal of detail in the boats, just their main shape is drawn.

Looking into the light creates a strong value contrast. The pencil lines of the drawing of the boats show through the wash so the hulls of the boats are painted with impasto. Although most of the hulls are white, they take on a deeper value as they appear in shadow requiring white, ultramarine blue and yellow ochre. It is almost impossible to connect a mast to its boat, so the masts are painted in as they appear, using a pointed sable brush and, for the smaller masts and rigging, a Gillott pen #170. Any bright or warm hues, such as seen in the superstructure, are seized upon as accents, to enliven this active fishing port where seasonal workers in the fish packing plant, seen at the left in the middle distance, live on their boats.

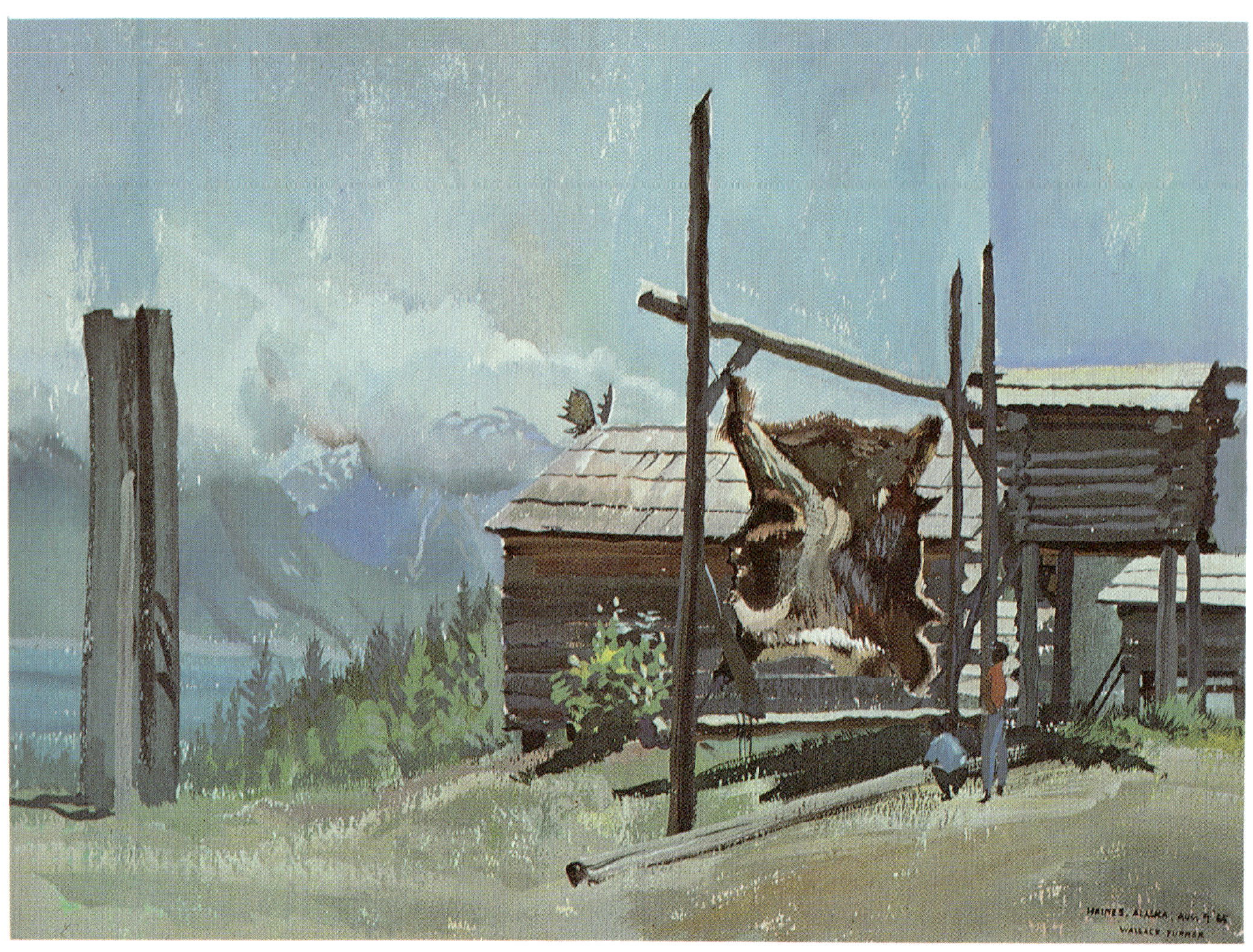

TANNING A GRIZZLY HIDE, PORT CHILKOOT, ALASKA.

In this painting, it was the shapes that appealed to me; the jagged-shaped Grizzly hide; the simpler rectangular log buildings in the rear, all meshed together by the calligraphic scaffolding supporting the great bear skin. Also, the perpendicular lines of the monolithic totem pole at the left repeat in the scaffolding and the stilts of the storehouse. It is a good idea to first look for the basic shapes underlying the surface material, the "bare bones" of the composition.

Studying the color of the locale before starting to paint helps to simplify the procedure. Here the color scheme is based on the hues of the log buildings. The roofs give the highest lights, painted with heavy white and yellow ochre. Though we are looking at the inner side of the hide, texture, hue, and value changes are painted to contrast with the simpler textures and flat horizontals of the buildings. Heavy impasto was used on rough watercolor paper with Designers Gouache.

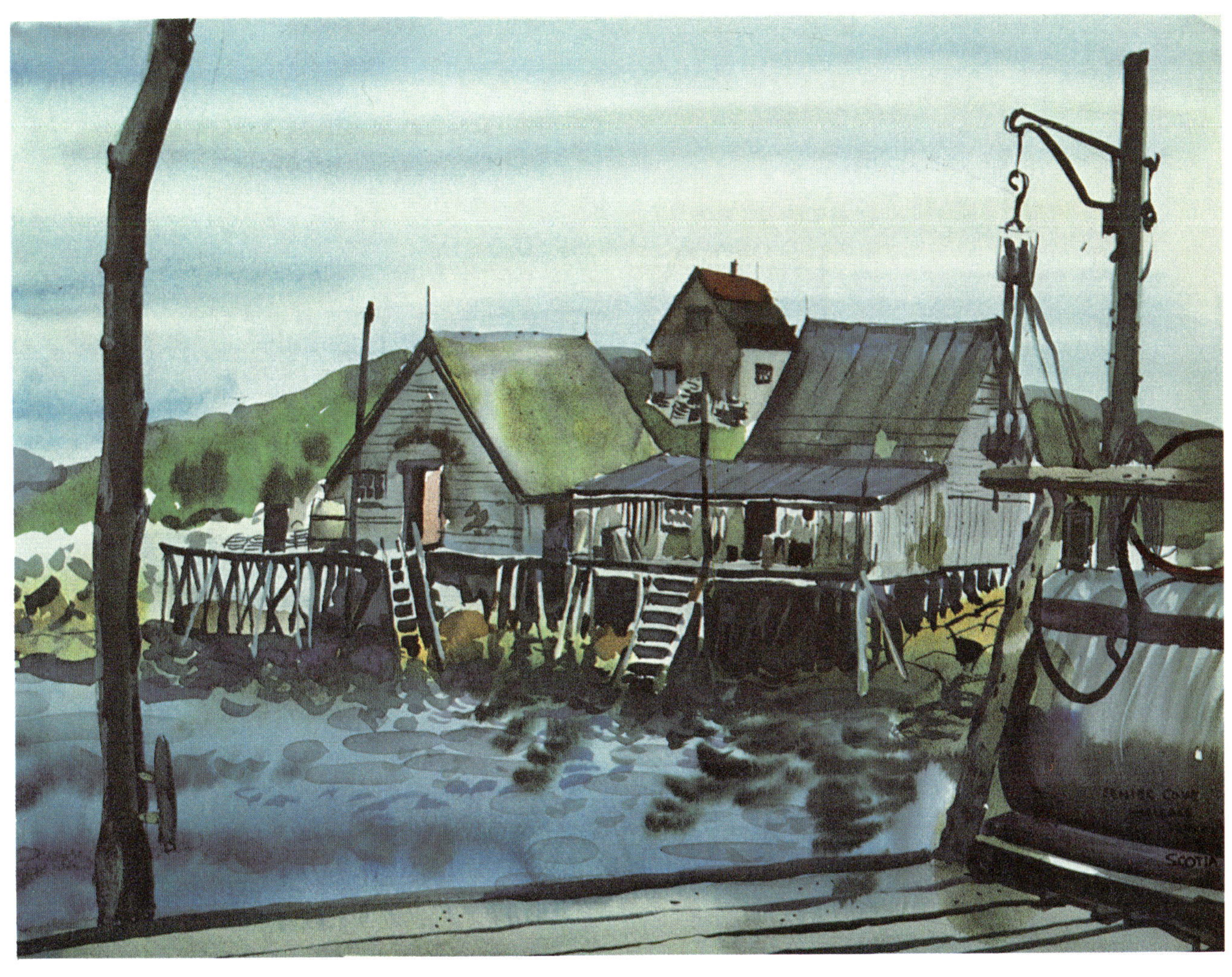

CENTER COVE SOUTH SHORE

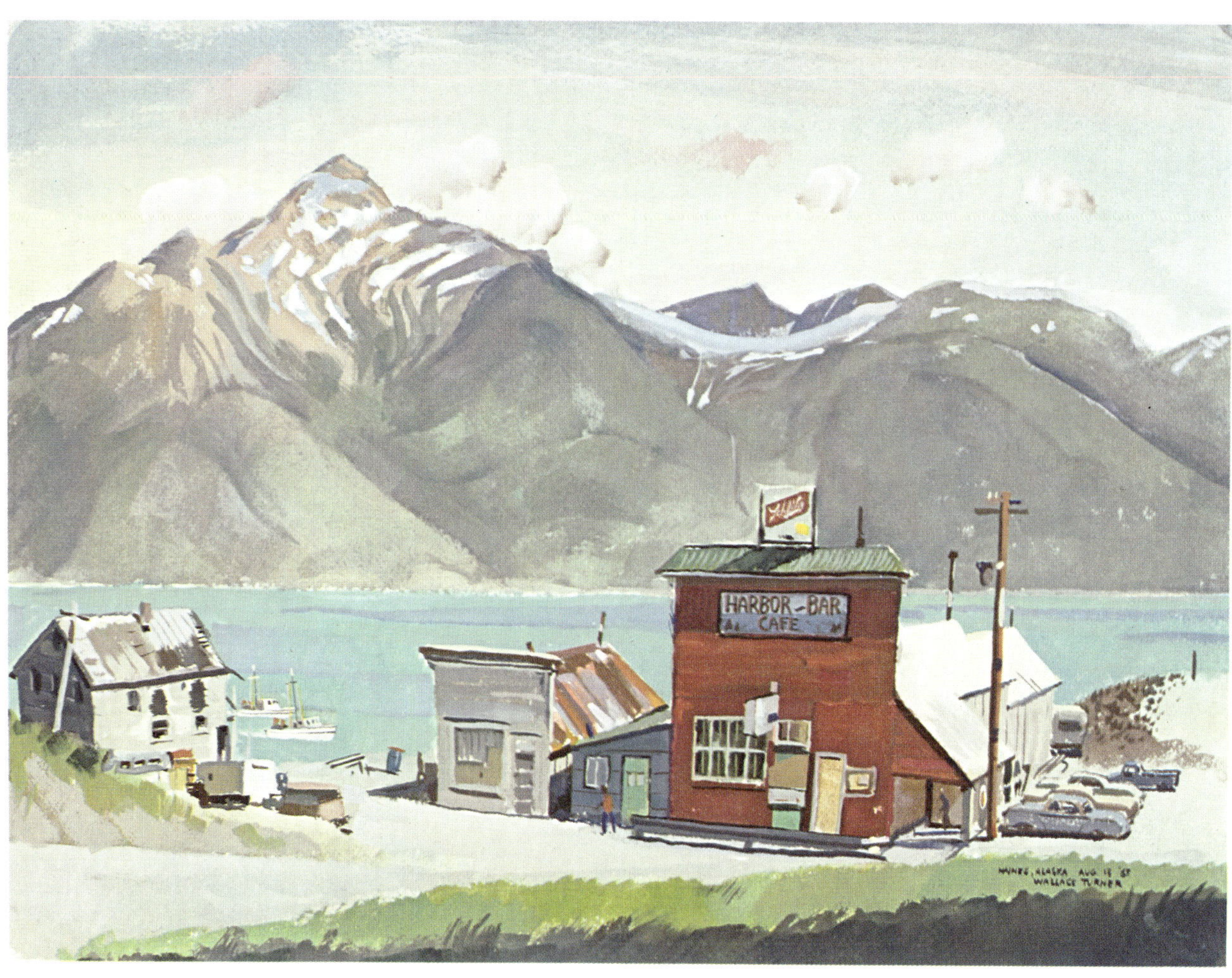

HARBOR, HAINES, ALASKA

When painting in Alaska, you will often find that the far distance consists of a mountain range, as in this painting. It was a warm day in southern Alaska. The mountains were bathed in a soft sunlight, giving them a greenish yellow ochre color. Value contrast is observed in the lighter color of the blueish-green water of Ellis Sound at the base of the mountains and again in the tall red building with its metal roof which helps to hold the interest in this area. The muted colors and shapes of the buildings in various degrees of disrepair, add variety and interest to the middle foreground, while the lower foreground is more open.

I planned my composition, placing the horizontal line at the foot of the mountains below the center of the paper in order not to divide the picture into two equal parts. The perpendicular lines of the tall building and the telephone pole in the upper foreground break this horizontal line, while the curved lines of the mountains, the road, and grass lend contrast.

The color was applied quite thickly. Except for the thin washes of the sky, there is little of the transparent watercolor feeling. I might add that I used the technique of painting back to front, explained previously.

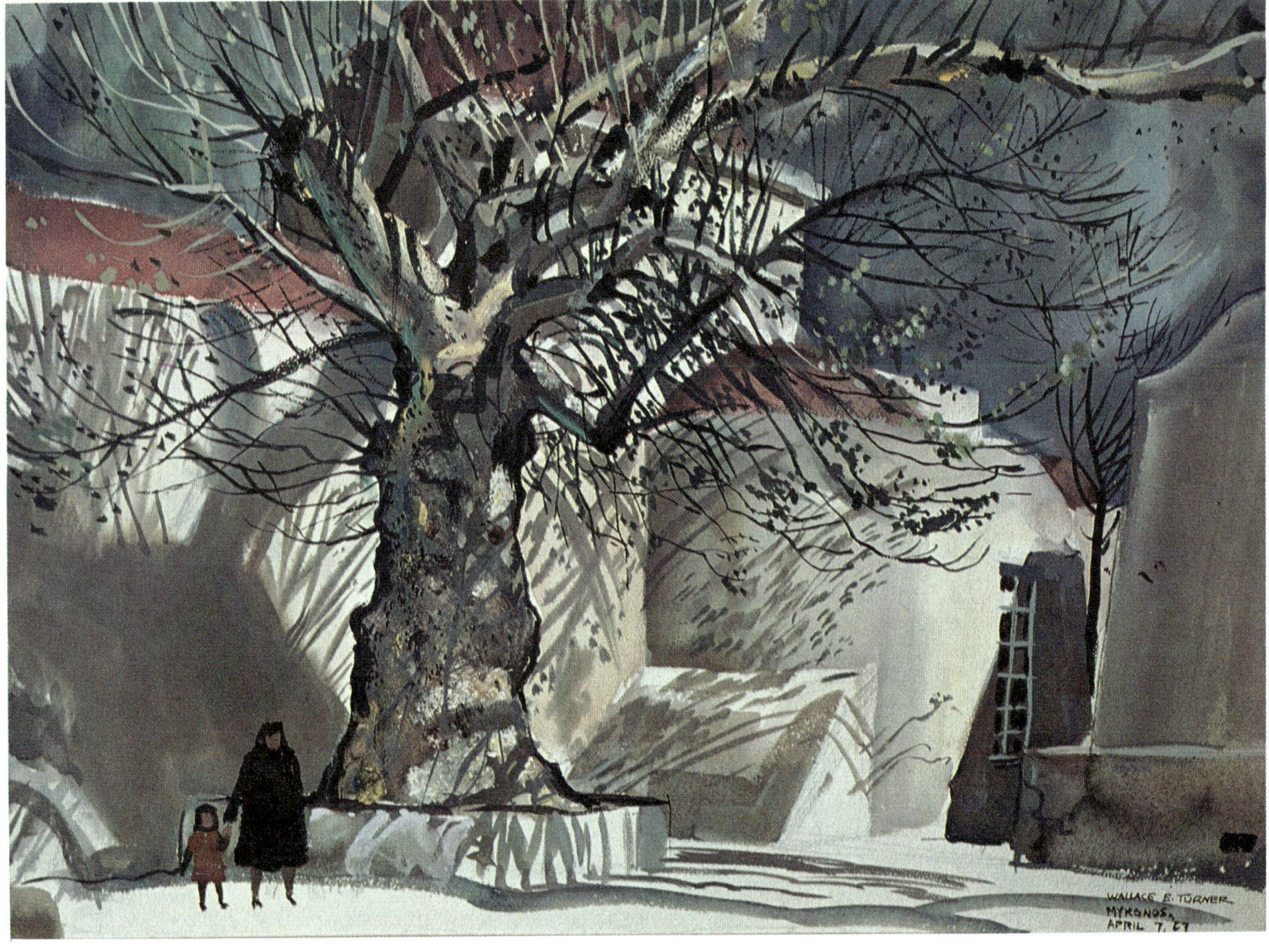

GNARLED TREE AND CHAPEL, MYKONOS, GREECE

The 400 or so chapels on the Greek island of Mykonos, although somewhat different in shape, have some characteristics in common: painted stark white stone and cement construction, heavily buttressed walls and domes or half domes painted pure alizarin crimson. They are all extremely paintable. The Greek sky is usually a deep blue, throwing these white buildings into brilliant relief. The old gnarled tree offered a great contrast to the smooth white walls behind it. The subject appealed to me, bringing to mind the concept that has been drummed into art students. Draw through.

Painting from back to front, I mixed a variety of blues, graying these hues somewhat so as not to detract from the chapel or tree. This is a high key painting with the strongest darks contained in the outline of the old tree and some of the overhead branches.

The heavily textured surface of the old tree was painted by using a stiff-bristled brush and dabbing on a heavy mixture of white, raw sienna, viridian green, ultramarine blue, and cadmium yellow. While this mixture was still damp, streaks made mainly with ultramarine blue were painted across the surface of the tree, catching the character of the branches which cast the shadows. The shadows of the branches were changed to a rich green and darker values as they were painted on the upper part of the tree.

About this time a grandmother and her little granddaughter came strolling into the scene, offering accents in both color and value. The grandmother's coat was painted with Payne's gray and the little girl's costume painted with cadmium red. These figures must have cast shadows on the stone street, but I forgot to paint them.

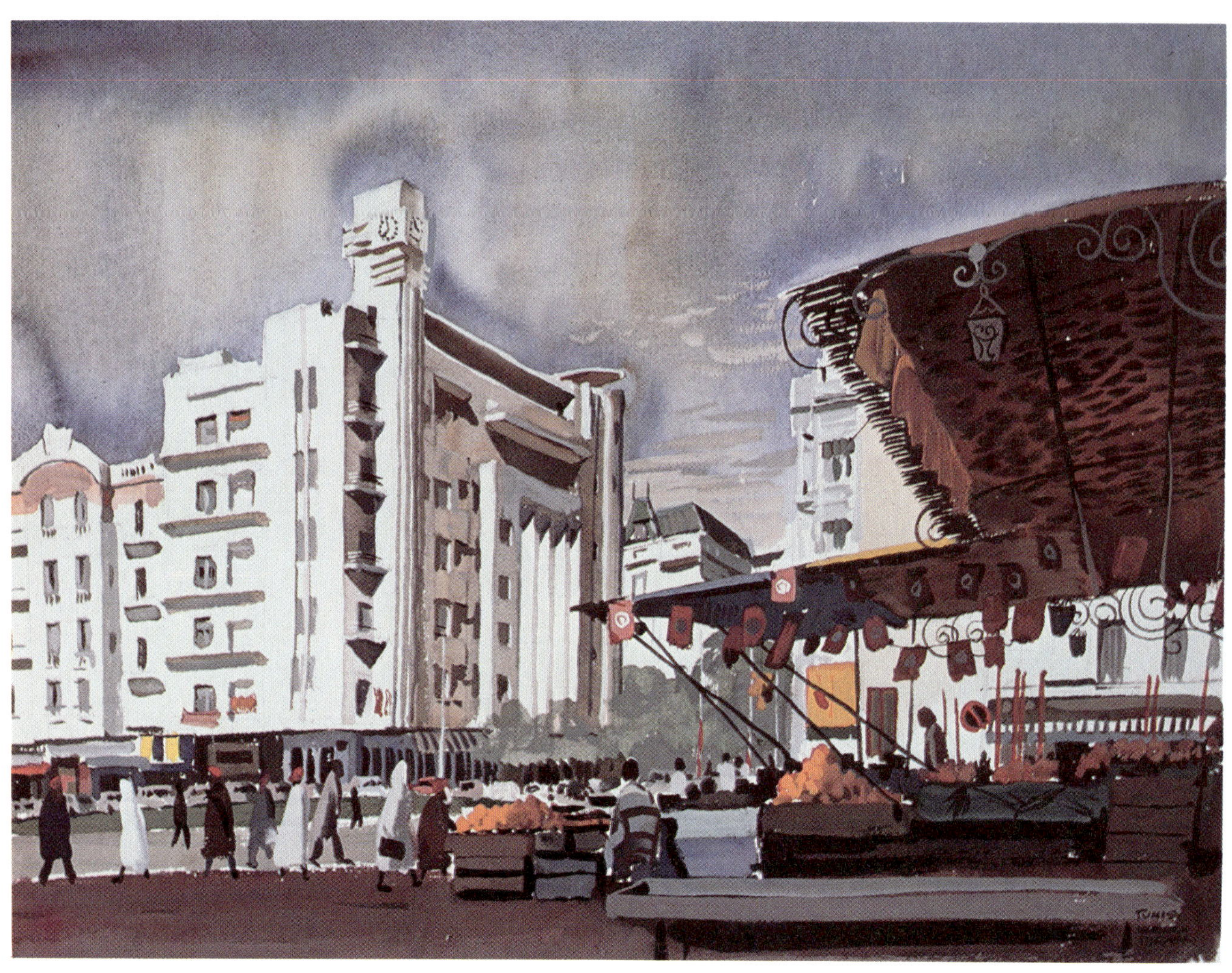

CITY SQUARE, TUNIS, TUNISIA

Painting a busy city street in any part of the world usually attracts a crowd. It was no different in Tunis, but by hiding a little behind a portion of the fruit vendor's stand I was able to work in relative peace. The spot also offered a little welcome shade.

The building across the street was done mainly in transparent washes. All of the white showing is the white of the paper. I like the shape of the structure against the dark awning over the fruit stand in the foreground. In general I think this picture captures the feel of the city and the place rather well.

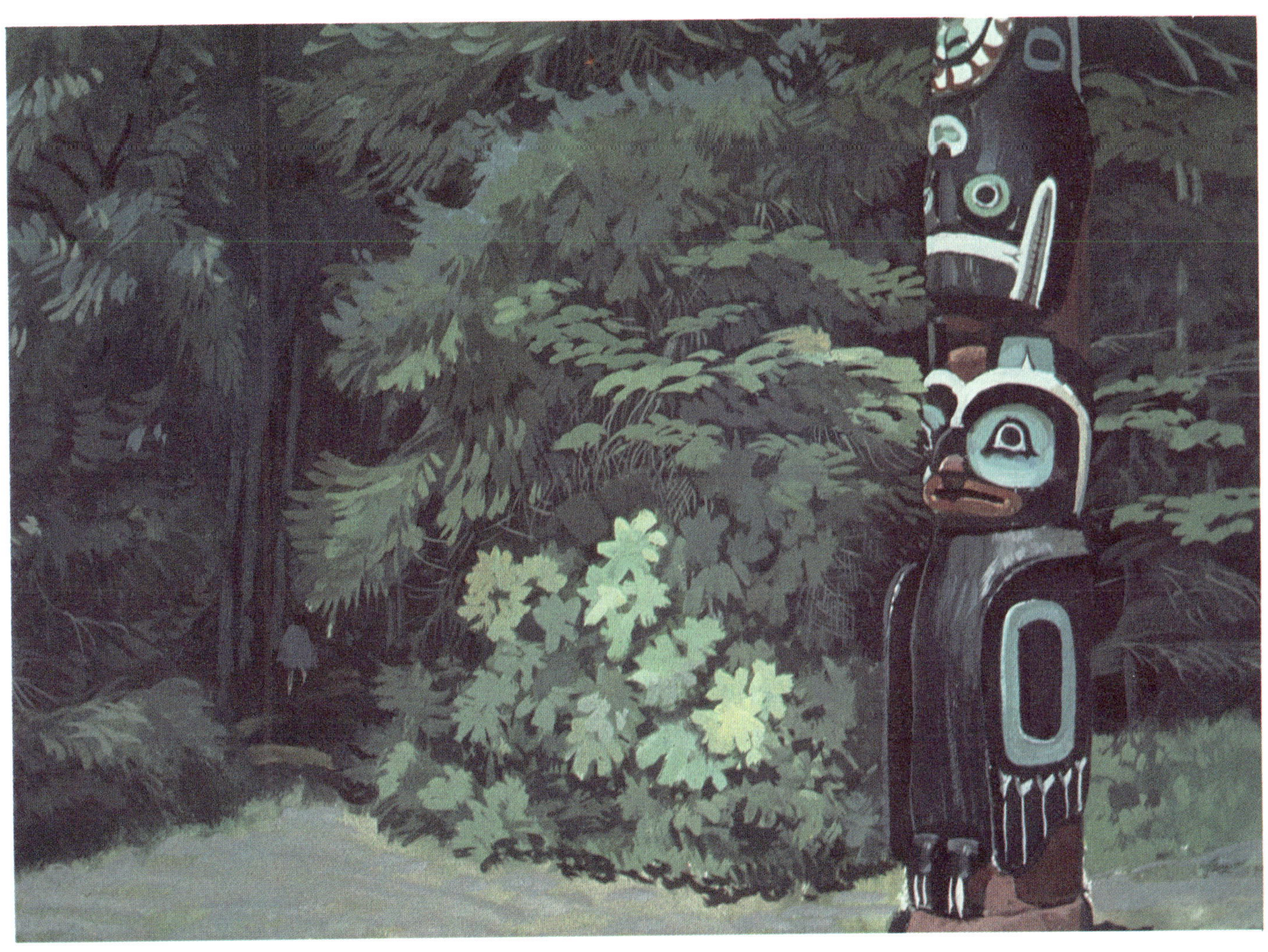

SITKA, ALASKA

I have always liked totem poles with their interesting carvings and bright painted colors. This one in Sitka seemed particularly appealing.

The main problem here was to incorporate enough interest in the background to make the composition work. By playing up the foliage and stressing the variety in the greens and the shapes of the leaves I believe it worked out satisfactorily. The path leading into the woods has become a secondary area of interest.

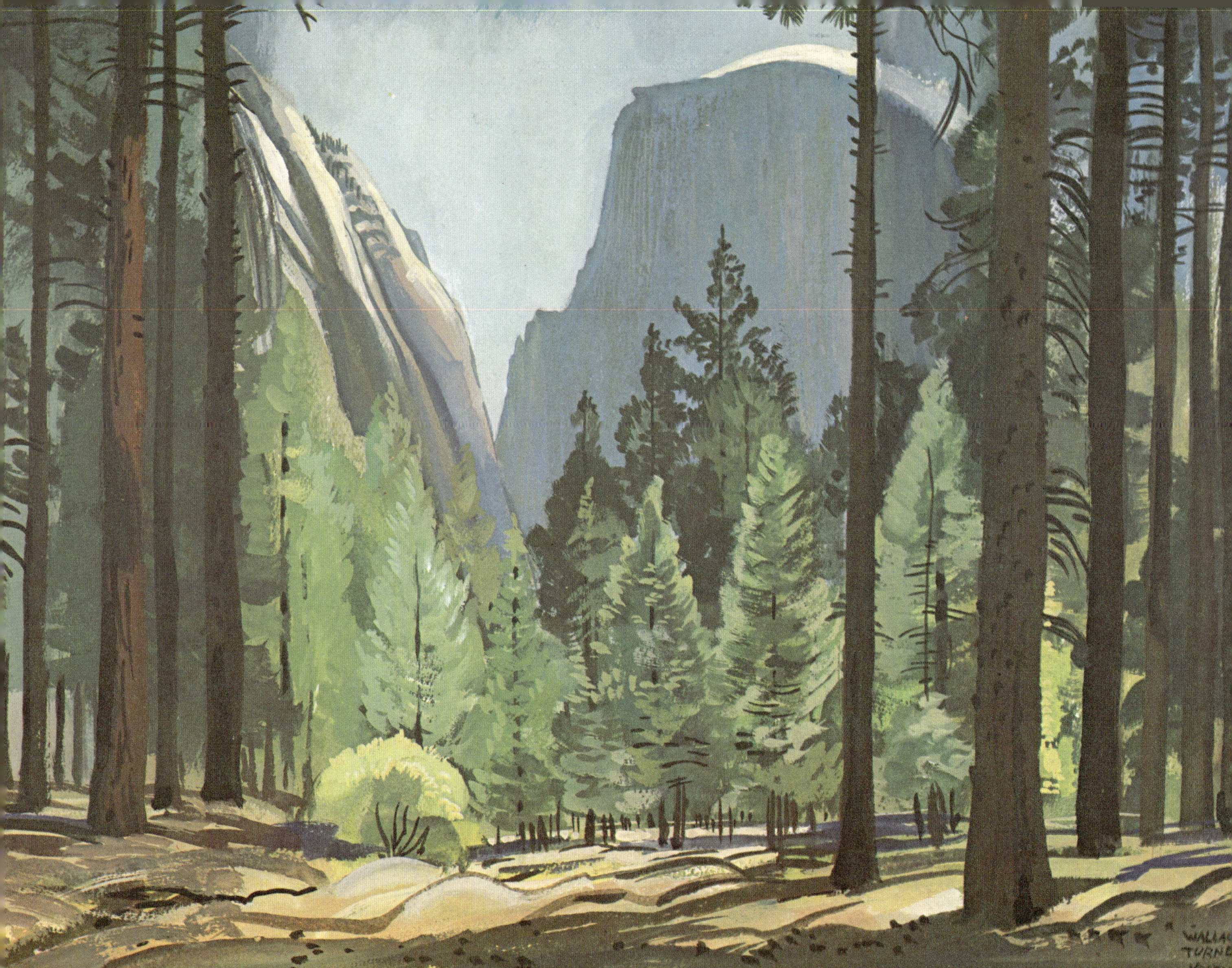

HALF DOME, YOSEMITE NATIONAL PARK, CALIFORNIA

Studying the great sheer face of Half Dome, I agreed with Josiah Whitney, who in 1874 said, "It strikes even the casual observer as a new revelation in mountain form." How could I capture the spirit of this awesome granite face in paint? Having painted boulders previously, the color and value relationship was evident. Many things were similar. Only the drawing and scale were different.

A blueish tone on the face, with mixtures of yellow ochre, suggested the reflected light that glanced off the face of this great rock. The stand of stately pines framed the towering granite face, the line of their trunks adding height, taking the eye upward. Lighter tones of green of the smaller trees in the middle distance provided an accent of lighter color. By these cone-shaped trees the eye was again taken upward toward Half Dome's lighted summit.

In order to concentrate interest on Half Dome, spaces between the trees on either side were darkened. If openings in the foliage of trees are painted the same value as the surrounding sky value, the tree forms are weakened. For this reason I usually make the foliage openings a bit darker than the sky value. To complete the painting, dark brush strokes to represent the shadows of the trees were painted over the ground area, being careful to follow the contour of the ground.

Although this has the appearance of a middle-of-the-wilderness painting, just a couple of hundred yards behind me was a luxurious hotel.

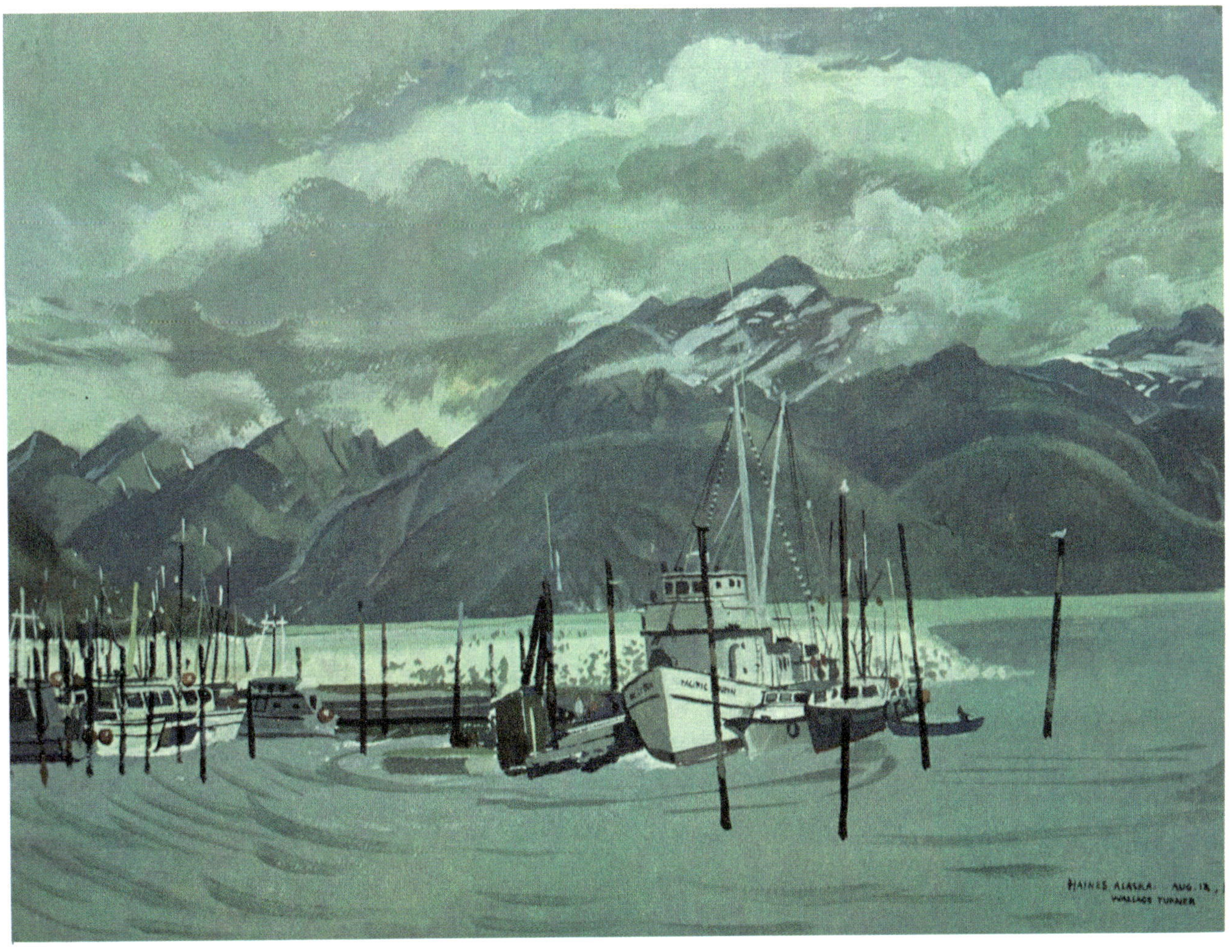

HAINES HARBOR, ALASKA

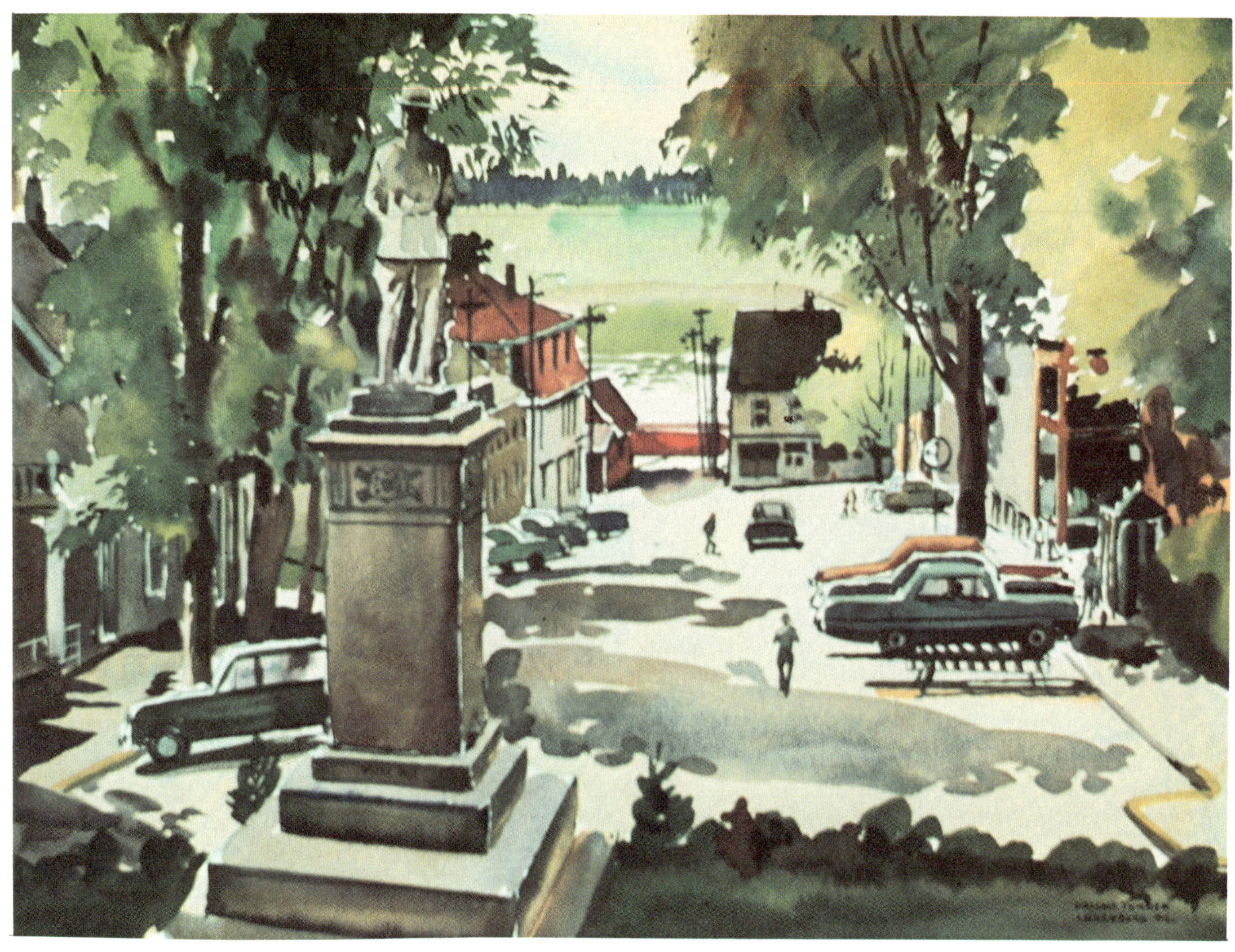

LUNENBERG, NOVA SCOTIA

I relied heavily on transparent washes in this scene to capture the feeling of a bright summer day. The strong contrasts between the cool shadows and the warm highlights are the main ingredients that make it work. The Lunenberg Park is a lovely area to sketch.

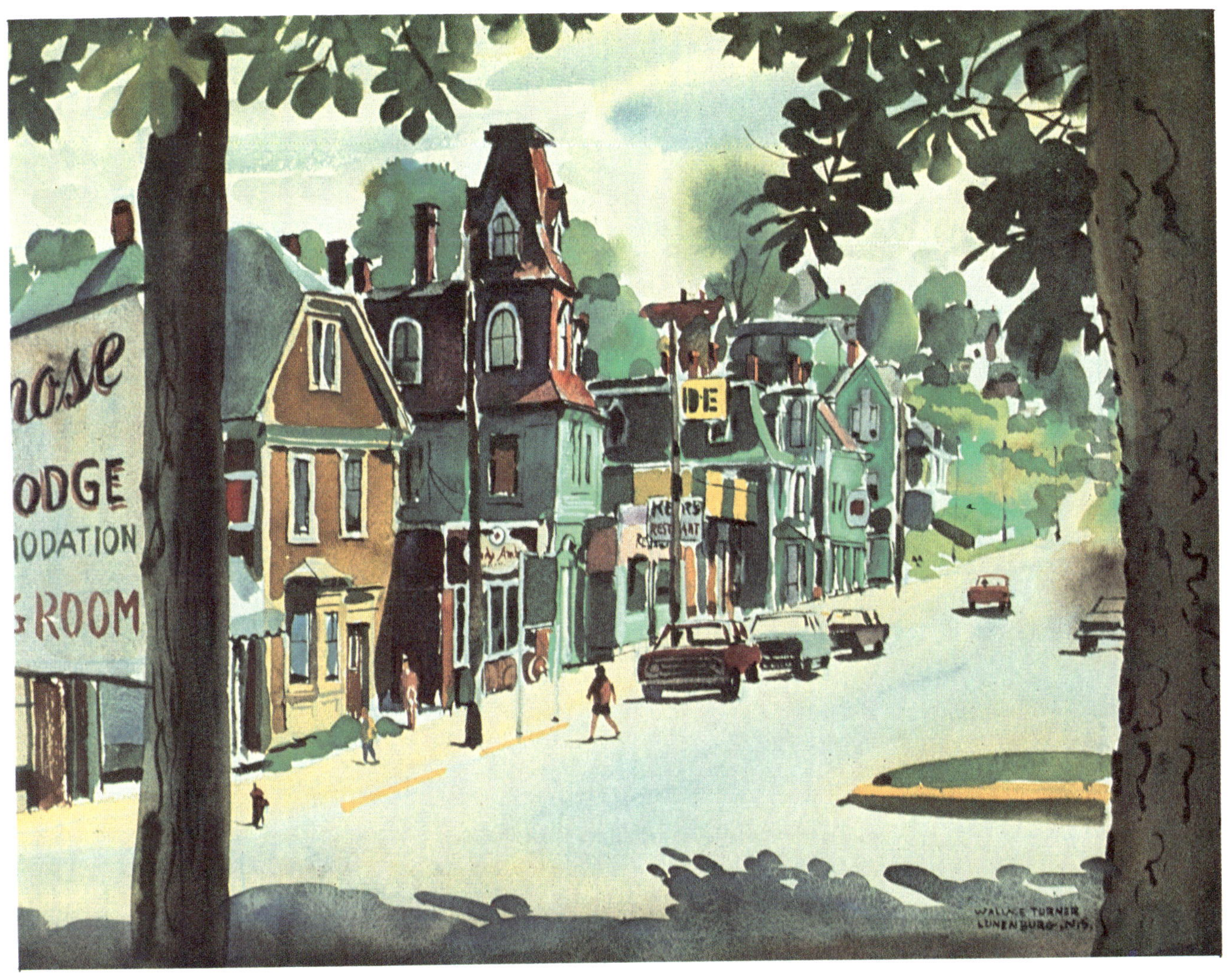

LUNENBERG STREET

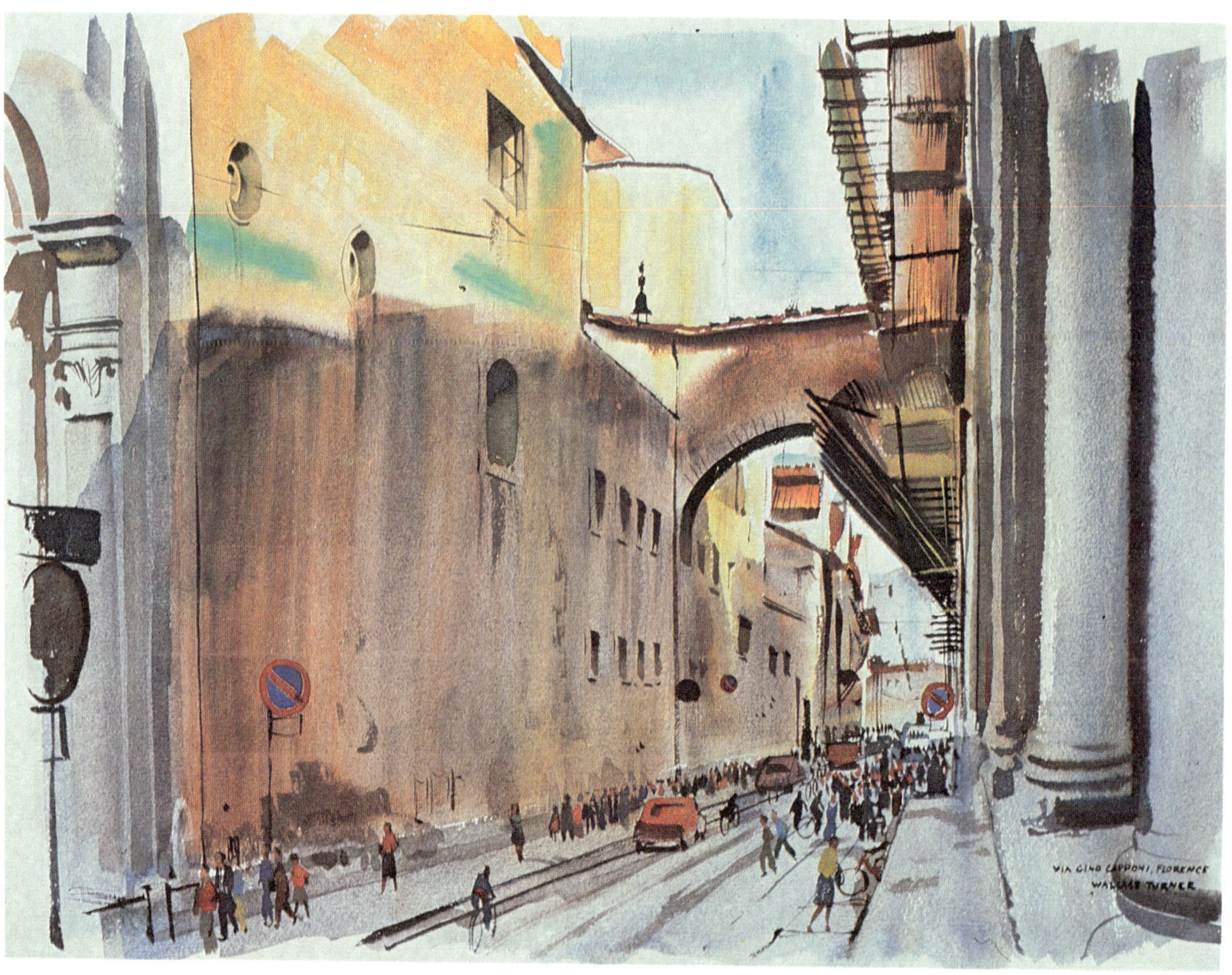

VIA GINO CAPPONI, FLORENCE, ITALY

The teeming street in old Florence with its warm yellow and yellow ochre buildings, the luminous shadows cast by them and the hurrying crowd at lunch time presented a real challenge to paint. Realizing that the light would change swiftly, speed was required, so transparent watercolor handling seemed best. The values in this street scene were more important than the colors, so I concentrated on them first.

Quickly the main areas were sketched in on a sheet of Fabriano with an HB pencil. The mellow-looking buildings on the left were then wet with a big brush. While still wet, the basic warm yellow was flooded into the shape, covering the shadow area as well. Loosely mixing the darker-than-life shadow color, I started with the distant buildings through the arch. The value just under the eaves was pulled down to the street level while forming the lost and found edges. The shadow mass, though quite luminous, was composed mainly of burnt sienna, ultramarine blue, and raw sienna. I picked up more blue on the downward pull so that the greatest cool-warm contrast was at the top of the cast shadow. As the wash rolled downward on the slanted paper, more burnt sienna was added. The blue color moving down the general wash gave a weather-stained appearance to the old buildings. A heavy wash of burnt sienna with a touch of blue was then laid on the still damp archway. The columns were painted with a gray made of yellow ochre and ultramarine blue. Some yellow ochre was then added to suggest reflected light on the columns. To separate the columns, I used a heavy pigment of a strong dark burnt umber and ultramarine blue. With a small pointed brush the figures were swiftly dropped in, giving scale to the picture. I made the figures a bit smaller than they actually were in order to make the buildings appear more monumental. Bright red cars were added for color variety and interest.

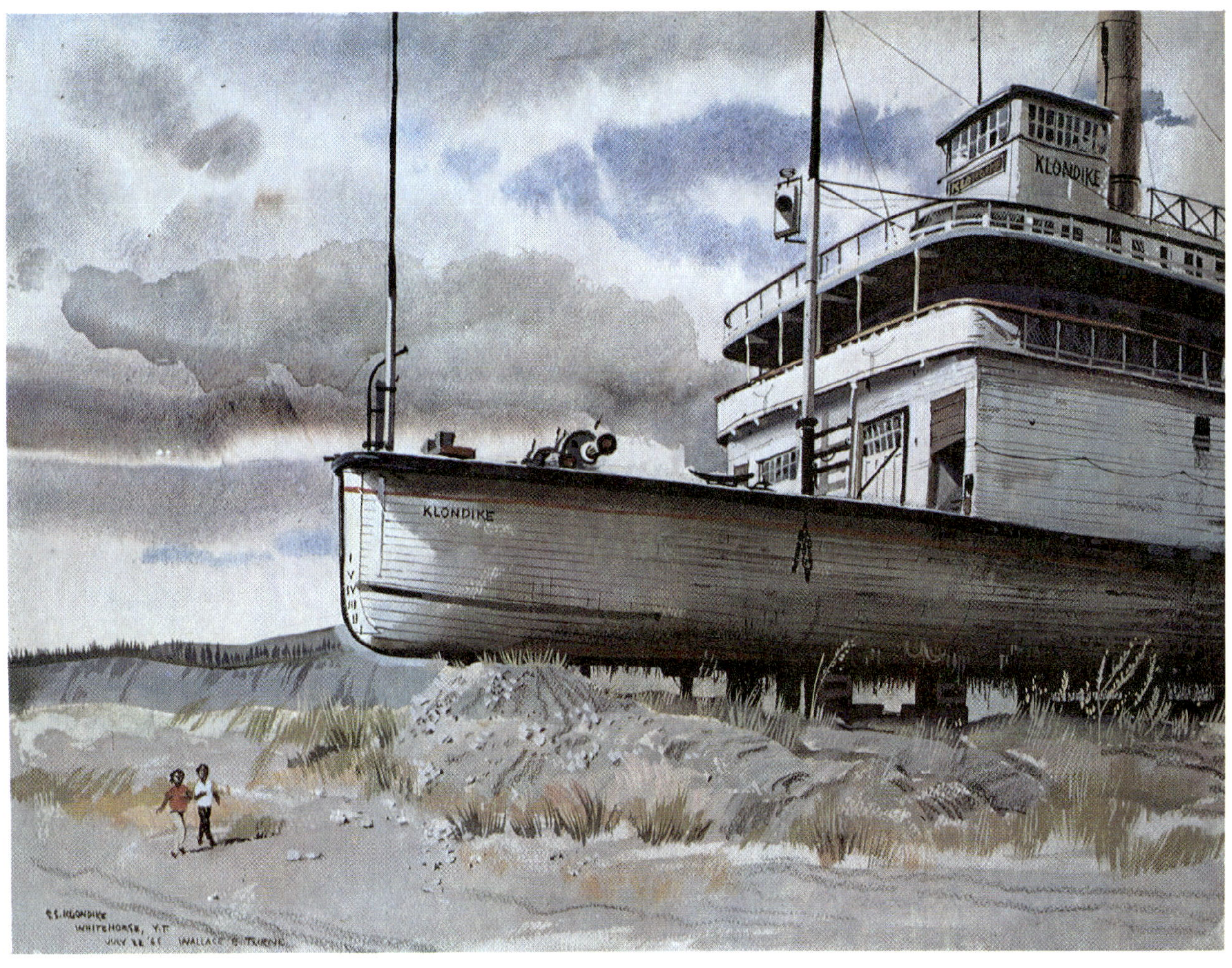

S. S. KLONDIKE BEACHED, WHITEHORSE, YUKON TERRITORY

This is another one of the rotting wooden hulks of an old paddle-wheeler to be found along the banks of the Yukon River on the outskirts of Whitehorse, retaining its dignity despite the ravages of time and weather. Since this painting was made, two of these historical boats have been destroyed by fire. Even though the drawing of the boat's construction is simplified, the forward section dominates the composition. The painting is reduced to mainly two values: the ship with its shadows the darker value; the sky and foreground the lighter value.

The importance of the prow of the Klondike as the center of interest is emphasized by the strong darks of the winches and other equipment indicated on the deck. This is a somewhat static composition with the grays reinforcing this feeling, though offset by a lively sky. The wet-in-wet technique is used liberally in the sky treatment. The washes here of Payne's gray and yellow ochre were kept thin.

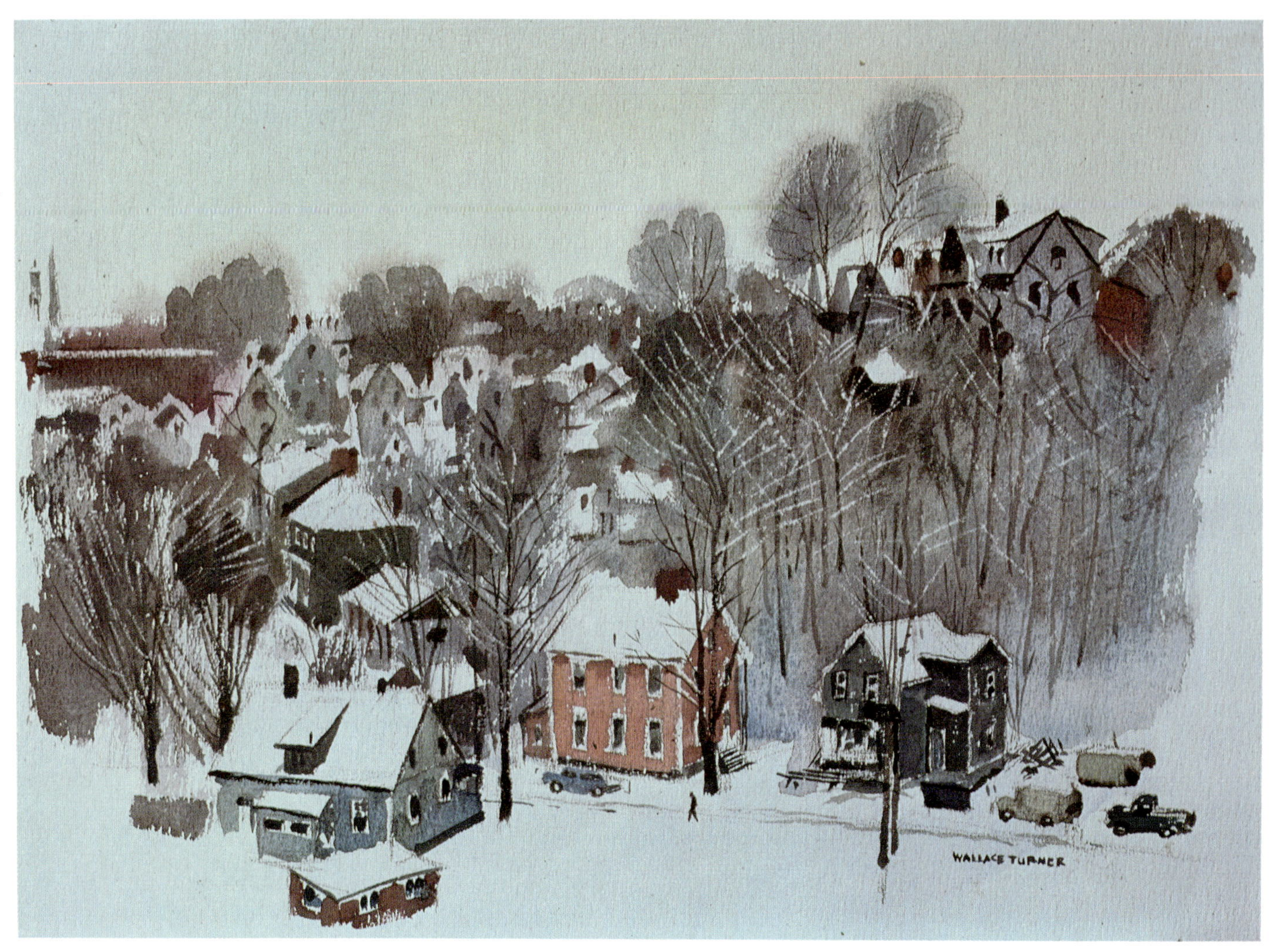

WOLFVILLE, NOVA SCOTIA

Earlier we discussed a painting I made from a view out the window of my house. Here is another view, only this time it is winter. With all the colorful leaves gone, many more houses can be seen.

This painting is almost all transparent washes. The tree branches were indicated by scratching into the moist surface of the paper. I like gray, wintery days as the local colors stand out so well. Notice how little light and shadow is indicated; an indication of an overcast day.

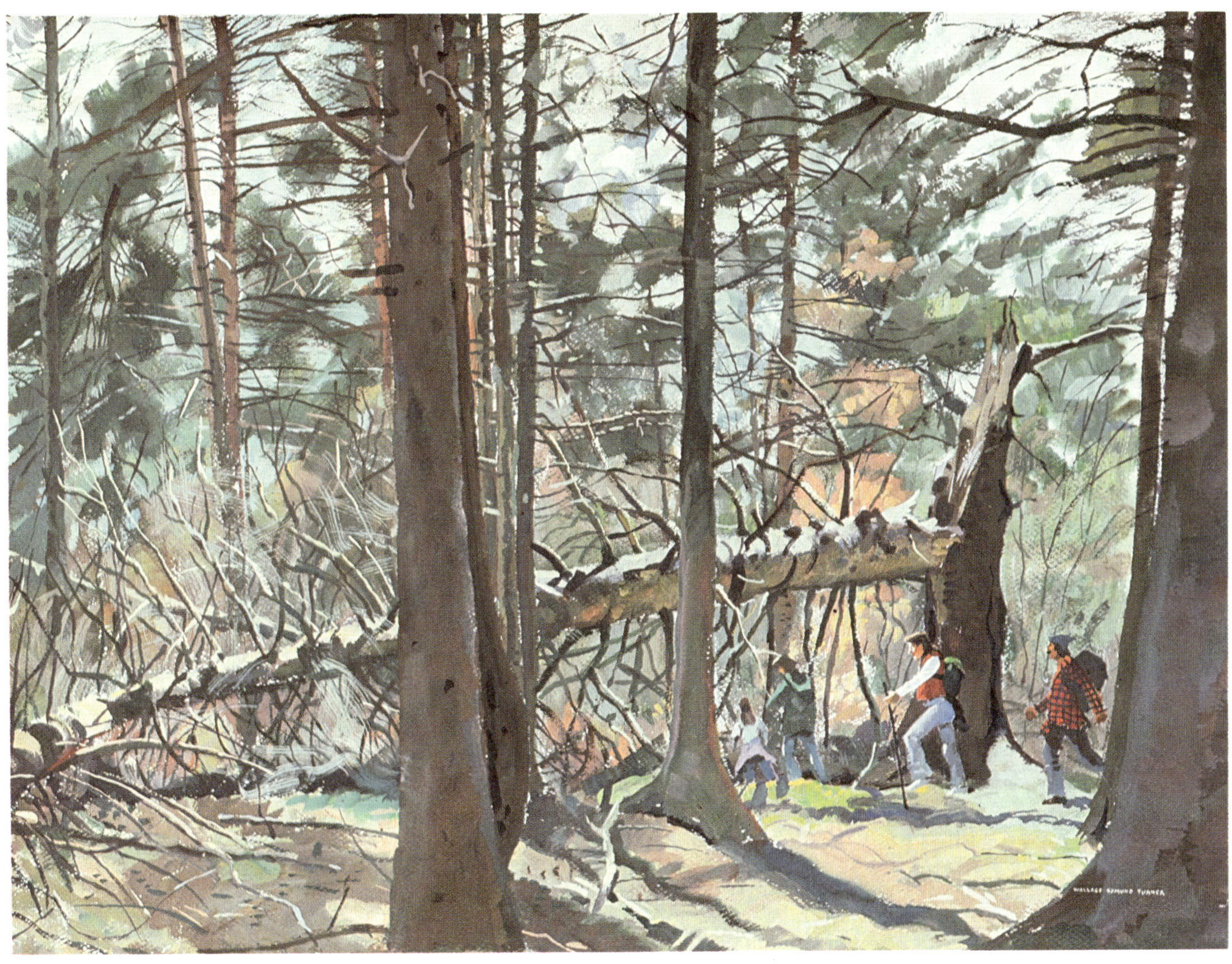

NEARBY WOODS, WOLFVILLE, NOVA SCOTIA

You can travel the world over and discover many exciting places to paint. But, don't overlook the obvious. There are meaningful pictures to be painted close-by wherever you live. All you have to do is recognize them and paint them in your own way.

Here is a scene nearby my home. It is not the great mountains of Alaska or the high Sierras, nor does it have the romance of the Pacific islands or the banks of the Nile, but it is paintable, and it is obtainable.